Mark Kollar

KIRSTEN

ഗ

JADRO

- 2019 -

- KIRSTEN -

In 2019, JADRO Publishing released

ISBN 978-80-89426-58-4 (print version)
ISBN 978-80-89426-97-3 (PDF)
ISBN 978-80-89426-98-0 (EPUB)
ISBN 978-80-89426-99-7 (MOBI)

Sometimes,
when we give up immediate success
in favor of another person or a more suitable time,
the result can be better
than we ever hoped for.

Table of Contents

Chapter 1

- KIRSTEN -

On the table lay a white envelope. It was clearly visible on the brown wood. Kirsten was getting ready for breakfast and packing her school bag. She walked around the table and glanced at it occasionally. It was still sealed, but she knew what was inside. She didn't have to open it. And she didn't want to. Even closed, it stirred the same feelings of uncertainty in her. She couldn't escape them. And when she managed to forget about them, more envelopes arrived the following month.

Since the very first envelope arrived, nothing had changed, and Kirsten wanted to keep it that way. She didn't want to pay much attention to it. She wouldn't let it distract her. It caused wrinkles on her forehead too. She didn't want to lose the life she had been living. She was afraid it would change, and she was afraid the envelope would change Kirsten forever. In the past few months, she had been very fragile and vulnerable.

He packed his lunch and watched her. She was eating bread, her gaze fixed on the wooden table. She looked as if she was studying its structure. Deep in thought and calm. This was his Kirsten. The number of thoughts in her head was immeasurable, and if they could generate electricity, the whole small town they lived in would be lit up. She was probably thinking about school again. Or the piano. So many changes had happened lately that he wasn't surprised she was constantly absorbed in herself. It worried him. On the other hand, he knew she could handle it. He could certainly help her somehow. But he also knew that Kirsten wanted to help herself. She always said that when she helped herself, the problem wouldn't be a problem the second time. But if she accepted help from someone else, she would show weakness and would have to, or even want to, rely on others for help. That's how she has been since she was little. Always bringing home cats and dogs that needed help, of course. She was always there for her friends. They often sat together on the porch late into the night, discussing relationships or just philosophizing about life. Kirsten thirsted for experience. She helped because she learned to understand problems. To find solutions to unsolvable situations. Somehow it enriched and fulfilled her. Although she seemed fragile, her determination and patience often triumphed over this envelope.

„Is everything okay? Do you need anything?“ Sam asked.

„Well, I don‘t know. I‘m just thinking about today,“ she replied as if she didn‘t hear the question. „I‘ll somehow get through it. I‘m going to Belinda‘s in the afternoon. I‘ll be home around half past six,“ she said, lost in thought.

„Okay. I‘m going to Mrs. Stewart‘s. Her faucet broke again. Last time, it was the fridge, before that the door. Either she wants to marry me or the whole house will fall on her head soon,“ he said, and a smile crossed his old face, smoothing out the wrinkles on his forehead.

Even in these days, he looked optimistic. A lot had changed in their lives after the funeral. For Sam, it was now most important for Kirsten not to lose her ground. She was at that vulnerable age where she was no longer a child but not yet an adult. They tried to fill that emptiness together whenever they entered the kitchen or sat down at the table. When they smelled the aroma of their favorite meal together. They didn‘t want to forget these moments, and at the same time, they didn‘t want to constantly think about them. They evoked sadness in them. Sam knew that the emptiness would eventually fill itself. He took care of the house and the household. Kirsten helped him and enjoyed spending time with him.

He still watched her. She took a bite from the edge of the bread and glanced at him briefly. He knew that after her mother‘s death, she grew up faster, unlike her friends, and that often led her into complicated situations. She finished breakfast and put her snack in her bag.

„Hi, see you tonight,“ she said, opening the door of the white wooden house and stepping onto the veranda. The sun was just setting over the lake, creating a beautiful sunny day. The weather was always pleasant in the south. It was always warm, and winters weren‘t as harsh as in the north. Nature was almost always in bloom. She looked towards the red house that Sam had renovated into a shelter from the outside world. She had also moved the piano there so she could play in the garden. It gave her energy when she played, and the sound could be heard all the way to the veranda. Sam would always sit in his armchair and open a beer or light a cigarette during these moments. In such moments, they were grateful for everything they had. They didn't let themselves be broken by what had happened to them. They tried to become stronger because of it.

Sam took his snack, keys, and wallet from the table. He closed the door and walked down the stairs to his van. He opened the side door and looked inside. He checked the tools and materials. Someone else would surely get a new one. It had already been through quite a few years. But he had installed various shelves, boards, and improvements in it, so he didn't even consider replacing it. And besides, it was running reliably. There was no reason to think about getting a new one. Everyone in town knew him and often customers would wait for him right by his car. As a general repairman for everything that could break, he had to be prepared to fix anything from a socket to plumbing. In the small town full of older people, he never knew what else could go wrong. It wasn't a modern metropolis, but an old town full of small houses that had memories of several generations. It had its charm. That's why they had moved here. Time had stood still here and it suited both of them. They needed to settle down somewhere where they would have more time for each other, wouldn't have to travel long distances, and where nobody knew them.

Edwood was a charming place. One square with a small park, a few benches, and a fountain. Shops lined the square. Since you could get anywhere on foot and there were enough parking spaces in town due to the small number of residents, parking spaces stretched across the square in front of every shop and office. Everyone was like one big family. Everyone knew everyone by sight.

He checked his tools. He had just been to Mrs. Wortingher's. She wanted him to fix the wheel on her big cabinet. Little did he know that the cabinet contained everything that could fit in there since the fifties. And when they threw everything out and turned the cabinet around, he realized he needed a special key that was made in those times. Mrs. Wortingher's coffee and cakes were always a pleasant way to spend the morning.

He closed the doors of his van and checked his house and surroundings. A white house with a front veranda that extended to the left side. From there, you could see the lake. A stone path ran from the mailbox by the road to the door. Flowers in front of the house. Many flowers. Kirsten was always planting something and it was starting to show what it would actually be. It was nice and it reminded Sam of a woman‘s touch in the house. Next to the house was a large garden with apple trees. He backed out onto the road and headed to Mrs. Stewart‘s. He waved at Kirsten.

She ran down the stairs to the car. The doors opened slowly, but that‘s exactly why she liked it. It was a gift from her parents for her birthday. She wouldn‘t trade it for any other. It was full of memories that no new one could ever give her. Those memories couldn‘t be bought now. Not without Mom. She still saw the envelope in front of her. And she knew she still couldn‘t open it, no matter how long she stared at it. She drove onto the main road and headed to school.

Chapter 2

- MATCH -

„Kirsten must be somewhere around here," said Sofia as she got off her bike. The school parking lot was full. Everyone was looking forward to sports day - a chance to escape from classes, play soccer, lounge around the school grounds, and disappear somewhere for the whole day. Each student had found their own little corner on this day.

„We have to win today. That‘s why we came here, and that‘s why the sun is shining today. That‘s the goal of the day!" announced Sofia. Emie was still catching her breath and looked around.

„What‘s that?" Sofia exclaimed in surprise and brushed her short black bangs back to see better. „Someone wrote the word ‚Whiners‘ on several cars near the right rear light," Sofia added and turned to Emie.

„Well, who else? Are you new to this school?" Emie remarked.

„No, Angela wouldn‘t stoop to such pettiness. Let‘s see who we‘re up against today. I just hope I don‘t find the same thing on my bike, or on yours," Sofia replied, placing her bike next to Kirsten‘s car. She threw her backpack in front of her and rummaged through it angrily.

„Come on! The match will start before we find everyone," urged Emie impatiently, wondering what Sofia was looking for in her backpack.

„Hah, I knew I had it with me!" exclaimed Sofia with sparkling eyes, holding a marker in her hand.

„Really?" asked Emie in amazement.

„Really!" replied a grinning Sofia. She poured some water on a tissue and wiped over the writing on Kirsten‘s car several times. Under the tissue, a blurry smudge appeared. Sofia put the marker in her mouth, opened it, and triumphantly closed it again.

„Well, are you satisfied now? Can we go?" asked Emie, looking at the rewritten message on the car.

„We‘re not whiners, but winners!" Sofia exclaimed and grabbed her backpack from the ground.

„Wait for me!“ Emie called out to the fleeing Sofia with outstretched arms. Sometimes she couldn‘t keep up with Sofia‘s energy. Sofia was like a swallow, flying from side to side, as if she never felt tired.

She quickly made her way through the crowd of students to the bench by the soccer field.

„Are we all here?“ both of them asked, looking across the field at the bench of their opponents.

„We are. Adam is somewhere around here. But the four of us are all here,“ Kirsten replied, scanning the crowd to see if she could spot Adam.

„Oh, and Angela, of course, is here,“ Sofia added sarcastically.

„That wouldn‘t miss an opportunity to rub it in again to someone. Miss Amazing,“ Emie added, watching the bench on the other side. Angela grinned at them, and who knows what she had planned. Her team, of course, consisted of several good players. Angela was their leader and captain. Even in her jersey, shorts, and pink cleats, she looked stylish. And her long blonde hair.

„When I look at those familiar faces from school soccer, this looks like a tough match. Not that I don‘t believe in us, but let‘s face it...“ Emie assessed the situation.

„And do you think they joined her team for her blue eyes or whatever she has?“ Sofia laughed.

„Her fan club came too. Well, now we‘re all here,“ Sofia added ironically, looking at some trendy-dressed classmates who stood right next to Angela‘s bench, following her everywhere like on a leash.

„No matter why they joined for whatever reason, what‘s important for Angela is the result. No one will remember who was on the team in eight years. But that the team won. It will be recorded in the yearbook. I assume Angela will attach a suitable photo of herself to the team photo and the result,“ Kirsten smiled.

„But that‘s not important. What‘s important is that we‘re here, that you came. Today will be a great day. I can feel it! Something that money can‘t buy,“ Kirsten smiled, and the three of them fist bumped. Adam walked across the field. The early sun lazily rose behind him, so Kirsten shielded her face with her hand.

„Hey! Are we ready? We won‘t play Angela‘s game, but our own. Let‘s have fun with it. The outcome doesn‘t matter. Well, the outcome is already known. It‘s definitely going to be less embarrassing to lose than to play against a professional football team that played in a stadium with 80,000 seats yesterday,“ Adam said with a half-smile.

„Let‘s do this!“ he exclaimed, extending his hand in front of him. Sofia‘s eyes lit up as she slapped her hand against Adam‘s palm. Emie calmly placed her hand on Sofia‘s, sealing the bond with Kirsten placing her hand on it as the last one.

„Hurrah!“ they all shouted in unison, looking at Angelina‘s team bench. Everyone stood there like robots, seemingly unable to wait for the moment when they would finally crush them. The game could begin. The field was lined with students, and there was a pleasant atmosphere filled with cheers and adrenaline. They were playing on one half of the field with small nets, so two or three matches were happening simultaneously. Kirsten knew that this setup didn‘t suit Angelina very well, as she wouldn‘t be able to shine as much. She would get lost in the crowd, and it would definitely make her nervous. The opening kick-off sounded, and the field and the stands echoed with cheers and encouragement. It was one of those ordinary days that were happening all over the country. Kirsten ran across the field, realizing that she was gaining something that couldn‘t be bought in any store. She looked at the red faces of Sofia and Emie and knew that they were creating some great memories and moments. She could chase the ball all day long, as long as she could spend it with these amazing people. Even Angelina‘s presence didn‘t bother her. She still had a lot to learn from her. She watched her game, her decisions. She tried to compare them with her own. She tried to put herself in Angelina‘s shoes and wondered how Angela would handle being in her position or if Kirsten would become Angelina. What options did she have?

„3-0,“ Emie interrupted Kirsten‘s contemplation, panting. She took a glass of water from the small table and wiped her face.

„And that‘s just the first half,“ she added with a depressed tone.

„If I could, I would run towards their goal myself and score against them!“ Sofia said, rubbing her dirty cheek with her hand.

„Does it hurt?“ Kirsten asked, after the ball had landed on Sofia‘s face.

„I should have defended better,“ Emie said, leaning on her knees, still breathing heavily.

„Does it hurt? This?“ Sofia laughed, and Kirsten knew where she was heading.

„You can‘t stop them anymore. You‘re flying around like a rag. They‘re just too good. But if we could at least score one goal...“ Sofia contemplated aloud.

„Sofia, keep going for the balls like you‘ve been doing. Only three of all those shots have passed you so far. Emie, don‘t give up and keep cleaning the space in front of Sofia. I‘ll try to move the ball as close to their goal as possible. They‘re still coming after me. Let‘s use that,“ Adam outlined his plan out loud.

„I‘ll be in the right place at the right time,“ Kirsten added.

„Alright. Let‘s do it!“ Adam called, and everyone dispersed to their positions.

The second half went on in a similar fashion as the first. Angel‘s team pressed Kirsten‘s team so hard that it was almost impossible to get in front of the goal and score. Kirsten noticed that Adam was getting tired. They were swarming around him like bees. He was the strongest player on the team, so every time he had the ball, they tried to eliminate him. What started as a friendly game turned into a battle for life and death.

„I‘ve got it!“ Emie shouted and ran towards a pass that was heading straight towards the net, where another attacker was already charging. She slid right into a puddle of mud, splashing her face. She kicked the ball directly to Adam. He sprinted all the way to the right side. Kirsten instantly understood his plan. She ran alongside him on the opposite side of the field. Two players ran towards Adam, and that‘s when Angela read the play. They approached Adam, and just as they were about to take the ball from him, he seemingly kicked it into an empty space. Kirsten sprinted, and it was clear that she would reach the ball before Angela. A chance to score. She knew Angela wouldn‘t allow it. She was probably already disappointed that Kirsten‘s team wasn‘t losing by at least 10-0. Kirsten took the ball and ran down the left side towards the goal. Angela ran towards her. Kirsten kicked the ball around Angela and tried to outrun her. It seemed like she was a step ahead of Angela, with a clear shot at the goal. That‘s when Angela took two desperate steps and pushed Kirsten away from the ball. Kirsten felt herself losing balance. She crashed into the aluminum table with cups of water and ice tea, which spilled all over her face, hair, and clothes. She didn‘t mind. She was sweaty from running like a mouse. The other students murmured. She wiped the plastic cups off herself and wiped her face with her hand. Angela got up from the ground and came to her. Kirsten was expecting a sarcastic remark, but Angela extended her hand and said, „I‘m sorry, I don‘t want to hurt you." „I just want to defeat you," said Kirsten dryly as the referee raised the yellow card. She pulled herself up and walked away. Kirsten leaned on her knees and took deep breaths. She looked at Sofia and Emie, who were standing in surprise, waiting. Adam approached her from the other end of the field.

„Go for it!" she shouted and ran towards her half. Adam stopped. He wanted to make sure she was okay, but her shout motivated him enough to continue the match. The rest of the game proceeded in the same spirit. Only Kirsten and Angela were fighting on a different field than everyone else.

ഗ

„4 : 0. Not a single goal!" grumbled Sofia, scooping up cake with her spoon.

„And I came here to win today," she shook her head incredulously, while the filling melted on her tongue.

„But it could have been worse. Actually, you held up well. I don‘t know what you‘re blaming yourself for," Adam reassured Sofia.

„I feel like after a military warm-up. Barbie and her team really gave us a hard time," Emie added with flushed cheeks, looking at her bottle of cold pink drink.

„Barbie, but with a brain. She had a plan, and it worked. Angela isn‘t stupid. We would be wronging her. It‘s better to live with the truth than to die in self-deception. There‘s something about her. When I ran past her, she wasn‘t just a doll. She exuded focus from her eyes. On that field, she knew exactly what she wanted and how to achieve it. With such an opponent, it‘s not shameful to lose, but it‘s honorable to fight," Kirsten concluded and took a sip of her coffee, staring ahead without blinking.

„Are you defending her now? Hello, Kirsten? Are you there?" Sofia grumbled and tapped her on the head.

„Oh come on. You weren‘t unfairly punished. We just lost one game. Not the first and not the last. We can win the next one. And we‘ll do everything we can to win it!" Kirsten added more seriously. Sofia pouted for a moment.

„I'm saying we'll do everything for it!" Kirsten repeated and clenched her fist. Sofia smiled and bumped fists with her. Kirsten hugged her briefly like a cat. She looked around Belinda's café. She looked at all three of them and smiled: „Why are you all so disappointed? We won, after all."

„One nice experience to add to the collection. It doesn't matter what will be in the yearbook, but what you take away from the playground," she said, placing her open palm on her chest.

„Let's promise each other that we'll meet like this even when we're grown up. No matter how much we change and no matter what we experience. That nothing will divide us. And that we'll never meet in a smaller number than all four of us. Let's promise," Kirsten said with a slightly desperate tone in her voice. Outside the window, four close souls sat, and on the table, four hands were joined into one. Tiny droplets of mist, foretelling the upcoming autumn, fell on the café. School days would be longer, duller, and dragging, the opposite of what was happening in Kirsten's life right now. But she was looking forward to school herself. To blend in among the flesh and bones of people, to make time for feeding the questions that emerged like hungry fish from the ocean, demanding answers.

Chapter 3

- SPEARS -

The first class went by quickly. Kirsten rushed into the restroom just before the bell rang. She stood by the window, frantically scribbling notes on paper in a worn-out dictionary. She wanted to finish the middle part of the composition so she could practice it today. She made sure her tears didn't smudge a single line. She didn't notice if anyone else was in the restroom. In fact, she didn't notice anything at all. Only the tones that were born in her head. The more upset she was, the more emotional the composition appeared in front of her eyes. She could cry all day and write a beautiful song, but Kirsten didn't want to cry anymore. However, the past few months hadn't brought her much comfort. She understood that everyone thinks their life is the hardest, but this year was a turning point for her. She had experienced too many situations to just move on from them. That's why she found solace in music. It never betrayed her. She could communicate with the world and herself through it. Release her emotions without worrying about the response from the surrounding world.

Perhaps someone was next to her in the restroom and heard her emotions hitting the ground and shattering into countless droplets. But Kirsten didn't let herself be disturbed. Once the tones and notes started flowing, she wanted to forge them into hot refrains. Whether they evoked negative or positive feelings in her, she didn't think about Angela. She didn't deny that Angela was some kind of motivation for her. She couldn't understand her world, and Angela's world seemed to Kirsten like a creature that Angela chews on like a tasty morsel every day. That's why Kirsten was so reserved around her. Her eyes were still a little teary. She felt that something was changing or about to change, and nothing would be the same as before.

The notes she drew on the crumpled paper were very important to her. But it wasn't about the notes themselves or the composition itself. It was about what she wanted to express through it to Sofia. Somewhere inside, she was glad she was upset because Angela had saddened her again.

At least for these short moments, she stops being anxious and can feel something. Kirsten really wanted Sofia to feel these emotions from the composition. The piano was like a cooking pot for her, and she could work musical wonders with it. Unfortunately, so could Angela. Both of them were excellent piano players, albeit in different ways. Kirsten learned to play on her own, and her playing was smooth, as if one had fallen into six layers of fragrant feathers. Just close your eyes. Playing the piano was a social obligation for Angela in the wealthy family she grew up in. Her parents had no problem paying for the best teachers. Her playing was precise like a Swiss watch. Sometimes it seemed like a robot was playing the piano. At first listen, there was no difference in their playing. Both were exceptional pianists. But music connoisseurs could tell them apart. When a professional jury visited their school to evaluate them for the district competition, one part of the jury liked Kirsten‘s playing, and the other liked Angela‘s. This battle had no winner yet, but Angela was trying very hard. This parquet floor was one of the few things that Angela didn‘t have full control over. She never left the battle defeated. That was Angela. Wise, wealthy, educated daughter of a millionaire family.

Kirsten really wanted to win this competition. She was torn by her conflicting thoughts about her duet with Angela. Can she separate herself from their personal competition at the competition, or will Angela make her make a mistake? Angela would sacrifice even losing in the district competition for this win. The more Angela played against Kirsten in rehearsals, the more it inspired Kirsten. Angela forced her to reach the absolute limits of her abilities. And Kirsten was doing the same. That‘s why it didn‘t bother her. She was just afraid of failure because of Sofia. They didn‘t play poorly or out of tune in rehearsals. But they played against each other. Kirsten had never imagined that was possible. Both of them constantly challenged each other in rehearsals, to the point where they completely ignored the sheet music. All their performances were actually brilliant improvisations. Many times, their classmates were left in silent awe after rehearsals. But that‘s why they have a chance to win. Their mutual competition had already surpassed the boundaries of the school. That‘s why everyone was looking forward to the final round. They would compete against the most talented students from the wider area. Every school had been diligently preparing for this competition all year. Winning this competition would be a great honor. Especially this year. Various rumors circulated around the competition, and the whole rivalry gave it an incredible charge. However, Kirsten wasn‘t fighting for herself. She wanted to win mainly for Sofia. To give her the strength to keep fighting. Sofia must fight!

Many times she looked into her piercing blue eyes and told her as if she wanted to kill the illness inside her with words.

ꟹ

Just then the bell rang. The school bathroom quickly filled up with teenagers, and they filled the entire space with their „grown-up" problems up to the ceiling. They closed the door behind them to make sure no word escaped into the hallway. Kirsten continued writing. She was in a perfect state of mind. She was like the best golfer in the world who knows before teeing off that they will hit the hole on the first try. She perfected the notes on paper with every stroke of her hand.

Only the scratching of the pencil on paper and the hurried footsteps in the hallway, heading towards this confessional at the end of the corridor, could be heard. A strand of hair slipped out from behind her ear and partially covered her eyes from the sun that shone sideways through the window. It was as if it wanted to peek at the paper - at the composition taking shape. Just like Mrs. Miller found her notes on the bench. It was as if she had found a rare gem in the jungle. Kirsten didn‘t even have to sign up for the competition. Mrs. Miller signed her up.

ꟹ

The first girls rushed into the bathroom and the space filled with noise.

„Kirsten, I don‘t know what to say. Come take a walk, you‘ll distract yourself," Sofia insisted. She looked into Kirsten‘s eyes and smiled. A petite, kind girl. Kirsten liked her a lot.

„I‘ll go with you. Just a few more notes," Kirsten replied, straightened her long hair, and quickly wrote down the final notes on the paper.

„Why don‘t you confront her and say something?" Sofia continued. „She keeps insulting or embarrassing you. If it weren‘t for her paid friends, she‘d be standing in the middle of the class like a thorn in the side. She‘s only popular and arrogant because of her money..."

„I know she‘s not clueless. Angela is not stupid. She‘s aware of everything. And she benefits from it. Maybe you have to grow up in pretending to not be bothered by her and know how to live with her. Despite that, we have something in common. I don‘t want to ignore her. There‘s something I can learn from her," Kirsten humbly remarked.

„I feel like she‘s not the same girl we see every day at school. At school, she‘s just who everyone wants to see. Living like that must cause suffering, and I don‘t want to add to it. Maybe one day we‘ll have a time when we can be ourselves. For now, she‘s not my friend, but she‘s not my enemy either," Kirsten said, while continuing to jot down her notes.

ᔕ

Sofia remained quiet for a moment, watching Kirsten scribble down her hieroglyphics in her dictionary. She reflected on Kirsten‘s words. Kirsten was probably the only one in their class who had a different perspective on all those ordinary, everyday, and obvious things. Sofia‘s life hadn‘t been ordinary or simple for some time now, ever since she learned about her diagnosis. Kirsten‘s words had started to hold greater meaning for her. Life seemed to flow more pleasantly with her. Sofia wanted to repay her friendship. That‘s why she always stood by her.

„When she insults you, it‘s like she has no soul. As if it doesn‘t even bother her. She‘s like the devil herself," Sofia couldn‘t come to terms with it.

Kirsten laughed. „You know what‘s funny? That‘s exactly what my essay for literature class is about. Everyone has a soul. Even Angela does. Some people know about it, some don‘t. But we can still find a thought, an emotion, or an action with which we write into other souls. Everyone has the power to say something to someone that makes them feel better. Why should I choose words that hurt someone? I can tell them the truth, but they have to be ready for it. Because that hurts the most," Kirsten looked intently at Sofia. Girls were running around them, unaware of what they were talking about. They washed their hands and rushed off to deal with their everyday teenage matters.

ᔕ

„You know, it‘s not that simple. When you hurt someone, you‘re hurting yourself first. Before you say that negative thought to someone else, it exists in your head for a moment too. And when you have so many of those thoughts, you eventually realize that you only have those left.

There‘s no room for creative ideas, funny memories, dreams, desires. Just everything that can make us a beautiful and interesting person. The most amazing thing about words is that they can change someone else‘s life just with a few sounds. Isn‘t that incredible? I want to have only pleasant thoughts in my head.“

„So that there is no space left for the bad ones in me. So that my emptiness is not filled with anger, despair, and desperation. And it‘s up to me how much empty space remains there. It‘s my head, and what I let in is up to me. Only I have the keys,“ Kirsten concluded and immediately wrote more notes on paper.

„Angela knows how to use words like a dagger. It stabs deep into you. It stays there for a week and I can‘t seem to pull it out. I couldn‘t get rid of so many of those thoughts, so I accepted them within myself. Later, I realized that they probably landed exactly where they were supposed to, hitting some emotion, feeling, or opinion that had been troubling me for a while. When I come to terms with them, those spears will fall out of me on their own. Why were some able to stab into me, and many others not? Because they found a weak spot. My Achilles‘ heel. And I want to know where I am vulnerable, where I need to be careful with the places of my soul. I will need that. To be strong. Let those hammer blows shape me. After what has happened in the last few months, I feel like a piece of glowing iron. And now is the time to forge while it‘s hot. I don‘t want to harden into shapeless mass. And Angela is that hammer. Emotions are very important to me. I‘d rather accept whatever life brings me than start resisting. After a while, I would realize that I‘m resisting everything. That I can no longer distinguish between good and bad. When you build tall walls around yourself, they protect you, but at the same time they prevent the beautiful things from entering that get lost underneath them. I refuse to refuse. Every action causes a reaction. It makes me who I am,“ Kirsten concluded and added the last note.

Sofia knew that it wasn‘t just about Angela. Everyone knew what had happened. Kirsten needs time now.

ഗ

„But you know that you‘ve pulled out some spears from me as well? Many words, sentences, and experiences don‘t hurt me anymore. You picked the spears, but the holes remain,“ Kirsten finally smiled. She put the papers on the radiator and hugged Sofia tightly like a favorite doll, until her eyes widened and she smiled. She knew that Kirsten was a very emotional person and could always surprise her with similar outbursts.

„Well, alright, I'm glad," Sofia nodded, feeling embarrassed.

„Close those smiling eyes, or I'll drown in them," Kirsten laughed. She held her close like a sister. Sofia felt that Kirsten, whom she loved so much.

The embrace was brief, but they both felt they needed each other. This was not the type of movie where the screenwriter writes an interesting plot. Where the main and supporting characters smile in the end credits. Their fates did not follow any rules or logic. Sofia had come to terms with her illness. She wanted to accept it, get used to it, and eventually forget about it. When she fought against it, she felt weak. She felt like the illness was winning. The more attention she gave it, the stronger it became. That's why she decided to take the opposite approach. Not to dwell on it and let it take the wind out of its sails.

ɕ

Kirsten helped her come to terms with it. She had experienced similar pain, so she could explain to Sofia that what was happening to her could motivate her. That right now, time is precious, not annoying or sad. Because everything is valuable to us only when there is little of it left, we lose it, or we have already lost it. Suddenly, there were more birds, flowers, more sunshine and beautiful things around Sofia. She was a little scared that she had to thank her illness for all of this. But she understood that this was how she could defeat it. Just like Kirsten had defeated Angela. Although she didn't want to defeat it, just find a way to coexist with it. Sofia couldn't understand that Kirsten didn't despise her. She knew she could still learn a lot from Kirsten. It seemed to her as if she had matured overnight. But it wasn't because of her mom's death. It was as if she had come to a new outlook and attitude towards life. What was worse, she was more scared than content.

Kirsten stopped writing for a moment and looked at Sofia. Sofia had no idea that all those characters on the paper were arranged for her. Kirsten was composing a new piece and looked at Sofia like a painter when they portray a person on canvas. She examined her like that painter. And she infused every emotion she saw in her into the notes. She smiled with the corners of her lips. The tears disappeared, and a sense of contentment washed over her. Kirsten grabbed Sofia's hand, and they rushed out into the hallway.

„I'll just go exchange some books and then come to class," Kirsten smiled at Sofia.

„Yeah, I'm going to grab a snack. I didn't have much for breakfast," Sofia said and turned right.

Kirsten walked towards the lockers. She was wearing a dark fitted shirt with no pattern, jeans, and knee-high boots. Blending in with the high school color palette, she looked around at her classmates. They had only recently moved to the city, and many people didn't know them yet.

Mostly just classmates in the class. Adam was already standing by his locker, which was near hers. All lockers were in one long corridor, so they almost always ran into each other there. She didn't know much about him. His family invested in the town and owned some businesses. They owned a large wood processing factory where most of the town's people worked. The nearby forests provided job security for many years. She approached her locker, opened it, and smiled at Adam. They exchanged their belongings and he ran up to her.

„Hey, you have another test today. I'll come and see. Last time with Angela was amazing! You can definitely win. At least a few people would be able to locate our town on the map," said Adam, and his rebellious eyes sparkled. Kirsten felt a bit uncomfortable with his interest. She brushed her hair back with both hands and casually tossed her braid over her shoulder. She knew that their shared sympathies were unacceptable.

„Yes, this afternoon. Mrs. Miller wants to make sure we can handle it. Whether our duet is really suitable for competition," Kirsten replied hesitantly, but she knew that their duet sounded as if she and Angela had played together a hundred times before.

Not much happened in Edwood. A small town, a motel, a small square, a church, a factory, and a farm. All surrounded by omnipresent forests.

„Come, I'll be glad," she clutched her books in her hands. Adam was not like the others. But that probably stemmed from his upbringing. He was probably raised in a business-oriented world of money, so that one day he could take over the family business. Just like it often happens in these families.

„I'm going to class, see you," she turned around and Adam just watched as her braid slowly unraveled on her shoulder and her brown hair covered her back. He still felt that she was somehow unapproachable, but he knew it wasn't just for him, but for the whole world around her. He was glad she said more than three words, which was quite enough for a Monday. Kirsten was content inside. She felt like there was a cold copy left on the floor in the girls' restroom after they left. She clutched her dictionary in her hands and was grateful that she had managed to finish that important part of the composition. And it was still only Monday.

Chapter 4

- SOUL -

Kirsten sat quietly in her seat, as if waiting for a storm that would leave nothing dry. She wasn‘t nervous, she just didn‘t want to be in this class right now. In her thoughts, she strolled in front of the red house and wrote down more notes in her notebook. She pushed her hair away from her face with a nod of her head and looked out the window. If only it were evening already. She wanted to sit in her little house and play for herself. At school, she „had to“ play for everyone around her. She was, of course, glad that many people liked her music, but at home in her little house, she could be herself. Alone with herself. She needed these moments now more than ever. The School was quite okay. She enjoyed going there. It was like an encyclopedia that she could never finish reading. She studied all those friendships and relationships, getting to know new people. Today, she finally wanted to break the curse. She tried to write the essay as best as she could. Hopefully, she will finally convince Miss Wurm. The lessons with her were unbearable. Not just for Kirsten. She wasn‘t a confrontational type, but people like Wurm knew how to create conflict on their own. Whenever she looked at her, she understood that the worst emotion is no emotion. And since Miss Wurm couldn‘t create the nice ones, she at least created the negative ones. As if that‘s when she found meaning in life and didn‘t feel empty. Everyone in the class suffered in her lessons except for Miss Wurm. She enjoyed it. But Kirsten saw it differently. It wasn‘t everyone else who suffered in her lessons, but her. And that was liberating. She was as prepared for this lesson as she was for others.

For her, learning was about discovering something new. She was very interested in literature and all those amazing stories she could experience with a book. In moments like these, her imagination painted walls on the walls and ceilings of the rainy sky.

The chair was a stone bench, next to which sat the main character. Of course, she was reading girls' books in her little house. She loved escaping into fairy tales and other worlds, different from her own. But she never dreamed. She liked it here in this world. There was no reason to escape into fictional stories that ended on page 300.

Angela sat on a bench behind her. It seemed like she deliberately moved closer so she could spy on her and make her nervous. However, Kirsten didn't let herself get distracted. Angela didn't know, but these situations helped her strengthen her willpower and self-control. They toughened her. That's why Angela's proximity didn't affect her. Angela might have sensed it, which is why she kept pushing the boundaries further and further. Maybe one day she could sit right next to her.

When Kirsten first entered the classroom, Angela wouldn't have bet a penny that she would last longer than a few days at this school. She looked like a troubled girl, waiting for an unpleasant experience after which she would run home and lock herself in. Angela and her friends made bets on how many days Kirsten had left before she broke. Angela herself waited. She didn't want prey, but a challenge. She admitted that there was „something" about Kirsten from the very beginning. Her face reflected her inner self. Soft and gentle, but if a fist were to land on her, she would break her fingers. Kirsten sat in her seat and became invisible. Lost in thought. Angela didn't know about her past or her thoughts. She wanted to let her mature. Maybe she would bloom, or maybe she would wither. She didn't know yet that she had lost her mother.

Two benches down sat Hans. A shy, unassuming classmate who didn't talk much. He wore stretched-out sweaters to accommodate his overweight figure. Kirsten saw him as a cold rock in the middle of a desert. She couldn't figure out what kind of person he was. He was facing Angela's direction in his seat. He looked at her, and it was obvious that he liked her. Angela, of course, had no idea he existed. As if to say: he's out of her league. That's when Angela turned towards him and froze when she noticed he was staring at her.

„What? Do you need something? Don't look at me like that, it makes me uncomfortable. I'm not a piece of meat," she retorted in a calm voice, though offended.

„I hope you're not thinking that you and I..." she gestured alternately to herself and to Hans.

„Oh, please. I really hope you're not thinking that. And if you are, why don't you do something about it? Do you really want to spend your whole life just staring? Before you start staring at girls, maybe you should take a good look at yourself first."

Like this: this doesn't work, and the world out there will chew you up with a reel. If you don't have respect for yourself, how can you have a handful of respect for someone else? Isn't even the most beautiful girl worth a change?" Angela smiled and let her classmates speculate on who she meant by that.

„Listen! I won't belittle you, people belittle themselves. I will just speak the truth, take it as you want. Do you seriously expect rewards without effort, pain, and sweat? Look at how you look! Overeating is just a consequence. The cause is your inferiority complex, stemming from a lack of positive qualities, goals, and dreams. You are just being. Like many other people. If you want to look someone in the eye at a higher level, you have to climb a lot of stairs. Are you listening? Climb," Angela emphasized.

„You won't get anything for free. Nothing! And every day, repeat to yourself in the mirror in the morning: No one will help me. No one. Ever. No one will ever help me! And when you realize that, things will start to change. Stop lazily reaching out your hand, because someone might spit in it. Only weaklings wait. They fear responsibility, decisions. And I don't like such people. If you're content with yourself like this, fine. Grow old behind the fence of your house, but don't drag me along with you. So, please, don't look up, but ahead, or even down, to find a suitable victim who will endure your life with you. Or you can change and start chasing your dreams. Now you only see their dust in the distance. Can you see them there? How they're getting farther away from you? But you'd have to want it and not look for fraudulent shortcuts, right?" Angela concluded.

Hans just sat in surprise, speechless, searching for words. Kirsten understood what Angela wanted to say. She just said it without mincing words. One felt as if they had been splashed with a pot of hot oil. But maybe that was her way of expressing herself, so that everyone could understand her thoughts clearly and comprehensibly. She didn't want to explain everything twice, and that‘s why she hoped that the situation with Hans wouldn‘t repeat itself. A grave silence fell in the classroom, and no one knew what to say.

However, Miss Wurm just entered the classroom. No one wanted to catch her eye. It could mean being called up to the board and getting another bad grade.

Miss Wurm was already retired. She could stop teaching anytime. But she used to be the school‘s former principal. She had a special position here, and no one dared to fire her. She teached foreign languages and was needed in the school.

She quietly sat behind the lectern. The atmosphere was akin to the view from the window on a typical sunny morning when we notice an approaching storm on the horizon. It was a peculiar atmosphere, one that crawled under your skin. With a glance, Wurm surveyed the class, as if choosing her first victim. In reality, she already had her pick.

„Kirsten! Read your essay. I‘m sure it will be as profound as the last one, about sitting on a bench in the park,“ Wurm said with a smile that was both playful and serious, recalling the last class. The essay was supposed to be about our inner and outer selves, and the difference between the two. Kirsten had written hers in a slightly depressive tone, with no other option after her mother‘s funeral. Wurm took pleasure in being in control, when she had the upper hand. So Kirsten‘s confession was opportune. She already knew how Kirsten felt and where her vulnerabilities lay. Kirsten calmly opened her notebook, looking at the inked lines at the top that read: „The most precious thing in my life.“

Kirsten could have written about many things, people. About her mother, Sam, about music. Many ideas crossed her mind. They all had one thing in common, and so in her essay, she mentioned everything that mattered to her. From that one thing, all her love and joy emanated. She looked at the lines and then briefly at Wurm, who was waiting to seize on something else. Wurm had a similar nature to Angela‘s. She preferred to revel in others‘ misfortune rather than her own happiness. She was retired, with no children or family. Angela had inspired Kirsten to write this essay.

The soul is a marvelous creation. But not everyone has one. We can write into it with our thoughts. Best of all, into someone else‘s. Even better, into one we know. We know what to write to make it smile. We know how to tickle it to make it feel better. Sometimes a few letters are enough, and other times, even complex sentences are inadequate. Sometimes a person writes, but the letters get lost in the distance, and the sentence cannot be finished. Some people know how to place hard dots after a sentence. It hurts a lot when they drive the thought deep into the soul. Especially when it‘s a bad, malevolent thought. It hurts and sticks out like a splinter that you can‘t seem to remove even after a week.

We live with it for a long time, so long, until we accept it. And then someone comes along and suddenly picks it out and rewrites the sentence. A beautiful feeling. Sometimes it seems to us that there are only writers around us, who scribble nonsense on our soul. And they put that painful period after every sentence. We become immune and our soul hardens. It resists the onslaught of barbaric thoughts. We contemplate whether to turn the page, or if there‘s a blank one left. Usually, we succeed. However, it is then imprinted with the previous one, and it‘s difficult to write on it. You can still see sentences from the previous page. But it‘s clean, so it works. The next pages are cleaner and more balanced, and slowly we forget. It just takes flipping the pages until we turn the one on which we can‘t read any previous word anymore. We look for warm thoughts and warm up our soul. It needs care. When it‘s warmed up, so are we. When it‘s hot, we love. Each of us should choose from the wide selection of lips those write the most beautifully. With feeling, tenderness, and understanding. Those that don‘t want to write pages of meaningless text at any cost. Those that are satisfied with one sentence, and the ink lasts for years. At the end of life, when we reach the print run, we flip back and read only the most visible texts. We ignore the faded ones, we don‘t remember what was written on them anymore. We run our hand over the soul and feel the bump here, the cold there, the warmth or the beauty of the smooth page. We stop and sprinkle it with a tear. Our eyes moisten, the corners of our mouths widen, and we look at what was good. We try to give as many pages from this book to our loved ones as possible. Pointing with our finger at the stylish pens that only we know. We will never tell them about those terrible periods that were once there. In which heavy thoughts were stuck, which we could only pull out with difficulty. They don‘t sting anymore, but the holes remain...

ꕥ

Kirsten finished reading without even blinking. The classroom fell silent. She became uneasy. She heard a girl's voice from behind: „Can you lend it to me after class?" Wurm searched for words for a moment: „Average. Unfinished thoughts. It felt like a poem. Metaphors shattered and hard to understand. What did you mean with this essay? It lacks a clear point," she replied and tapped her pen on the table.

Kirsten looked at Wurm and said, „Anyone who values their soul above all else will understand these lines. The point is that everyone has a soul, even if they don't know it or others think they are such a bad person that they don't have one. That they are like soulless," Kirsten concluded, and Wurm's chair almost broke under her: „Are you trying to tell me that I'm the only one who didn't understand your essay? That I don't have a soul or what?" She raised her eyebrows in surprise. This time Wurm didn't get what she wanted. She needed to elevate herself above Kirsten, but Kirsten indirectly condemned her in front of the whole class as incomprehending. This battle was supposed to have only one winner. And that winner felt defeated.

„Do you really think everyone in the class understood it? From a literary point of view, your piece didn't mean anything to anyone," Wurm continued her angry monologue.

„I'm sorry, I didn't mean to portray you as a person without a soul," Kirsten apologized and didn't take her eyes off Wurm. She didn't even blink, as if she wanted to see every emotion that crossed her face.

„Now it's your turn. Let's hear your essay on ‚What is most precious to me,' Angela," Wurm said with a calmer tone.

Angela took a deep breath and said, „Success."

Kirsten stopped listening. She looked around the class with her head lowered. If her gaze met anyone's, she could sense their disagreement with Wurm. She didn't want to recruit the class for a crusade against her, but she was slowly doing it herself. Maybe she wasn't even aware of it. Or maybe she just thought she had the situation under control. Kirsten was only worried about one thing. That everyone would involuntarily place her at the forefront of the expedition. She wanted to avoid it. But for now, she didn't know how. She hoped the situation would develop differently, and she was already looking forward to spending the afternoon with Belinda.

„Kirsten! Kirsten!" Emie poked her from behind.

„I liked it. I know what you were trying to say," she smiled.

Finally, time returned to its usual course, and the hour passed more peacefully. Everyone wished it would end soon. In the remaining minutes, Kirsten locked herself in her subconscious with a sense of lethargy. She wasn't in a bad mood about the class. She had written the essay as well as she could. She would keep it with her other papers at home and occasionally read it in the red house at the lake. Wurm wasn't her biggest problem, even if Kirsten wished she were.

She didn't have negative thoughts in her head. Whenever they came to her, her „positive thoughts" light would go on, signaling that it was time to think about something positive. Many times, it was during these moments that she came up with an interesting refrain for a song, or she would mentally compose a piece.

The bell rang, and Kirsten blinked as if awakening from a dream. She could already see Angela coming towards her peripherally.

„Why didn't you say anything to her? After all, she's nursing her old maid and old bachelor complexes on you! Next time, I'll stand up and say what I think. She won't say anything to me. She likes to attend the parties our family throws. Money has its power. If you had it, you would understand my words. But you don't. So, you'll have to find another solution before Wurm completely crushes you. But I'm disappointed in how weak you are. I hope it won't affect our competition, because you'll really mess up behind that piano. Pull yourself together, you're capable of it! Otherwise, I wouldn't waste my time with you now. You know, I'd like to open you up with a can opener and pick out those tasty morsels that you're hiding so stubbornly," Angela tried to extract some emotions from Kirsten.

„And would it be okay with you if you only won over Wurm because of money? Wealth? You wouldn't really win. It wouldn't matter whose words they came from. You would be inconsequential. And one day, if the wealth disappeared, the bubble around you would burst too. And you wouldn't be prepared for that kind of life," Kirsten retorted.

„First of all, no, money won't disappear. I'll always be rich. We have so much of it. Just imagine. And secondly, yes. It wouldn't matter how I won. The important thing is that I would win. That's why you won't win over me, for example. You lack the element of money power. Based on that, I make my decisions. It gives me a sense of security," Angela smiled.

On the contrary, Kirsten saw insecurity in money. That one day she wouldn‘t know if she was looking at the real world. If everything and everyone around her weren‘t just a parallel dimension that differed from the reality in which everyone else lived. In the end, she saw Angela living like this. Completely detached from this reality. And she didn‘t even know how many friendships, experiences, smiles, and relationships she was missing out on and had missed out on. And this fact horrified Kirsten. She pitied Angela. She must have different values that she gained through her wealth. But Kirsten didn‘t see any of them. She couldn‘t see anything valuable in Angela‘s life. That‘s why she was afraid to enter this kind of life.

„Well, in any case, I‘m curious to see how the situation with Wurm develops. I‘m enjoying myself. If you need my help, just let me know. Whether Wurm wins over you, or you over her, for me, both situations will be a victory," Angela smiled and suddenly stood up. She winked at Kirsten and went after her friends. As soon as she joined them, they were waiting for Angela to reveal the topic of their conversation. However, she just waved her hand and seemingly changed the subject. Kirsten knew that Angela wasn‘t superficial enough to gossip about someone or demean others in front of them. She was a lady who valued her intelligence and position. She didn‘t want to stoop to the level of a gossiping market lady. Instead, she forced the victim to demean herself with her actions. What bothered her more, though, was that she didn‘t pour water, but oil into the imaginary conflict with Wurm. She felt that she couldn‘t win this battle alone.

Chapter 5

- AGREEMENT -

The car stopped in front of a large iron gate. A villa with a magnificent view of Edwood stood atop the hill. The gate slowly opened, and they entered. The driveway lined with white pebbles was bordered by neatly mowed lawn, with tastefully placed trees nearby. On the right side, there was a small pond with a bench, and on the left side, a meadow and an orchard. At first glance, it was clear that the owner was willing to pay extra for any beauty that could represent his successes in this garden. They passed by a fountain and turned towards the house. They stopped right in front of the main entrance. Kirsten got out of the car, and under her feet, she felt the crunch of fine white gravel. The garden was quiet. The sun was shining through the trees, not a single leaf moved. She felt comfortable in this place. She looked around and saw numerous elements and inspirations that could complement her own garden at home. However, all this beauty seemed purposeless to her, soulless, with strict instructions. Everything had its place here. She remembered the red house by the lake. She felt a sudden urge to play the piano.

„I'll just grab a few things, and we can leave. Now you know where I live. You can come visit me anytime. I left your name at the gate," Adam finished, and he started walking up the white stairs towards the large wooden entrance doors, which were dark in color.

„Okay, sounds good. If I run out of sugar or vinegar, I'll come around," she smiled.

Adam stopped on the stairs and looked at her. „Was that a hint of a joke from the mysterious Kirsten?" he raised an eyebrow in surprise.

„Come on, I want to show you something," he took her hand. This time, it was her turn to raise an eyebrow. He led her through the splendor and wealth. It felt like a privilege. Not many teenagers would get to go beyond the doors of this house.

However, even without the gate and the fountain, Adam was a boy who stood for friendship. Kirsten felt like he wanted to rid himself of this world. As if it was a burden to him. They lived in a similar environment with Angela, but Adam never identified with it. It was like a small coat that weighed on him at every seam. He wanted to put on a loose sweater that wouldn‘t hinder his movement.

They walked past stone pillars. The architecture, walls, columns, and furniture were all coordinated in white. Everything was clean and tidy. Kirsten felt like she was in a museum. Adam opened another wooden door. In front of them was a grand entrance hall. Prosperity in every corner, a large bouquet of flowers in the middle. Stairs lined the sides, leading up to the next floor. Sunlight streamed through the glass ceiling. Its rays passed through the crystal chandelier and refracted on the numerous sparkling diamonds scattered throughout the room. This sight must have impressed anyone, and it certainly impressed Kirsten. The opulence she had seen so far was in contrast to what Adam carried inside him. The villa exuded a sense of superiority. Kirsten again felt a sense of artificiality and excessive linearity. As if she had overeaten the most delicious ice cream. She stood there in a white blouse, blue jeans, and brown riding boots. Her hair was loose and cascaded over her shoulders. Her face exuded calmness and humility. When Adam looked at her, he felt that she had brought freshness, color, and vitality to this villa. She was like a sprinkle on a cake. A frame in the picture.

They entered the adjacent room. It was slightly smaller, but it didn‘t look much more modest than its larger sister. Opposite stood a stone fireplace, and on the right were large windows with curtains. The kind you would see in historical movies, perhaps five meters tall. In the middle was a comfortable seating arrangement, of course, in white, and a massive table. And in the corner... a piano. It was enormous. Adam stopped and let go of Kirsten‘s hand. Her knees buckled. She opened her mouth wide like a little child seeing an elephant or a large double-scoop ice cream cone in a cone.

„Oh my goodness! You never told me you had something so amazing here! It‘s beautiful! I‘m at a loss for words," she laughed.

„I wanted to surprise you. And I wanted to see your reaction," Adam continued to chuckle.

„Well, you certainly succeeded. It‘s gorgeous," Kirsten replied, running her hand over it. She treated it like her child. Adam could swear there was some kind of connection between them.

It‘s beautiful. But... it‘s just for decoration. My parents forced me to take piano lessons. You know how it feels when you have to do something but you don‘t want to. Something stuck with me, of course, but I‘m not blaming you for it. Well, nobody does," he chuckled, and Kirsten shyly denied.

„His parents have it more for the show than for music. It impresses everyone. It looks like a parked Cadillac in the living room," he continued, examining the piano as if it were just another piece of furniture.

„Well, it is," she agreed, and walked over to the chair that was geometrically positioned in front of the piano, as if waiting for someone‘s hands to give it meaning in time and space. She looked at it with interest. It gleamed all over the surface. It looked like every pianist‘s dream. It radiated incredible power. A majestic colossus ready to serve its master. She was fascinated by it. Adam smiled. He knew that both of them were slowly approaching the inevitable moment. He leaned against the couch and watched what would happen.

Kirsten approached the chair. She stood in front of it, but didn‘t sit down yet. She wanted to savor every second. An airport spread out before her. Ready for any hands that would land on it and bring forth the notes.

„May I..." Kirsten asked Adam, but the question sounded more like a fulfilled desire and a thank you.

„Can you? You must," Adam laughed. „May I?" He gestured with an open palm towards the piano.

She sat on the chair. Adjusted the height and tested the pedals. She was starting to get a sense of how the great virtuosos must feel. Just sitting at such a piano would make an ordinary person feel like a promising pianist.

Kirsten didn‘t consider herself a prodigy or a genius, just someone who loved music. The piano gave her the opportunity to express herself emotionally. To sort through all the scattered and jumbled thoughts in herself and arrange them neatly in order. When she needed to concentrate or ponder something, she played. She felt hypnotized while playing, with a clear mind. She gently placed her fingers on the keys. Slowly, she began to play one of her favorite pieces. It sounded like a newly lit fire crackling and coming to life. Gradually enveloping the logs with flames and covering the whole room with warmth and radiance. The music reverberated through the walls and permeated the entire house like a summer mist in a forest.

The piano was truly tuned perfectly. Just like Kirsten. She glided over the keys, completely absorbed in her music. Adam sat down on the couch and leaned back. The notes pressed into him entirely. They filled him with a sense of joy and serenity. He liked the composition. It was like Kirsten - calm, occasionally dynamic, occasionally relaxed, and he never knew what note would come next. Perfect harmony. Upright like a candle on an altar with a flame burning inside, driving her hands. Adam looked at her from the side. Her face was slack, as if in a trance. Her mouth slightly open, her eyes focused... Although the room was filled with furniture, flowers, and decorations, at that moment there was only Kirsten and the piano in it. He had never seen her play live by herself before. Only during rehearsals, where it felt like an obligation. Only now did he realize that he didn't really know her. She had never opened up to him like this before, never seen so much emotion and passion flowing from her. It was through this moment and the composition that he gradually got to know who she really was. He saw her exposed and vulnerable. No mask. He saw into her inner self. Suddenly Kirsten quickly ran across the keys and laughed. She slowed down the tempo and the piano gradually fell silent. She continued in these musical pirouettes, clearly enjoying herself. Adam settled in more comfortably and noticed the housekeeper at the door. She stood there with a cloth in her hand, in a similar trance as Adam on the couch. From her face, he could tell that she had never experienced this before. Such a performance was probably unheard of here. Adam was amused. They were all part of a small informal concert. He gazed at Kirsten. He would love to hear her like this in a hall full of people and excellent acoustics. That would be a musical treat.

Kirsten picked up the pace and experienced every beat. She played for only a few minutes, but Adam knew he could listen to her compositions for hours. He felt good. In the end, she snapped out of her trance and looked at Adam, smiling from ear to ear. She looked like a little child on Christmas. He had never seen her like this before. Due to whatever she had gone through in the past months, she had been lost in thought at school all the time, and Adam had no idea what was on her mind. But it must have been something big that she couldn‘t handle on her own. But now she was the real Kirsten. For a moment, the music drove away all the bad demons, consuming thoughts, and memories. She simply played and played. The room turned into an amphitheater. Everything was saturated with music. Adam would swear that the flowers on the table had started to bloom.

Suddenly, silence fell. Kirsten finished playing and slowly lifted her fingers off the keys. She kept looking at them. She ran her index finger over their surface. It seemed like she wanted to embrace the piano.

„If you like it, you can play it every day if you want," Adam tried to comfort her.

„The piano is fabulous. Perfect. But almost too perfect. I don‘t feel like myself when I play it. It‘s like receiving a gift that I don‘t deserve. I know that one day we could become one soul with this piano. But I would like to try different pianos first, to understand them. To know the differences in playing, the tones. To find out which one I like the most. I can say right now that it‘s definitely this one. But if you had only met one girl so far, me, could you say that I‘m the most beautiful?" Kirsten tried to explain to Adam how she felt.

„Yes, I knew that from the moment I first met you, and I still know it now," Adam smiled.

Kirsten raised an eyebrow. Her question was rhetorical. She didn‘t expect an answer. She also scolded herself a little for choosing such an example. She didn‘t want to delve deeper into her feelings and emotions towards Adam. She knew that they weren‘t „compatible" yet. And she didn‘t want to appear as someone who is with Adam only because of his status. She needed to decide how her life would continue now. She didn‘t want to unnecessarily provoke Adam. She valued their friendship, which was more than just love for now.

„I‘ll go upstairs for my stuff and we are ready to go," Adam got up from his chair and rushed to the hall. Kirsten straightened her back and started playing a slow melody softly to herself. At that moment, the doors on the other side opened and Adam‘s mother entered the room.

Kirsten stood next to the piano. „Hello, Mrs. Mackenzie," she greeted timidly, bowed her head and ran her fingers through her thick hair.

„Hello. You must be Kirsten. I just had to hear that beautiful piece and based on Adam's words, I guessed it must be you. You're Kirsten, right?" She asked kindly but also with a hint of scrutiny.

„Yes, I am," Kirsten replied, looking Mrs. Mackenzie straight in the eyes.

„But it's not about the music that I came to talk to you. I have something on my mind. I really hope you'll understand. It's not easy for me to say this, and I can't influence how you'll react. I know that you and Adam are close. He talks about you every day," she changed the tone of her voice, but still appeared calm.

She holds the trump cards not Mrs. Mackenzie, but Kirsten. Some decisions inside were not yet matured. She couldn't yet judge whether she would gain with them or lose them. Mrs. Mackenzie looked into Kirsten's eyes and pitied her. Several people will be unhappy just because of the money. And just to make many more people happy. And they won't even know about it. This is what a sacrifice would look like if it materialized into flesh and bones. She hoped the deal would close soon. Until then, she would still be tormented by guilt. On the other hand, she wondered at the calmness with which Kirsten accepted this request. As if she had made similar decisions in her life several times before. She felt like she wasn't talking to a teenager, but to a mature woman who understood the power of money.

„Thank you!" Mrs. Mackenzie breathed a sigh of relief. They heard footsteps on the stairs. Adam rushed into the room and slowed down. He was surprised to see Kirsten with his mom.

„Well, I see you've already met," Adam said timidly.

„Yes. I couldn't resist the piano, have fun," Mrs. Mackenzie smiled and slowly left the room.

„I'm heading to the factory then. I don't know when I'll be back. I'll settle accounts with Angela and give you a call," Adam said to his mom and turned to Kirsten.

„Is everything okay?" Adam asked.

„Everything's fine," she replied.

Chapter 6

- SKELETONS -

Kirsten looked down from above through the glass panel at the workers processing wood in the hall below. Dust was everywhere, and the work was demanding. She couldn't blame Adam for feeling weighed down by the burden. Deciding the fate of so many hardworking people carried a great deal of responsibility. He wasn't yet an adult, so Mrs. Mackenzie made all the decisions with him. After losing his father, he became the man of the house. Kirsten walked around the office, and her gaze stopped at the carved furniture on the shelf. They were small chairs for dolls, dollhouse furnishings. She picked up a bed. The wood was smoothly finished and pleasant to the touch. Kirsten immediately went back to her childhood room. How much she had wished for such furniture in her dollhouse back then.

„Don't judge me, please - Angela made it," Adam chuckled.

Kirsten raised an eyebrow and looked at Angela.

„Well, what? Do I have to be constantly portrayed as that heartless and emotionless witch? It's my hobby. Other millionaires collect stamps, breed horses. Boring and awkward. It's fascinating how you can materialize perfection. Bring out what's hidden in you. Touch it. See it the way others see it on you," she retorted, taking the small wooden bed from Kirsten's hands.

„Angela, you know this diagnosis has its number? These are not your children, but pieces of carved wood," Adam looked at Angela with a raised eyebrow.

Kirsten took the bed, and as Angela watched, she placed it in its place silently. She examined those beautiful pieces of miniature furniture in awe. She hadn't expected Angela to have this side to her. She heightened her attention. What else was she missing?

„A few more minutes, and we can go," he said from the table, still watching the screen with numbers.

Angela sat a few meters away, focused on her screen. „I don‘t know if it will be ready in a few minutes. We have to finish that report if we want to provide all the documents for that investment," she said dryly.

„Well, I didn‘t ask for this factory. I didn‘t have a choice. I was simply born into it. Into a family that owned the factory. And now I feel like the factory owns me. It stands with me with every decision I make, watching over me. I have no life. Just this factory," Adam said in a frustrated tone.

„You suffer because you‘re too soft and compassionate. See it as a job that puts food on the table and cars in the garage. And you‘ll see it in a more positive light," Angela smiled.

„I‘m not a robot like you. You know... That‘s the difference between us. I still have red blood flowing in my veins. Yours is green. You‘re intoxicated by money like it‘s some kind of drug," Adam continued in a bitter tone.

„Well, you have no right to talk about drugs," Angela retorted dryly.

Kirsten stood surprised beside them, feeling like she had no right to interrupt the conversation. Adam glanced at Kirsten with a hint of annoyance, but she knew that look was intended for Angela.

„What? You didn‘t know? Adam went through rehab. He probably didn‘t tell you..." Angela added with a more serious tone.

„So what? Should I have mentioned it casually? Kirsten, you look really good today. You know, I had a problem before, went through treatment, and now I‘m clean. I don‘t plan to go back to it, and that phase is behind me," Adam replied measuredly to Angela.

„That‘s fine. I have no right to judge anyone. Everyone has the right to do what they see fit with their body and life. It‘s admirable that you‘ve managed it and were able to close that door behind you," Kirsten replied and gave Adam a fleeting smile.

„Admirable? The admirable ones are those who never started in the first place," Angela retorted, stopping her data entry into the computer.

„We can cheer for Adam and commend him for it. I don‘t deny that. But he‘s a hero in second place. The stronger ones who never started are the real heroes. What‘s worse is that these people don‘t get attention. You shout to the crowd that you‘ve never done drugs, and the crowd barely responds with a whisper that they don‘t care."

And when you say that you used drugs and ended up clean, everyone applauds you. It should be the other way around. How would people look at someone who takes drugs every day? They would turn away...

The line of emotions towards such people is actually a sine wave. But in the case of someone who has never used drugs, the line is... well, just a line. You feel the same emotions towards such a person all the time. And that‘s the problem. The line is boring. And the sine wave has nice curves. It‘s more appealing. That‘s why, at least in my eyes, the hero will be the one who has never used drugs or drank alcohol. And the one who quit comes second. Of course, you can only judge such people if you haven‘t done the same. Solving a problem by creating another problem is schizophrenic masochism. Expecting support from family and loved ones is inconsiderate and superficial. Support is a precious gift and one should not rely on it. Force yourself to receive it. It‘s a gift. We should receive it when we value ourselves. What does the family have to support you for? After all, such a person doesn‘t stand alone! Support from family should be given only when one takes the first step themselves. And that applies to all life situations.

I have found myself in various difficult situations. Just like many others out there. And no one knows about it. Not that I‘m hiding it, but I was able to deal with it myself and in a short time. I didn‘t torment anyone with my feelings. I can also live with myself, because I value myself. When you hate yourself, you will continue to harm yourself. And no family support will help with that. I don‘t want to harm myself. I want to move forward as fast as I can. Because life is really short. I won‘t stand in one place and wait for someone to push me. And I won‘t risk that there won‘t be anyone to do it. And I‘ll die two steps from where I was born. Life is not fair to anyone. And that‘s what‘s fair about it!“ Angela finished and looked back at her computer.

„I agree with you. Just don‘t run so fast that you end up alone in the middle of an empty field. But yes, I didn‘t value myself either. And I went for treatment only when my mother found out about it. I was hurting myself and it didn‘t even hurt. But it hurt when I hurt her. And the lost time when I wasn‘t with her was punishment enough for me. You‘re enjoying your dominance now.“

„If you didn‘t have money, you would be quiet in a corner and who knows if you would be able to do anything,“ Adam replied, and Angela had an immediate response ready.

„But I do have the money! Period. I will be here without you, but you won‘t be here without me,“ Angela retorted.

„Are you threatening me? You‘re not that irresponsible. Emotions are secondary to you. That‘s why I will remain calm,“ Adam added in a composed voice. Kirsten remained silent the whole time, as if waiting to see how the situation would unfold. As if she had a backup plan prepared.

Adam got up from the table. „We will continue tomorrow. You can perhaps dig up some more skeletons from the closet. Your own, for a change,“ he said, put on his coat, and slammed the door behind him.

„Well, then. Shall I make you some tea? He probably won‘t be in the mood for anyone now. He slammed the door right in your face,“ Angela replied and conjured up a smile on her tired face.

„That must be love. Italian-style. Or like in a soap opera. But if you two are Maria and Juan, searching for 256 parts of each other‘s path, then I must be the witch who ruins it all for you, and for whom the soap opera actually has so many episodes,“ she laughed.

„You know how witches end up in such soap operas, right? And that in the end, Maria and Juan stand together in the middle of the hacienda, happy and rich?“ Kirsten added sarcastically.

„I know. But then you also know that one day you‘ll catch that witch with your Juan, when she‘s having a weak moment? When she takes advantage of it and grins at the camera,“ Angela added.

„We‘ll see each other at rehearsal tomorrow,“ Kirsten said calmly and closed the door behind her.

Chapter 7

- STARS -

She pulled into the parking lot. There were already several cars parked there, as always at this time. Couples seeking some privacy. From the top of the cliff, Edwood offered a panoramic view. The city shone in the midst of the forest and rocks, as if nature itself held it in the palm of its hand. This place was a sanctuary for abandoned and kindred souls at the same time. Nobody wasted time here drinking alcohol or making noise. Only those who wanted to escape from these things and everyday life came here for a moment. This place was like the back pew in the local church. Always reserved and occupied. Occupied by someone who didn't want to be seen, but wanted to be there.

She got out of the car and slammed the door. The sound echoed through the surrounding woods. As she walked past the car, the fine pebbles under her leather-soled boots made a soothing, crunching sound. She climbed onto the bed of her pickup truck. She tossed a soft sleeping bag onto it and put another one, still wrapped, under her head. She turned around and looked at the stars. That's probably how it looks in her head right now. Countless thoughts lost in space. Thousands of tiny lights in the pitch-black darkness forming patterns together, which she didn't understand yet. She reminisced about past events. She felt like a piano out of tune... She had so many possibilities within reach, yet she was afraid to reach out. Up here, alone, she lay down to mature like the last raspberry on the bush. That's how she felt. As if all the others had already ripened and she was the last one left. The one who ripens later. And will shine alone in the background of green leaves. The one that will put a smile on someone's face when tasted and remind them of the days that have passed. She hoped she would be sweet and tasty for anyone who tasted her. She felt she was changing and that change was necessary, but at the same time she wanted to remain the same person she saw in the mirror every day. And that was a very demanding task. She knew she couldn't complete this transformation on her own. That she would need those closest to her to create a mold around her, into which she would bake into a golden shape and not overflow into an unattractive form.

Kirsten looked at the stars and thought about everyone who mattered to her. She saw them against the dark sky, shining even on a sunny day. They were her motivation and inspiration, perhaps without even knowing it. Including Angela. Only now did she realize that something only has value until it‘s obtained. And once it‘s obtained, it loses its value in an instant and becomes ordinary. Whether it‘s something tangible or even love. And what had the most value for Kirsten was something she was currently losing. Life slipping through her fingers like sand, and she couldn‘t hold onto it. However, she had come to understand one thing. She won‘t be rich when she has everything. But when she doesn‘t need everything. Maybe it‘s a good thing that so much of life is slipping through her fingers now. Those are probably the insignificant parts she can live without, and in the end, she will be left with a few grains that she will close in her fist. And she will hold her life tightly in her hands.

Another car parked next to her. She didn‘t turn around. The doors opened and immediately slammed shut. Footsteps approached her.

„Hi! I was expecting you to be here. Actually, I was hoping for it," Kirsten raised herself up and spotted Adam leaning against his car, watching Edwood.

„Hi! You know all my hideouts. Were you in the red house too?"

„No, this was my first choice. If I would‘t find you, I wouldn‘t have declined solitude either. We must know how to be alone with ourselves. If we can‘t, something is very wrong, right? When they can‘t stand their own consciousness and conscience," Adam looked at Kirsten and squinted his eyes.

„Get in," Kirsten made some space on the sleeping bag and folded her arm behind her head. Adam jumped in beside her and lay down. They both watched at the same dark sky full of stars.

„I didn‘t want you to see me like that. I‘m sorry. It must have been awkward to be alone with Angela. I exploded and was rude. Up there in the office. I don‘t know how far it will go. And how long it will last. Everything is so complicated. If someone thinks that a lot of money simplifies life, they don‘t know how money can hurt. Simplify the life? Rather complicate it. Our family is wealthy and still has problems. And above all, responsibility. It‘s very binding. I feel like I‘m on a leash. And money is my master. I go wherever it pulls me. I‘m like an ordinary dog. I have a master who will take care of me. His shine blinded my vision.“

„He gave me a roof, food, and toys for it,“ Adam started talking as if he were alone, just speaking into the wind.

„Be glad you don‘t know too much about money. And be glad you don‘t have too much of it. You‘re a wonderful person even without it. I know few people who have remained true to themselves even after becoming wealthy. Stay as you are. People get more benefit from you this way than they would from your money. On the contrary, I feel bad for how I‘m treating you. But believe me, there are reasons for it. I really wish you would be patient. A lot of things will change soon. Then I‘ll explain it to you,“ Adam apologized for his coldness. She remembered her conversation with Mrs. Mackenzie, and in a corner of her soul, she was grateful for this situation. She was going through a complicated period, and this relationship with Adam suited her. She needed someone experienced with a cool head whom she could rely on. A friend. The best one.

„You haven‘t done anything you would regret later. We have mouths to speak what we want, not what we don‘t want. I don‘t want it to seem like I‘m demanding your attention. Your friendship means a lot to me. I don‘t want to change anything, so be at ease,“ she spoke without taking her eyes off the sky. She didn‘t even blink.

She understood why Angela was so reserved towards her. She was fighting with her for Adam. She wanted a trophy. Him and her. She felt, she had him within reach. And knowing Angela, she relied on money winning in the end, and Adam would stand by her side. Kirsten felt sorry for Adam. She also wanted to regain her position as the favorite, which she now shared with Angela. Kirsten would like to return it to her, but she had to do it personally and publicly. This fact annoyed her. She just wanted to be friendly and have a few friends. But she ended up with more labels than she expected. Others labeled her without her desiring it. And that bothered Angela. After all, Angela was just one and only original!

ഗ

„Have you ever thought about what kind of person you would be if your family wasn‘t wealthy? Would you be someone else?“ Kirsten asked timidly, still looking at the stars.

„You know... the most depressing thing about it is that I don‘t know. I was born into wealth, and it shaped me into who I am today. I lost a whole other life. The one where you have emotions and feelings untainted by banknotes locked in a safe. Where you experience honesty.“

„May your days be good or bad, but they are honest. You don‘t have to distinguish truth from lies or falsehood. It offends me when I am just a transparent statue that everyone talks to. They look into my eyes, but I can see that their gaze goes beyond me. To where the wall is covered with banknotes. And against this background, I am just a figure made of green pieces of paper. Those people don‘t talk to me, but to the money. They don‘t want something from me, but from them. When you talk to someone, you focus only on what you want to say. When I talk to someone, it‘s communication full of obscure turns. You never know what lies behind the nearest one. I literally have to wave in front of people‘s eyes to make them not talk to my money, but to me,“ he concluded and fell silent for a moment.

„I think the one who becomes richer during life will always be richer than me. They will have something that I will never have. Life experiences from before they got rich. And that can‘t be bought. They can compare two worlds. It‘s as if half of my brain is missing. Or as if it‘s there, but I‘ve never used it. I feel it there like a piece of stone. If I used it, I would definitely be a different person,“ he added and ran his hand through his hair.

„I‘m afraid of that too. That I will lose my face. That one day I will look in the mirror and someone else will be standing there. Or I will remain the same, but others will see someone else,“ Kirsten pondered.

„You? You will always be our Kirsten,“ Adam turned around and smiled in the darkness. „You‘re not rich like our family. But you‘re wealthier. Trust me. I already feel a strong personality in you. You‘re an amazing person! Since I‘ve known you, you‘ve always been that way. And you still are,“ he added and looked back at the stars.

„I don‘t want all the beautiful things around me to suddenly disappear. The ordinary, mundane life that I love. Just spreading butter on a slice of bread while looking out the window at our lake. Or moments like this. I know I‘ll gradually lose them. I‘m trying to come to terms with it in advance. Explain it to myself. Accept the fate that will come,“ Kirsten finished speaking and didn‘t expect a response from Adam. It was as if she was comforting herself.

„Do you mean with age? Yes, everything will pass eventually. Although you can spread that slice of bread anywhere and anytime you want. The state of your mind is what matters. And in your mind, you can stay as long as you want. Be with whoever you want, wherever you want, and how you want. That's something no one can take away from you. It shouldn't be nostalgia. That's sad."

„They are supposed to be memories. Ones that will be like warm icing on a pudding. Spreading all over the glass and bringing a smile to your face. And this feeling will spread within you every time you stand by the window and remember how you spread that slice decades ago in a completely different house, in a completely different place. And you will be standing there again. We may have a lot of money, but for me, the greatest wealth is experience, adventure, and knowledge. No one can steal that from me. I won't lose them even in the stock market. Only death can take them away," Adam stared at the stars, as if trying to determine when his time would come.

„In your next life, you will experience many new things. How do you know right now that they won't be pleasant? How do you know that you're not about to encounter something beautiful right now..." Adam didn't have a chance to finish his sentence before Kirsten interrupted him: „Because we are here together! I don't need anything more right now. I'm not losing anything, I'm gaining," she calmly but firmly replied.

„With time, I'll get used to the new things that come. They will make me a different person. I'll move on to something else. But I'm afraid of going too far. I want to stay on the ground. In this world. I don't want to become someone else for others," Kirsten whispered.

„What if you don't become a different person, but a new one? Who people will love just as much, if not more? I understand what you're trying to say. When I fly in business class, I can't imagine ever flying cramped with others again. And I'm not saying this as a snob. It's just that my standard of living has gone up. And yes, I'm no longer compatible with the lives of ordinary people. But I don't have to be. On this new level, new opportunities have opened up for me. Opportunities to change the world. When I don't have to cook and clean at home, but can focus on my investments, projects. When I can influence many people. And I try to do it in a way that makes those people happier. That's why I don't fall into depression over not being in a good enough economic class," Adam smiled.

„The same will happen with your life when you move to the city, start working, maybe even start a business. Yes. Many things will change soon,“ Adam punctuated the conversation with a tone of voice.

Kirsten listened and felt that this conversation was calming her. They were lying there together in the middle of the night, and the voices around them were filling the silence with a similar sense of mystery.

„I wanted to be alone, but you convinced me that I didn‘t actually want to be,“ Kirsten smiled.

„Do you have a wish that I could fulfill for you, something that money can‘t buy?“ She turned to Adam.

„I do, but I can‘t say it out loud, because it won‘t come true,“ he smiled and kept looking at the sky.

In the darkness, Kirsten felt Adam‘s hand and slipped hers into his. Adam squeezed it in agreement. Neither of them moved. They fell silent, looking at the dark sky and the stars. They absorbed together the atmosphere they had just created. Both knew that such moments don‘t repeat themselves and that this one was unique. There was no need for more words. They already felt like one soul. In their hearts, they danced and contemplated each other. At the same time, doubts and fears about what awaited them mingled with these thoughts. They wanted to behave responsibly so that no one around them would suffer. That night, some dreams came alive and some desires died, so that they could rise again later. This night was destined not to end. It would linger in their minds until it was replaced by another, even more beautiful one.

„You know, I have enough money to lead a completely ordinary life. If I lived like many others here in Edwood, it would certainly be enough for me for a lifetime. If I had a regular job, I would definitely not be in poverty. Many times I‘ve thought about running away from everything and simply starting a new life. Somewhere where they don‘t know me. And experience what all normal people experience. Real life. Crazy, isn‘t it? Almost anyone would trade places with me. And I would trade places with almost anyone. I need to get out of here. At least for a moment. Actually, I don‘t know how long for. To be someone like you. To have my life firmly in my hands. To know how to experience emotions. Not just survive them. When a child has a few coins in their hand, they know exactly what to buy. And when they buy that gum or ice cream, they truly enjoy it. Give a child a banknote, and suddenly they won‘t know what to buy first. They'll buy useless things that will bore them and pile up. Rich people simply have the misfortune that it's very difficult for them to create any emotion. A homeless person is satisfied with fresh bread. A wealthy person needs even the tenth car in the garage. And when you add a little fantasy, the intelligence of a rocking horse, you have a simple recipe for making tabloid headlines or an empty liquor cabinet at home in the office."

„Tell me, do you think we will ever be able to be together? Without anyone suffering because of us?" Kirsten interrupted Adam and turned to her side. She propped her cheek on her hand, as if waiting for an engaged response.

Adam didn't take his eyes off the sky and calmly replied, „I don't know, it's written in the stars."

Chapter 8

- QUESTION -

Angela sat in the courtyard at a wooden table, having lunch with two friends. Kirsten had been attending school for a few weeks now, and it seemed like the school had gotten used to her, or rather, hadn‘t even noticed her. Angela didn‘t know that Kirsten had been observing the details of her new life all along. She noticed people, analyzed situations, and familiarized herself with the environment. She didn‘t need any special detective skills to understand who Angela was. Angela was like an open box of chocolates, offering herself with grandiosity and boldness, the exact opposite of Kirsten. That‘s why Kirsten knew she would have answers for her, unlike many others.

She approached Angela and said, „Hi, I need some advice," looking at Angela calmly. Angela looked back at her, and there was no sign of surprise on her face. Maybe she was expecting it.

„Well, not many people ask me for advice, especially those who barely know me. Most people just kiss up to me, their knees buckle in front of me. But you seem bold. Are you often this spontaneous? You walk with confidence. That‘s not a sign of maturity and adulthood," Angela smiled.

„Yeah, I guess I‘m acting like a lovesick teenager now," Kirsten pondered aloud.

„That‘s all of us. Sandra, are you a lovesick teenager too?" Angela turned to the girl next to her.

Sandra understood the game Angela was playing, „Sure! Forever in puberty, forever in love," she laughed.

„I don‘t think so Kirsten," Angela dismissed this fleeting excuse.

„I expected you to want to join us and share lunch together. Slowly worm your way into my presence and take a piece of my cake. Be a part of my world. Many people want that. Too bad you didn‘t take the tasty bait. I still don‘t have you hooked."

„Well, I guess you don‘t see the value in material things. At least I know where our battleground is now. So I won‘t waste my energy on unnecessary fronts. But I admit that you asked for the most precious thing I can give. Go on," Angela replied, looking Kirsten straight in the eyes.

„You've experienced a lot, and I know you have an answer to my question. I would need to know how a person can remain human and down-to-earth even after their bank account grows by millions," Kirsten presented her question as if she and Angela had known each other for eternity.

„I'll try not to take this question as a provocation. You're not that primitive to try to insult me like this. I don't know why you're interested in this particular question. If you're serious, then you have my attention. I'll answer it when the time comes. I don't think you'll understand the answer right now," Angela replied in a serious tone, and at that moment, the bell rang. She got up and walked silently with her friends from the courtyard to the classroom. Kirsten stayed there among the last ones standing. She knew that besides one answer, she would also learn another one that Angela wouldn't have to say out loud. Are they equals, or does Angela simply see her as an inexperienced child wandering in the room, unable to open the door?

Chapter 9

- MRS. MILLER -

Kirsten walked down the hallway, tucking her hair behind her ears and looking forward to her audition. She had put her long brown hair in a braid to keep it out of the way while playing, dressed in a grey shirt and jeans. She mentally went over the keys with her fingers, the abstract music relaxing her and filling her with zest for life. If anyone at school could match her talent, it was Angela. Like other children of the wealthy, Kirsten had been taking piano lessons since a young age, and of course, she had the best grand piano money could buy at home.

„Hello Kirsten," greeted Mrs. Miller. Today at two o'clock, but you won't forget that, I'm sure. I'm looking forward to seeing you. Both of you," she added with a smile. Kirsten liked Mrs. Miller's natural demeanor. She had lived her whole life with music, and her face and soul expressed how it had enriched her. Students often heard her playing in the auditorium even in the early morning hours when they were still groggy. She played with closed eyes in the dim light. She was a local legend and added to the school's cultural heritage. Kirsten looked up to her with respect and admiration.

„Yeah, we're practicing today. I'll be there. Although I can't imagine it with Angela," Kirsten said, raising her eyebrow in concern.

„Why? You're both really good. As a teacher, I can't complain about anything. Such exceptional talents at one school! And specifically at the one where I teach piano? I hope you'll find a way to work together. At least for the competition," she smiled. Mrs. Miller was thrilled that their school had a real chance of winning the national competition this year. She was more nervous than Kirsten and Angela combined. The two of them hadn't realized it yet. They were competing against each other. And Mrs. Miller hoped that they would join forces and compete against other schools, not against each other. Their joint performance was truly unique. In her years of experience, life, and teaching, she had encountered various talented students and victories. But what she was experiencing with Kirsten and Angela was incomparable to anything from the past. It was a gift for her. Their joint performance and friendly rivalry fascinated her.

She had never experienced such energy while playing the piano. When they practiced, tears often filled her eyes, as she experienced emotions such as fear and sadness. She had entered them both into the nationwide competition. It wasn't just about winning for herself. She wanted to share this budding miracle with others.

Kirsten played from the heart, losing track of time and space during her performance. Angela complemented her with her flawless, almost robotic perfection, akin to artificial intelligence. As she listened to both of them, she couldn't decide which performance was better. Each was perfect in its own way. She didn't mind their competition, as it was the spice that made their music an otherworldly experience. She didn't want to change that. On the contrary, she let them grow and wanted to be surprised by how far their musical relationship would go.

ꕥ

Angela trained hard mainly because of Kirsten. She admitted that Kirsten was her motivation. There weren't many students at school who could compete with her. Angela needed nourishment for her ego. She didn't want to be average, but better than the best. She saw many mediocre lives around her, which she despised. She wanted to be exceptional. Dragging the average behind her. Changing the lives of others, shaping the reality around her, and erasing the everyday banality like an eraser. But Angela was angry that Kirsten wanted the same thing. She just did it differently. Angela was like a draft in a musty pantry. Or rather, a strong wind. Many didn't like it, but she had a great influence in school and the town thanks to her money. She knew that money and power would shape the environment around her into the form she desired. She didn't care what means she used to achieve what she always intended. And money was always the fastest and easiest way.

The competition was approaching, and Kirsten was trying to come to terms with the situation. She thought about Sofia. Each thought softened the situation she found herself in. Mrs. Miller could see that they were both struggling within themselves and against each other. She tried to understand their inner selves and adjust the exams accordingly. And the performance itself. So that they could channel their emotions through the piano. Kirsten wanted to win the competition not only for herself but also for Mrs. Miller. She felt that she needed to fulfill her efforts in her life. For all that she had sacrificed. She herself often said that she would do it again and again, even if it cost her her career. She would exchange it for her parents' lives anytime.

Kirsten knew that playing the piano was not her only talent. There was another pianist before her, a girl named Mrs. Miller, who had won all the regional competitions and was on her way to winning at the national level. It was just a matter of a few months. However, due to her sick parents, Mrs. Miller had to go back home to take care of them. The other pianist eventually won the competition, but with a different teacher. Of course, all the credit was given to her, and nobody remembered Mrs. Miller anymore. She missed out on many opportunities in life and ended up teaching at a school, as if she was stuck in time. She looked at Angela with a smile as she explained something to her about the piano. Kirsten could see in the corner of her eyes and lips that there was still a small piece missing for the smile to be truly genuine. It was like it was stuck at ninety-nine percent. It should have made Kirsten nervous and anxious, but the thought of her winning the competition and stretching her lips into a perfect smile motivated and encouraged her. Maybe something would happen that would bring her and Angela closer together. She walked further down the hallway, relieved that she only had one more class left. She was looking forward to an afternoon in the café.

Chapter 10

- PIANO -

Kirsten parked in the city center parking lot. She got out of the car. Autumn was just starting, and the weather was quite pleasant, in complete contrast to her inner state. The wind blew and carried the scent of summer. As if it was playing with it one last time before covering it with a blanket of leaves. Kirsten stood on the parking lot for a moment. She liked these moments. Everyone was rushing up and down, seeking refuge from the weather in cafes and shops, and no one wanted to talk to the rain on the streets. Kirsten needed exactly what the shops and cafes couldn't give her. The feeling of being flesh and bone. Feeling the cold, feeling the sun on her face. All those „worthless" things that money couldn't buy. She needed to know that there was something between heaven and earth. Something that couldn't be bought. And yet, it evoked more emotions in her than a new handbag or shoes. As she stood there, everyone else hurried to gather those ephemeral possessions that would bring them temporary joy. She knew that there was no difference between having little and having a lot of money. Every need would be satisfied sooner or later, and then a step higher would be taken. So that she could shine again in the distance like a lighthouse for her satisfier. Showing him the direction to take to satisfy her. And she also knew that this road had no end. If all her material dreams, desires, and goals were fulfilled in one second, she would feel emptiness. Is that all? Is that what she lived for? And now what? Double the effort and the results? Until when? Why was she always rushing somewhere? She felt disappointed. And she also realized how much precious time she had wasted. Time that she could have spent with her mom, and that couldn't be bought with any amount of money. On the street, she felt like a snail in an airport departure hall. She didn't believe that anyone besides her had noticed the fragrant breeze.

She saw life passing by in front of her eyes on all those people. For her, as an observer, it was meaningless. She didn't know why so many people rushed somewhere. It was a waste of time. Our lives must look the same way to it. Maybe it sees exactly what we're missing and what it offered us. And we didn't take it from it. She stood there like the last blooming poppy at the end of the field. One decision could now change whether she would ever see Belinda and her café again. She would love to work there forever. She had pleasant memories of moments spent there. Another one of those things that money couldn't buy. She crossed the street. In the distance, she could already see Belinda's Cafeteria. It was all white with large windows. On the covered terrace with three white columns, there were three small tables with chairs. The doors were open, and a bell above the entrance jingled, welcoming every customer. They said it had been hanging there since the first day. Belinda's Cafeteria was a personal matter. Both for Belinda and for the customers. Anyone who spent a few minutes there came back after a few days. To hear the fleeting creak of the floor, the bell on the door, and to see the smiling Belinda. Kirsten sat down on a comfortable chair and, with a cup in her hand, momentarily left everything behind the door.

Kirsten helped Belinda several times a week after school and on weekends. The café was also her personal matter. Even though she hadn't worked there for long, she loved it. It gave her Sofia and a reward that she wanted to use to buy a special gift. She passed by it every day on her way here. And Belinda was also glad to have someone reliable and kind by her side, who had become so perfectly acquainted with the café. They drank hot chocolate or coffee together and talked about their problems and joys. It was like a cheesy script where the writer skimps on the characters and lets them just be friends. And that's why they liked it. It was just... friendship. Kirsten enjoyed being able to talk like this with an older and experienced person.

Mainly now, she needed to gather adult opinions and experiences, and she needed to hear a sober view of the world she lived in. To come to terms with what had recently happened to her. Belinda was glad that her old-fashioned habits were softened by a young soul. She was a widow. Her children had left the town for work and careers. She didn‘t know what would happen to the café when she was no longer around.

Kirsten was one day closer to her coveted new piano for every day she worked at the café. Well, it wasn‘t new. It was older and had an incredible sound. Kirsten hurried along the sidewalk and stopped in front of the display. She had a few minutes left before she needed to bring more coffee beans from the back for Belinda. It stood there in that small display and almost filled the entire space. Surely many hands had played on it. It had survived many joyful and sad moments. It had lived with its owners. It played their lives, their emotions, absorbing their feelings with its keys. And that‘s how it gained a musical soul.

The shop owner didn‘t really want to sell it. That‘s why it was still there. It was more for decoration. But when Kirsten touched its keys for the first time, she immediately knew that she was looking at an exceptional piece of musical instrument. Her fingers sank into the keys like into a fruit jelly, and every tone was like a bite of a juicy peach. Maybe only Kirsten felt it this way. Maybe their souls tuned in together on the right wavelength. She definitely didn‘t want to leave it alone like an orphan or just for decoration. She wanted it to come to life again and please many ears with its tones.

So, she made a deal with the owner to sell it to her. He couldn‘t even set a price. No one was interested in it. Eventually, they agreed on a reasonable sum, and Kirsten would be able to buy it in a few months. Every day of waiting was now like a new note in a composition that was being created. When she writes the last note, a beautiful composition will emerge, bringing a smile to her face. There was another way to get the piano, but she didn‘t want to deprive herself of all these sincere emotions. She wanted the piano to have an immeasurable value for her. The value of memories, imaginations, dreams. She gradually became friends with it and formed a bond that would be necessary for their mutual and perfect harmony. Only then would Kirsten truly feel the music on the piano. She already knew that she had gained feelings that she would have missed out on if she had bought the piano on the first day. And she would have missed out on moments with Belinda. Those were the realities that were worth more to her than any amount of money. It was something that Angela didn‘t understand.

Despite her wealth, she was impoverished in these values. Kirsten was glad she had met her. Even in moments like these, she could make decisions confidently thanks to her. She had nowhere to rush. Now was the time when she was becoming a person. When she was no longer a child and needed to lay a solid foundation for her future life, which she believed would be exceptional. And which she still feared for now.

She looked away from the shop window. She tucked a strand of hair behind her ear and walked past several stores. She passed tables on the terrace and entered inside. On the left side, there was a counter with a cash register, a display case, and cakes. Opposite was a box of cakes that Belinda baked herself. The box was still full, and the cakes were fresh. On the right, there were several tables. A young family sat at one, apparently celebrating something. Two older gentlemen sat at another, explaining something over coffee.

Suddenly, the coffee grinder rattled, and the smell of freshly ground coffee spread through the room. It still looked the same as the day Kirsten met Sofia. It was two weeks before the end of the summer holiday. Sofia was actually the first young person Kirsten met in Edwood. It seemed a bit funny to her because the way they met and Sofia herself, in connection with this town, were exactly the familiar clichés Kirsten had read about in so many books. Suddenly, it didn‘t seem ordinary and dull. It had its charm. Their first meeting was warm and natural. Sofia was an ordinary decent girl. The one who stands on a break in the yard, leaning against the wall and watching what‘s going on. Enjoying her snack calmly and waving to anyone who waves at her. She‘s like soil into which, when we put a kind word or trust, friendship grows. A lifelong friend. Her illness was an unwanted gift. So that someone would finally notice her. As if she was worth noticing and could change someone‘s life. Or maybe both were true.

They met at Belinda‘s. Kirsten was standing at the counter, in front of the large glass windows. Colorful signs of cocktails, sandwich pictures, and whipped cream desserts were shining above her head. When she entered the café, she could order food just by the smell that filled the air. Belinda was behind the counter, addressing everyone by name. People felt really good in the café. Not exceptionally, not uniquely. Just good.

When Kirsten first sat on the brown wooden chair with a checkered cushion, she felt that she would feel fine in this town. If there‘s a café like this here, then there are people who enjoy this atmosphere.

She knew she would feel great with them. Edwood was a prime city for creating big problems. At first, Kirsten felt bored there. Later, she realized it wasn‘t boredom, but peace.

The brown wooden tables with cream tablecloths looked like perfect oases of relaxation. The sun didn‘t shine directly into the café. It always cast an angle, and the surrounding buildings prevented it from shining inside with full intensity. So, the café always looked like sunset or sunrise.

She looked at the counter full of sandwiches, bowls of wrapped fruits and vegetables. Right next to it was a glass cake tower, and behind it, the coffee machine was bubbling. There were tables on the sides. Various objects related to Edwood hung on the walls above them. A wooden block sign that read „Take a bite“, lamps, an old radio. A television with no screen, but a hand-drawn picture. The whole room was decorated in brown shades and exuded a pleasant warmth. A moment frozen in time. A black telephone with a rotary dial and old metal signs depicting advertisements from the 50s and 60s. Kirsten looked around like in a museum. In her hand, she held a cup covered in stickers from different places.

Throughout the time, she thought about Sofia - how they met in the café. About what happened on that completely ordinary day in this completely ordinary town. She looked at the spot where she stood back then. It was her first time in the café, and she was still in line at the counter.

Chapter 11

- GIRLFRIENDS -

„Hi, can I recommend something to you? Is this your first time here?“ Belinda looked interestedly at Kirsten.

„We usually treat every new customer with our delicious fruitcake. It‘s filled with blueberries, raspberries, and strawberries. Topped with forest fruit jelly and whipped cream from our farm. Can I offer you a slice?“ she smiled.

Kirsten laughed, „Well, can you really refuse such a cake? We moved here a few weeks ago.“ She found it endearing how Belinda was winning over new customers. After this experience, she already felt at home here.

„I think I bake excellent cakes. I see that they please both the stomach and the soul,“ Belinda boasted.

„What do you usually do to please your friends?“ Belinda continued the conversation, as Kirsten seemed friendly to her at first sight.

„Well, if playing the piano is comparable to baking cakes...“ Kirsten replied somewhat shyly.

„You bet it is! Did you know that we have a successful piano club at our school? Maybe you could play for us at a performance in the future. Or you could play for us sometime right here in the store. Mr. Newton has an old piano there. I don‘t know if it‘s for sale, but when we stop by after closing with some cake, he won‘t mind.“

„Yes, I know about that piano. I‘m saving up for it. I‘ve tried it already, and it sounds amazing! It‘s an older piano with a very distinctive sound. Mr. Newton has reserved it for me. When I buy it, I‘ll play it for you one morning!“ Kirsten smiled shyly.

„Well, deal! Your welcome cake is on the house. And eat it slowly! It would be disrespectful to it if you didn‘t savor every bite,“ Belinda handed Kirsten a plate with a burgundy cream cake.

„Thank you. I really like it here. I‘ll definitely be coming here often from now on,“ Kirsten said, looking at the cake.

„I‘m glad to hear that. What‘s your name? Unless it‘s a secret,“ Belinda asked, as she wanted to associate a name with the lovely face in front of her.

„Kirsten. My name is Kirsten," she replied and looked into Belinda's eyes.

„I admire people who can play the piano. When I see their hands running across the keys, I don't understand it at all, and I can't comprehend how they can remember which melody each key plays. And then to arrange them in sequence to create a melody. It's just wow. It's a miracle and an experience for me. How long have you been playing?" the unknown girl standing behind Kirsten asked. She turned around and looked at her. The energy radiating from her surprised Kirsten at first glance. She was about the same age as her. Short black hair, cut diagonally just below the ears, gave her a dynamic look, and her smiling lips expressed multiple emotions at once. And those mischievous blue eyes. Sharp, slender, dressed in a striped white t-shirt and jeans. She seemed friendly.

„Well, I've been playing, I don't know... since I was about four years old," Kirsten pondered, unable to remember exactly when she first hit the piano keys.

„That must be amazing! You must be really good by now!" continued the conversation the unknown girl. Her eyes sparkled as if she had met someone holy.

„I don't know if I am. You know how it is... There's always someone better. But when I play, it just brings me joy. Especially in the evenings at my little house by the lake. The music has a completely different color, taste, and scent then," Kirsten spoke passionately about her heart's matter.

„Really? Music can have a color? Or taste? That's amazing! I've never perceived it that way. I would like to taste music. Just be with it. When no one needs anything and I have time for myself or my loved ones. Lately, I've been seeking such moments. While there's still time," the unknown girl looked away from Kirsten and stared at the shop window in front of her. Kirsten became alert. It sounded like a revelation.

„Well, come see me today then. I would be happy to play something for you," she spoke to the unknown girl as if she were her best friend. She felt a connection with her. And she also felt something that she couldn't name yet. Something that convinced her to spend more time with this girl.

„I live by the lake. There's only one white house there. And behind it, right by the lake, there's a small red house," Kirsten explained.

„I think I know where it is. I can't do it today, but tomorrow would work," she thought out loud.

„My name is Sofia. And you're Kirsten. I'll come," she said, smiling as if she had just unwrapped a sweet candy. Belinda stood quietly next to them. No one else was waiting in line, and the day was slowly passing by, as if giving them more time to get to know each other. A smile spread across Belinda's face. This situation had put her in a positive mood. Two strangers had instantly become friends right before her eyes. How often does one witness such an event? It was magical. When she looked at them, it was as if they had known each other for years and were just pretending in front of her. Sofia ordered a cake and they left together to a table in the corner of the room, still talking non-stop. It seemed like they had a lot in common. Or maybe they had many experiences they could share with each other. They simply clicked. That day, they became an inseparable duo. They had known each other for only a few minutes, but Belinda already knew that they would trust each other with their lives. Two life paths intersected so that their threads would not be lonely in the universe, but would start knitting a long, colorful story together.

Kirsten remembers this moment as if it happened yesterday. She looked at Sofia and grabbed her hand, pulling her towards the classroom. They didn't really want to go, but reluctantly took a step forward. Sofia squeezed Kirsten's hand tighter. She didn't want to show her „dependence" on Kirsten and her positive mood. She didn't want to be a burden to her. But at the same time, she wanted to show how strong the bond between them was. How much she valued their friendship. It was strangely schizophrenic. Every day now was a gift. Sofia hoped that she would unwrap a similar gift tomorrow morning. Kirsten hoped for the same.

Chapter 12

- HEARTS -

They entered the classroom. It was time for the class with Miss Wurm. But Kirsten was not bothered at all. She felt numb somehow. She walked and pondered whether she had gradually covered herself with a thick skin like a hippopotamus, and Miss Wurm's words simply couldn't hurt her anymore, or if the words were still piercing her, but she just didn't perceive the pain. Today, she might have another chance to change something. She must be prepared. Soon she would have to distinguish these emotions. She still had many unexplored corners within herself. Maybe every day doors opened for her that she had never noticed before. Some were locked. Some were unlocked, and when she opened them, the room was dark. How many times had she tried to find a switch on the wall, but there was none. And sometimes she found a room with a lamp that was lit. But the room was empty. As if it was waiting for Kirsten to furnish it. But she herself didn't know how. She had no use for it. Kirsten felt like an incompetent real estate agent who didn't know how to utilize her free space. She couldn't sell it, rent it to interesting ideas, concepts, experiences, or emotions. Yes, that was it! She still felt a lack of emotions. She didn't know if she was resisting them herself or if they simply weren't coming.

„Oh no, another empty room," she thought. Emotions did come, but she felt like she was pouring a cup of water on a large, leafy tree.

„You deserve a heavy downpour of clouds!" she chuckled inwardly. At least she cheered up a bit at the topic that Miss Wurm came up with for them.

She didn't have to think long about what to write on the topic of „Love." Miss Wurm wanted to tease the youth a bit. She was probably already looking forward to enjoying some unsuspecting soul's take on love. What could she know about it? Kirsten wondered. She probably doesn‘t know anything about it. That‘s all she knows. But she didn‘t care. She wanted to write something for herself. From herself. And maybe for Sofia.

For Adam, it‘s not possible yet, but soon Adam himself will be that lush tree, behind which dark clouds full of water are already gathering. Ready for a change in air pressure. Just waiting for the warm southern front to drive them straight over its crown, where they will mix with the cold northern air current. The sky will be crossed by lightning, and the curtain will fall with a deafening roar. Kirsten realized that even while walking to class, she was writing lines of some unidentified literary genre in her soul. However, she knew that the literary genre she had written in her notebook would see the light of day in a few minutes during literature class. When she thought about the topic, the one thing that immediately came to her mind was the one that expressed love, both internally and externally, the most. Symbol. Miracle. The one that is present in every living and non-living entity in this world. She had heard countless times that even an ordinary street has it. Even Belinda‘s café has it.

ഗ

Some hearts are carved from stone, others are carved from wood. And some are modeled from fine clay. Ones in which we can carefully plant a thought, from which a flower will grow. The owner will cultivate it carefully. It will bloom right inside it and will have a pleasant scent to everyone around. Others really like people like this. Just turn in the wind, and we can sense them. Hearts of stone weigh heavily on their owners. They cool them on their chest and never beat even with a gentle touch. They are too heavy and clumsy. They just exist. Silently filling the cavity of their bearer. They don‘t even try to get rid of them. They drag them down to the ground and prevent them from perceiving life around them. These hearts can quickly break some other hearts. For example, those fragile ones that await gentle caresses. For some other soft heart that would envelop them, absorb them, and protect them from the pitfalls of the surrounding world. For the owner of the stone heart, breaking such a heart is a pleasure. The ringing shards cry, and the person becomes cold and immune to any emotions. There is no receptor for emotions, feelings, and sentiments. One that would capture them. It lies among the shards and waits to be put back together by something else. However, if the fragile heart is lucky and finds some soft, warm heart, it will never again feel the hard blow. It will always be surrounded by tenderness and love that will protect it from the harsh impacts of anger and hatred. They will beat together until the very end. The rhythm of each one will gradually synchronize with the other, and after a short time, only one strong heartbeat will be heard on the bench under the lamp in silence.

A stone heart does not receive a donor at birth. The heart hardens gradually throughout life under the weight of anger, sorrow, and emptiness. It creates a natural shell to protect itself from breaking. Hearts are not deaf or blind. They see, hear, and feel exactly what their owner does. They are not vindictive, they do not crave revenge, and they are not lazy. They are here with us and they wait for us to guide them. We choose the material and shape. We show them the way. All hearts have a chance to be soft and warm, even the stone ones. They can melt into soft, sweet candies that everyone will want to taste. It takes a lot of love, tenderness, and contentment. But it is possible. It just requires a lot of understanding.

Wooden hearts are also pleasant. They are ready to accept anything that grafts them onto a fruit tree so they can bear sweet fruits for their owner. Just like they bring joy to their owner, as well as to the gardener or carver. Just start carving them and they will yield. They are full of expectations and will accept any well-intentioned advice. They allow interesting thoughts to be carved into them again and again, until they become a complete work of art at the end of life. And when we run our hand over it, we can read it like a blind person reads braille.

A clay heart is similar to a wooden one. However, in the wrong hands, it can dry out or harden and leave its owner moments of solitude and emptiness. On the other hand, it is very sensitive to the warmth of human deeds and words. Just a small amount of warmth and positive vibrations and our hard heart will regain the right temperature. It will beat with happiness in all directions. It will not harden anymore. And if it does, it will always radiate warmth like a stove in a small cottage.

When we rejoice, the heart beats and is warm. If we have worries, it pricks and wants to escape. If we have problems, it cracks.

If we appreciate it, we are actually appreciating ourselves. If we value our heart, we will know how to value others‘ hearts as well. Even the stone ones...

ഗ

After reading Kirsten‘s work, there was silence in the classroom. She expected Miss Wurm to have nothing to add to her thoughts.

„A slight improvement, but it won‘t be an A today either," she concluded, and the class murmured uneasily.

„Silence! In the middle of the class, I demand silence. The educational process cannot be transferred from the teacher to the student if you are not focused. Everyone in the class knew she said it to stop the silent protest. So everyone knew that B on the essay was just out of spite. Kirsten didn‘t ask for any special attention. She didn‘t even expect her whole school year to be marked by B‘s. But she would be grateful for fair treatment. Somehow, though, she knew that her future life wouldn‘t be fair. Life, after all, is not fair to anyone. And that‘s what‘s fair about it.

She humbly watched the class from under her brows. She was a little disappointed, but she accepted the decision.

„Can I rewrite it again? I want to prove that I deserve an A," Kirsten said.

„You don‘t have to prove anything to me. I have a strict grading scale and today you simply got a B," Miss Wurm said uncompromisingly.

„Kirsten deserves an A!" came a voice from the back.

„Who was that? Everyone be quiet! It will be repeated and we will have a test. It was a B, and I‘m ending any further debate in this class. No one will undermine my grading. I will give each of you the grade I see fit!" Miss Wurm decisively put down the small rebellion in her class.

„The class gradually realized that Kirsten was being used as a sacrificial lamb by Miss Wurm to demonstrate her power. She was like an exhibit into which stones were thrown to intimidate the others. Wurm had thus acquired her authority. She thought that when others saw that one of the most capable students in the class couldn‘t achieve anything, it would demotivate the rest.

„If I have upset you in any way, I apologize. It was not intentional. I‘m sure you found something that speaks to your heart in that essay too," Kirsten defended herself.

Wurm got up from her chair. The class murmured.

„This topic is closed. Today we will move on to the next period of post-war literature," emphasized Wurm, signaling that the discussion would not continue. She had achieved what she wanted and didn‘t need to hear any more unnecessary questions.

Kirsten sat down and looked around the class. Everyone was disgusted. They had just realized what would happen if they weren‘t obedient. So most of them just listened to the lecture. Kirsten knew that the plan had failed again and a similar situation would likely repeat itself in the next class.“

Chapter 13

- ICE SKATING LESSON -

Kirsten packed her things inside the house and went back out to the veranda. The mosquito net banged lightly against the door, scaring away a couple of sparrows on a nearby tree. Evening was approaching and the nature in front of the house was becoming cozy. She looked at the lake, watching leaves falling from the trees into the water. Even the roof of the little house hinted that warm days were coming to an end. She sighed with concern and kept looking into the distance.

„Is something wrong?" asked Sam, still busy with something on the veranda.

„No, no. Nothing that can't be handled," she thought about Sofia. Her illness was perhaps the only thing she had no control over. Every day she waited for George to reach out.

„I know. Everything that happens has a reason. But I'm trying to change those reasons. To make everything happen the way I or others want it to. I want to be on the other side. Not just accepting the consequences, but being the cause of those consequences."

„So, in short, you want to motivate and inspire your surroundings," Sam added.

„Even before, a new bike or car never satisfied you. That's why I know your values won't change now either. You always sought out new stimuli to gain more experiences and knowledge. Those were always your wealth. Nothing will change about that. Only the way you will gain them now," Sam reassured her.

„You're right. Experiences and knowledge. No one can take those away from me. Except death. I hope I can still share them with the world before that," Kirsten stated, peeling off dried paint from the veranda railing. It was getting harder for her to create new emotions, to seek challenges. And when they didn't come, she felt like a withered flower in the desert.

„You know, I would like to help Belinda. She's worried about her café. She says the good times are gone. She feels that she's not enough for the new era. It would be a shame if she had to close it down," Kirsten pondered about Belinda and made plans on how to save her café.

„How was it on the piano? Still the same song? I hope you still enjoy playing music," Sam asked uncertainly.

„I don't mind that Angela is competing with me. I'm improving with every lesson with her," Kirsten replied completely calmly.

„It's interesting, others would have sent her away already, they would be angry. You find inspiration and motivation in her. You're like your mother," Sam reminisced sadly.

„Why should I be angry at someone who pushes me forward? She's not really doing anything wrong. She just shows me where I have gaps and where I can still improve. I definitely won't waste this opportunity because of primitive instincts and emotions. I would rather say it's exciting and every lesson is different. I was afraid I wouldn't challenge myself at this school. Whether I would find opportunities here. And I found what I was looking for. I have limited time and I want to make use of every minute given to me. Another 60-70 years or so," Kirsten smiled. Rather than thinking about Angela, she was thinking about Adam and the promise she made to Mrs. Mackenzie. Under different circumstances, this agreement would have troubled her, but these days it was a defensive shield against all the emotions that her relationship with Adam could bring. Currently, she couldn't divide her thoughts into multiple compartments. They were creating one complex program and she needed all of them in it. If she left them running outside the program, they would overwhelm her and the system would crash. They were all now in one big pot, simmering together. She herself didn't know what would come out of it and whether it would taste good to her and everyone around her. She didn't want to let anyone near that pot to avoid getting burned. Even Adam himself communicated with her wearing asbestos gloves. As if he sensed that it wasn't the right time. She felt that he was patient and waiting. He was smart and prioritized reasons over instincts. He knew that emotions were locked in a safe and no one else had access to them. He was waiting until he got the right combination. A new school year had started and she was facing a lot of new experiences and adventures. The hustle and bustle would help her distract herself and not think so much about her mother's death, moving to a new environment, and uncertain thoughts about the new life that awaited her.

„I went to fix Belinda's refrigerated box. She made me coffee, we talked. As you say, her sales are declining. She feels she can't compete with others. Do you know how we could help her?" Sam turned to Kirsten, but he already knew the answer.

„I know. But I don't think about the same thing as you," replied Kirsten confidently. She lowered her head and her face was hidden by her thick hair.

„I have a plan that could help Belinda. And without any scars on her soul. I will work on it until the café is back on its feet. I hope Belinda's experiences and my plan will bear fruit."

„Alright, alright, I just wanted to make sure you've considered all the possibilities," smiled Sam. „I know you're persistent like your mom. You won't give up until you've achieved what you've set your mind to," he looked at Kirsten and then back at the chair he was fixing.

„Yeah. I remember how she wanted to teach me ice skating in the winter and she taught me something else too. I was sweating and exhausted, but I learned to ice skate. But... when I fell on my butt countless times after half an hour, and I didn't want to get up anymore, she came to me and said something that I remembered for the rest of my life. It's as if she's standing right in front of me now. In that red hat with strands of hair sticking out on the sides: ‚Don't you want to continue? How do you know how close you are to learning how to ice skate? What if you're just a few steps away from the goal? We can go home. You can have a hot cocoa and maybe you'll never learn how to ice skate. Do you know how many times you'll fall on your butt in life? But you won't stay sitting on it, because it'll be cold soon. You'll just waste a lot of time. And that's the time when you could have changed your life for the better and reached your goal. Remember that. No matter how comfortable it may seem to sit on that butt, someday it will be cold. And your problem will still be waiting for you when you get up from the ice,' Kirsten finished.

„That's how it was. I got up from that ice right away and learned to ice skate that day. Since then, I've been careful not to have a cold butt. I miss her so much, Sam... She could have given me so much more. I don't even know what I've lost," she smiled and wiped away a tear.

„So now I'll try to teach Belinda how to ice skate. I think she's sitting on her butt on the ice right now. And I don't want her to feel the cold," she descended the stairs and headed towards the red house. The sun was just setting. The sky changed colors and the lake began to glisten. It was time for music. The small house was cozy at this time. Kirsten enjoyed the moments she could spend alone with herself. She wasn‘t afraid of being alone. These moments might be the last ones.

Sam watched as Kirsten walked through the meadow towards the lake. He stopped fixing the chair and began cleaning his screwdriver from oil. Kirsten was able to bring him joy every day. Thanks to her, he didn‘t withdraw into himself after the death of her mother. The days after the accident were difficult. Two people had died, and they would be missed for the rest of their lives on this earth.

He looked at his old hands, as if afraid that he wouldn‘t be around long enough to help her start a new life she didn‘t ask for. He knew he wouldn‘t be here for her forever. The first melodies began to spread from the little house. He smiled. He knew Kirsten already had a plan in her head to help Belinda. The music gave him inspiration, so he got back to repairing until it got dark...

Chapter 14

- SACRIFICE -

Kirsten entered the classroom. It was a few seconds after the bell had rung, but the teacher was not yet there. Sofia and Emie were sitting right by the door. Across from them, Adam had his chair turned around and they were talking. A few desks away, Angela was sitting with two friends. They all looked at the door in anticipation, expecting the teacher to come in.

„Maybe he won't even come," interrupted their conversation.

„He stopped me in the hallway yesterday and said that if he doesn't come to class in the morning, we should join another group from our class," said Kirsten and sat down in an empty desk behind Emie and Sofia. The class was divided into groups based on the subjects the students had chosen. Currently, they were divided into two groups. They knew that the other group had a geography class upstairs.

„I really don't feel like going to geography," Sofia yawned and looked at Emie.

„Don't look at me! If we stay here, I'm staying too. If we go, I'm going," Emie defended herself, running her fingers through her ear, where she had several earrings. Adam just raised his hand in agreement.

„What will happen if we don't come? Does everything always have to be so boring? So many rules. Maybe no one will even notice," Angela excused the situation, but Kirsten knew that if someone did notice, the blame would fall on her. She tried to understand whether Angela really didn't want to go to class or if she was trying to drag her into trouble.

„What will happen? We'll disappoint someone's trust," Kirsten didn't want to change the established rules of the school.

„Well, let's just go for the second half of the class. When the test is already over. And the wolf will be fed and the sheep whole. We'll say we were looking for them," Angela persisted. The others in the class agreed. Kirsten reluctantly, but agreed. She looked at Sofia and took out her vocabulary book. She turned to the last page and started writing notes to forget the sadness that always came over her when she saw her. The morning passed slowly but calmly. Kirsten wrote down the notes for half a page when Adam got up to signal their departure. They all packed their things and slowly walked to the geography class.

They walked through the empty hallways of the school, and Kirsten was focusing on her next exam with Angela. Adam opened the door and they entered the classroom. It was quiet, the teacher had already started a new topic. They sat down quietly and took out their books. The teacher looked at them, waiting for someone to explain the situation.

„Kirsten, as far as I know, you were supposed to come as soon as you found out Mr. Neeson didn‘t come. Where have you been for so long? He told me he informed you to join us,“ the teacher asked, a question that everyone was already expecting.

Adam raised his eyebrow and wanted to defend Kirsten somehow. He knew it was late. Angela remained neutral, waiting to see how the situation would unfold. Sofia and Emie sat quietly, feeling a bit scared. Everyone felt their share of guilt.

„Did you tell the others to join us?“ the teacher asked, to which everyone was already waiting for Kirsten‘s answer.

Kirsten looked at the others, lowered her head and said, „No, I didn‘t,“ and looked down at her desk. The teacher frowned in surprise. He didn‘t expect this answer.

„Alright then. Wait for me outside the classroom after the lesson,“ he said calmly and started writing new notes on the board. Kirsten looked at Sofia and Emie. They just stared at her with surprise and guilt. Kirsten smiled to soften the tense atmosphere. Angela pensively twirled her pen between her fingers. Adam sighed and started taking notes.

As unpleasant as this problem may seem to Kirsten, it was just a small grain of sand that was part of the desert storm she was going through. She needed to feel solid ground beneath her feet. She felt that her new situation was lifting her off the ground and trying to take her away somewhere into the clouds. From where she would never see all those beautiful things again. She was looking for an anchor to attach herself to in her home port. She already felt that she was seeing situations through a new lens, and rose-tinted glasses they were not. She needed to do something she used to do before. She took notes on the new material in the meantime. She drew the new furnishings of Belinda‘s café on the paper next to it, already had an anchor. It just wasn‘t heavy enough. She needed more. They were sitting right next to her. Each of these people were close to her in their own way. She was waiting to see how the situation with Sofia would develop. If there would be a cure that could save her. The clock was ticking against her. They were still waiting for the answer that seemed to never come. Hopefully it wouldn‘t be too late. The bell rang. Kirsten sat on the windowsill outside the classroom and waited. In her head, she had the notes, „Alone“ and the afternoon sun that was breaking through from behind the hill and dazzling the schoolyard.

She felt somehow numb. Even though everything was actually fine. She felt that she still had to think about a lot of things in order to find herself again in this new world.

„It was noble. But let‘s not repeat it,“ the teacher stepped in front of her and summarized the situation with a simple sentence.

„Don‘t you want to apologize?“ he asked.

„No. I can‘t. It was my conscious decision. I stand by my opinions and decisions. I apologize for my honesty,“ she looked into the teacher‘s eyes without blinking, as if searching for an answer in them.

„Well, alright. But I will forgive you only because that decision was based on your moral principles. You have gained respect in the class. I don‘t want to ruin that now. I don‘t have proof that you knew about it,“ he smiled briefly, shook his head at the whims of a pure-hearted student.

„Just be careful to earn it in the right places. You probably know how much energy and pain it takes to gain respect.“ Kirsten knew that, and she knew it very well.

∽

A brand-new radio was playing on the veranda. No one else on the street had one like that. It was small and could be taken outside because it ran on batteries. The music on the veranda always attracted other kids from the street, and in front of the house, it often looked like a school playground.

„We have a better one at home! Bigger! And it plays better music!“ boasted the boy who was new on the street, and Kirsten didn‘t know his name yet.

„We have a better radio, everyone comes to play at our place! We are richer,“ Kirsten shouted until her eyes were filled with tears of her long hair.

„No, we are richer, we have two cars!“ shouted the unknown boy at Kirsten. They argued while the other kids continued playing as if it didn‘t interest them. The door slammed behind Kirsten. She turned around and saw her mom. Only then did she realize that her shouting had probably interrupted her from her household chores.

She knelt in front of her and said, „Don‘t try to look down on people. Not for what you have in your room, not for who you are. If you have to force someone to believe that, it‘s not worth it. You may see it as superiority in your eyes, but in the eyes of others, you will be the one who humiliates yourself."

„Remember... you don‘t have to look down on people. They can humble themselves on their own. If you want to earn respect from someone, it must be through selfless acts. Trust me, you won‘t get anything by demanding it, and it may even hurt and require a lot of effort. But that‘s how you earn respect. Respect can‘t be bought with a radio or candies. It can only be earned. And don‘t argue. Rather, converse. Listen. You‘ll learn things you didn‘t know before. When you argue with someone, you‘re rejecting a gift they‘re trying to give you, and you don‘t want it. And if someone has made you angry, then they‘ve already given you that gift, right?" She smiled, stood up, checked on the kids playing in front of their house, and went inside to cook dinner.

The sun was setting behind the horizon, all the kids had run off somewhere, and Kirsten was playing alone on the porch. Suddenly, she heard a scream from behind the house. She quickly got up and ran down the stairs. She followed the scream, which came from two houses down. She jumped over a low fence that separated the two houses and turned the corner. She came face to face with a black dog. It was biting a boy with whom she had argued in the morning. She stomped her foot and yelled at the dog. She picked up a stone from the ground and threw it directly at the dog‘s chest, making a dull sound. The dog stopped biting the crying boy and ran towards the other kids. They scattered, screaming, except for Kirsten.

„Run!" she yelled at the boy who was getting up. The dog jumped and knocked her down. She quickly turned her face towards the ground and protected her head with her hands. She could feel the animal searching for a spot to bite. It only lasted a few seconds, but for Kirsten, it felt like an eternity. Suddenly, the dog yelped in pain and ran away. She turned around, propped herself up with her elbows, and saw an adult man driving the dog away with a stick. She straightened her dress. She had small cuts on her hands and scratches all over. Her mouth was slightly swollen.

She was jolted out of her thoughts by a voice saying, „You drove it away," the boy thanked her ashamedly.

„Friends?" he said and extended his hand. Kirsten didn't say a word and shook his hand in agreement. Their hands were covered with band-aids, representing what they had been through to end up being friends.

„We didn't mean to run away, Kirsten. We were scared," someone from the group of children said, and they all looked at Kirsten with admiration. She still remembers it to this day, as if it happened yesterday. She still sees those big dog eyes filled with anger. It was as if the dog represented the life that was pressing her down and searching for a place to sink its teeth into. She clenched her hands, and the scar showed where the pink bandage with little balls had been attached. Friendship signed directly on her skin.

ᔓ

Emie pulled a chair closer to Kirsten's desk: „I'm sorry. We're sorry."

„It was selfish of us. We should have spoken up and told you that we knew," Kirsten replied, and she could see that everyone felt a bit guilty.

„It's okay. I would have done the same. But I hope such a situation won't happen again," she smiled.

„Will you come to the farm this afternoon? We'll be harvesting more vegetables. There's a lot of work on the farm in the fall, but also a lot of sunshine and fresh goodies. I have to help my parents. They can't afford to hire help," Emie invited Kirsten. Their farm was located on the outskirts of Edwood, and they grew vegetables, fruits, and had fields of corn and wheat around their house, as well as chickens. Emie had been helping on the farm since she was little. That's why she was an average student. She didn't have time to study. She knew that one day she would have to take care of the farm herself.

„Yeah, sure. I'd love to come. Sofia will probably come too. We'll help you," Kirsten was excited. She needed to be in nature and with friends, because her head was about to burst from all the thinking. Emie happily sat back in her seat. Kirsten walked over to Angela and stopped by her.

„Are you coming with us to the farm this afternoon? We're all going. To help Emie and have some fun," Kirsten asked Angela, who wasn't expecting such a question at all.

„To the farm? Thanks for asking, but I have private lessons in economics and piano after school," she said, running her fingers aristocratically over her white collar. Her dark blazer with stripes, black skirt, stockings, and shiny shoes screamed that a person dressed like this simply doesn‘t belong on a farm. „And even if I didn‘t, what would I do there? Kirsten, I‘m not from your world, and I like it this way.“

„I‘m sorry for disappointing you. And I hope you don‘t feel too upset about the geography issue. You chose the answer. You could have said yes and we would all be in this together. Anyway, I applaud you for finding the motivation to say no,“ Angela blinked her eyes and smiled. As if she already knew in advance that she would be the winner in this micro battle.

„Have fun! There‘s plenty of work on the farm. You‘ll strengthen relationships and friendships. We‘ll have fun too,“ Angela continued to smile along with her friends who nodded in agreement. Kirsten sensed a hint of sarcasm in Angela‘s response, but she could see on her lips and in her eyes that Angela might have actually wanted to spend the afternoon with them. However, she couldn‘t even utter such words. She couldn‘t cut out a piece of her social status and stoop to such primitive fun as vegetable picking with friends, even if she might have enjoyed it. Kirsten had noticed something earlier. Angela was smiling all the time. She was constantly smiling. She didn‘t know if others had noticed, but she felt that the more Angela smiled, the more she was hiding something. She knew that people often show what they lack the most. They laugh because they lack laughter, they talk wisdom because they are foolish, they are aggressive because they are afraid. And Angela‘s smile seemed like a mask to Kirsten, behind which she was hiding tears. She didn‘t know if she was right, so she wanted to verify this intuition. Angela didn‘t give her a chance today either. Kirsten saw how bound Angela was by her status and money. She pretended to control the money, but the money controlled her. Kirsten couldn‘t reconcile with that. The fact that one day Angela would realize that all the decisions were made by someone else. Or something else. Angela was a sociological study for her, and she was grateful for the opportunity to peek into such a book. And to learn. Angela didn‘t pay much attention to her, so Kirsten turned around and walked back to Emie and Sofia.

Chapter 15

- RESTART -

Kirsten parked directly in front of the café and turned off the engine. The motor purred and died. She looked through the front window at people by the counter, grabbing cakes to go and heading to their tables. She would work her shift at the café until it was time to go to the farm. A plan was forming in her mind. She needed to find out a few more details before telling Belinda.

„Hello!" Belinda greeted Kirsten while sprinkling ground nuts on a cake.

„Hi, was it busy today?" Kirsten greeted back, walked to the end of the counter and headed into a small room in the back to change. It was cozy in there. On the shelves were boxes of vacuum-sealed coffee, cutlery, and all the things that every good mechanic has in their toolbox. The room was a palette that the café painted. Kirsten unpacked her things and tied on an apron. She ran her hands over it and smiled. She wouldn't trade this job for any other. As a bonus to her paycheck, it gave her a lot of positive emotions and, most importantly, experiences. Daily conversations with customers helped Kirsten understand the problems and joys of other people. It made her feel more human too. She was still afraid that she would slowly detach from the ground and one day find herself floating in the clouds, unable to return and land firmly again. And thanks to the café, she always felt the solid ground under her feet.

„Well, it was a bit busy in the morning when people were coming back from early mass. But then it was calm again. You know how it is... Everyone is at work, at school. People are scattered, the city is changing. Nobody has time during the week to sit down for coffee and cake. I remember the times when there were four of us working here, and we were still busy. People found a moment for someone close or for a moment with a cake. You know how it is? If you eat the cake at home where nobody sees you, then it's only half the calories," Belinda laughed and wiped the counter in front of her. She put her hand on her hip and leaned against the counter.

„But I don‘t have to explain that to you. You‘re from the same generation. You may be like all the teenagers around, but you‘re exceptional in some way!“

Kirsten hesitated for a moment and said, „I‘m not exceptional, and I‘m probably not special in any way. I‘m just not like everyone else,“ she concluded and paused to think. She looked around the café, observing a customer who had sat at the bar and unfolded a newspaper. He ordered coffee. An older gentleman. Mostly older people or children frequented the café. Kirsten noticed that the younger generation, always in a rush, seemed to have disappeared. Belinda was right. They simply didn‘t have time to enjoy a peaceful cup of coffee. They needed to have it with them while they were doing something else, whether driving, walking somewhere, or having it with them at work. Kirsten looked outside the door. There was a parking lot by the road that could accommodate about ten cars. It was never full. It would probably suffice for a short stop, for 5-6 minutes, so that there would be space for another car afterwards. And then for another. These pieces of information started to make sense to Kirsten. She smiled at the customer, took a cup in her hand, and started preparing the coffee.

„Are you saying that the café could go bankrupt?“ she asked softly. Belinda was putting pastries into the display case and couldn‘t answer her.

„Well, anything can happen. I hope not. But at the moment, it‘s probably no longer in my hands and power,“ she looked worriedly at the children playing at the table. Kirsten saw her like this for the first time, lost in thought. She knew Belinda was struggling, but she wasn‘t sure about these feelings until now. It was as if Belinda felt sorry that she wouldn‘t have the opportunity to experience similar moments anymore.

Kirsten would be sorry for the café, and not just her. Not so much because of the work itself, but Belinda‘s café had its charm. It added color to the town where everyone felt good. With every closed shop and shuttered corner, the town was losing its face. Like when a beautiful picture at home with grandma fades. When the picture fades, the space becomes sad.

It was clear that even if Belinda took out a loan or someone invested in the café, it might save the situation, but it would be the first nail in the coffin for Belinda. She didn‘t want to prop up the café with crutches. She wanted to give it new energy. It would be like losing her beloved child, seeing it suffer. She wanted to give her hope and help at the same time. Kirsten served the coffee to the old gentleman with a hat and wiped her hands on her apron. It was time for a change. The plan had matured. Next time, she would tell Belinda the whole plan. She hoped she would like it.

Chapter 16

- FARM -

Beyond the city, the countryside began to change like a cake in the oven. Edwood was a pretty town with a park and a square with concrete houses. And as she walked away from it, it gradually softened and took on colors. Before her eyes, it turned into a beautiful, fragrant, fluffy cherry cobbler. The road wound around a mighty tree and turned left behind the hill. That tree always reminded Kirsten of Emie. Solitary, with its feet firmly on the ground in any weather. She passed by it and down the hill she spotted the farm. Maybe today they would help Emie harvest so that she would have time for studying. The horizon was cut by a large red barn, a silo, and two large fields. They looked like colorful patches on the black, scorched Mother Earth. Next to the farm stood a greenhouse and a another house. In front of the house, a few meters from the road, was Adam's car. Kirsten felt the wind blowing away all her worries as she ran toward it. They disappeared high in the sky, where the wind carried them away. She was looking forward to helping Emie and being with her loved ones. Maybe Angela would like to join them too, but perhaps she was afraid she would enjoy it. Kirsten hadn't given up on trying to penetrate Angela's soul more deeply. But now she was about to connect with several other amazing kindred souls.

She parked the car next to Adam's and ran towards the greenhouse. There were always many empty crates near it, which they used as chairs and a table. And the greenhouse was always an endless supply of radishes, carrots, and cabbages.

„Hello Kirsten," Emie greeted her as she ran towards her.

„You're the only one missing now! Today we're harvesting lettuce," Emie said, braking suddenly in front of her, kicking up dust around their feet. Over her shoulder, Kirsten saw Adam coming out of the greenhouse with a crate in his hands. She threw her coat on the nearest crate, tied her hair in a bun, and put on work gloves.

„Phew, it‘s hard work here," greeted Sofia and Adam.

„Hi, we just started. We want to help Emie so she can have some free time tomorrow. At least she won‘t be dozing off in school again," Sofia smiled. Kirsten quickly nodded to Emie‘s parents, who were sorting something next to the house, and went into the greenhouse. It was humid and warm inside, like in a jungle. She admired Emie for having so much energy - working on the farm and managing school. Teachers often turned a blind eye to her because they knew she didn‘t have much time to study. She was smart, but her grades were average. Kirsten really liked that she never complained. She took life as it came and tried to make the most of every moment in a positive way. She had her dreams, desires, and goals. An ordinary girl with an extraordinary life. Kirsten approached the lettuce beds. They were beautiful, green, just the right size...

Emie cut the lettuce just above the ground and placed it in a prepared crate. When it was full, she took it to the yard and rinsed it off with a hose. She then carried the crate to the cold storage room. In the evening, they would transport them to the city warehouse. Kirsten cut off a head of lettuce and took a whiff. It smelled... well, like lettuce. She smiled, realizing she enjoyed this scent. It reminded her of Mother Earth. She loved everything natural and organic. That‘s why she felt so good on the farm. She could spend hours there every day, but other responsibilities didn‘t allow her to. She was afraid that later on, she wouldn‘t have time to spend even a few hours a month on the farm with everyone. Kirsten stood next to Emie, who smiled at her and handed her a head of lettuce. She placed it in the crate. Within a few minutes, it was full. She picked it up and nearly bumped into Sofia along the way.

„Wait, don‘t bother with the crates. I‘ll carry them for you, and you can spray them with the hose," Sofia said, stopping her.

„Well, of course. How should I feel as a guy?" Adam retorted.

„I‘ll carry the crates to Sofia. And then to the warehouse. You can pack the lettuce in them," he joined in the division of labor.

„Alright, so I‘ll cut and leave the lettuce in the rows behind me. You can pack them in the crates," Emie continued.

„Great! I‘ll arrange the crates right away behind the greenhouse,“ Kirsten exclaimed. Emie jumped behind the rows and started cutting one head after another. Since she didn‘t have to store them, her work was smooth and in a few seconds, a regiment of lettuce heads was left behind her. Kirsten placed them into the prepared crates. She felt Adam standing behind her.

„Here you go,“ she smiled and handed him a full crate before he could say what was on his mind. He rushed out of the greenhouse and Kirsten could only hear the water spraying from the hose. The crates disappeared from the greenhouse and piled up in the cooling storage. Gloves were damp with sweat and water, and everyone tried to make occasional eye contact. Kirsten placed another crate on the ground and leaned against it. She hadn‘t noticed Adam yet, and Emie was adjusting her headscarf. Those few seconds were currently the most enriching moments in her life. This moment couldn‘t be bought. Nor sold. It was an underground commodity known only to the initiated. No matter how rich Angela was, she was deprived of these moments. She had her moments, but Kirsten didn‘t know if they were similarly valuable to her or if she artificially overestimated them. Honesty was the key. So that the moment wouldn‘t be wrapped in a mink coat at a snobby party. But so that it would be an intimate moment alone in a meadow behind the forest. Where they would be themselves. Then everyone would know if they were looking at a dying carcass or a beautiful white horse on which they wanted to ride.

Kirsten thought of Angela and tried to quantify the value of this moment. She took it and stored it in the safe in the innermost room of her mind. Where no one would find it and she would occasionally visit this room. She would light a dim light, open the safe, sit on the soft couch, and revel in it. And over time, it would mature into a very valuable piece in her collection.

Everyone‘s work went smoothly, and soon everyone found themselves sitting on crates with a piece of vegetable in hand, watching the sunset. They all felt like they were working on their own farm.

„I‘m glad you‘re here. Tomorrow will be a tough day at school, and I haven‘t even seen my books yet,“ Emie smiled.

„None of us have,“ Sofia chuckled with a kohlrabi in her mouth.

„Is there any way to make the work more efficient? Machines would probably be expensive," Kirsten pondered aloud.

„Yes, that would help. Our family wouldn't have a problem accepting a partner on the farm. With machines, the yield and profits would increase. But as you can see, no one has been found yet. They say the return on investment is slow," Emie rolled her eyes.

„And maybe it's for the best this way. If someone invests in our farm, we will know that it's not just about profit for them. That they care about more than just money. That they love nature and enjoy seeing carrots grow in the field. I love the farm. But this world is unforgiving in some way. It gives you one thing and takes another. Since money is constantly being invested in the farm, there's not much left for my study fund. I wanted to study veterinary medicine. At this rate, I'll never save enough for school. But if all those machines were bought at once..." Emie didn't finish and took a bite of her carrot. Kirsten listened to Emie and chewed on the juicy pieces.

„You know what? I really like it here. I'm investing in the farm, and you'll become a veterinarian," Kirsten said without hesitation.

„Well, there you go... That's exactly the big heart that this farm needs!" Emie laughed.

„What can I say! I have the same problem, just from the opposite side. I have money, but I want to spend more time with you all. Somewhere other than school or private lessons. Like you said, life always gives us one thing and takes another. Balance?" Adam smiled.

„Emie, you deserve the life you wish for. Don't despair. Sometimes help comes to us on the wind. It literally hits us in the face, and we fall on our backsides and look at it from the dust as it extends a helping hand. And sometimes you have to walk towards it against the wind. Just like you're doing now. You don't give up and keep walking, even though the wind is really strong. But soon you'll catch a glimpse of shelter with squinted eyes. Hope dies last," Kirsten replied, and looked around the farm.

„But sometimes hope does die," Adam added.

„I hope not. But I don't want to be ungrateful. I'm doing what I love, dancing among the vegetables at home... Everything else will be just a dream," Emie said softly, lowering her head until her earrings tinkled in her ears.

„A fulfilled dream," Kirsten smiled. Adam and Sofia just listened, as if those two knew exactly what they were talking about. For them, it was a foreign, encoded language.

„If you don't need anything else, I'll go. Private economics lesson," Adam rolled his eyes in boredom, although he knew well that it wasn't a waste of time at all. He just wanted to lighten the mood.

„I'll go too," Sofia added.

„I'll give you a ride home," Kirsten gathered her things from the box.

„You don't have to, you're going the opposite way. I'll drop off Sofia," Adam offered.

„I'll keep an eye on him for you," Sofia smiled with wide open eyes and grabbed Adam's shoulder like a favorite toy.

Kirsten smiled through tired eyes. Sofia's carefree smile and cheerful blue eyes at the end of the day were the most beautiful gift for her. She turned to Emie and waved goodbye one last time. As they walked to the car, she turned around again. Emie was carrying tools in her hands, heading towards the house. They had bought her some time for herself and for studying. Kirsten smiled at her contentedly in the dim light.

Chapter 17

- STATUS QUO -

It was the end of the week. Kirsten walked down the school hallway with Sofia, the farm, and the café on her mind. She opened her locker and started exchanging books. She paused for a moment, looked ahead, and pondered. This year is different. One that will never be repeated. It's because of what happened and the fact that it's likely the last of its kind. Wurm was just a fleeting distraction compared to everything else. She closed her locker. She saw Adam approaching with books under his arm.

„Are you okay? You should have spoken up. Everyone can see that what's happening between you and Wurm isn't ok. We would stand up for you!" Adam said, quickly exchanging his books.

„If I spoke up, it would just be playing into her hands. I don't want to go against the tide. Waste my energy. I want to hide from it, take shelter until it loses its strength... Maybe it will subside on its own, or I'll dress better to confront it later," Kirsten stated.

„I understand what you mean. But this battle is getting on everyone's nerves," Adam said angrily.

„But the class is with you. You know that," Kirsten winked at Adam.

„Kirsten, you're supposed to go to the principal's office," a familiar voice sounded behind her. She turned around. Emie was standing there.

„Well, we're moving to the next level," Adam raised an eyebrow. Kirsten didn't even flinch at the comment. She was surprised herself. It was as if she already knew before Emie told her. Emie patted her on the shoulder and without a word, Kirsten headed to the principal's office. Emie watched her as she disappeared down the corridor from the lockers. Kirsten walked, and the closer she got, the calmer she felt. After all, there was nothing to surprise her.

„Hello, I was supposed to come," Kirsten greeted the principal.

„Hello Kirsten. Yes, please have a seat. It's about the classes with Miss Wurm. But you probably already know," the principal stated, and Kirsten nodded in agreement.

„Miss Wurm thinks that you are rude to her and distracting the whole class from paying attention. She says you undermine her authority. I wasn‘t there, so I can‘t judge who is telling the truth," he replied and settled more comfortably in his chair.

„But Mr. Principal, what am I supposed to do? I have no idea what Miss Wurm wants from me. I‘m trying really hard, and deep down, I‘m glad I have the motivation to improve. I want to prove to her that I deserve an ‚A‘. On the other hand, I understand why she‘s behaving this way. But I can‘t give her what she‘s looking for in me. She has to find it within herself," she said, looking directly into the principal‘s eyes.

„I know what you‘re trying to say. And I won‘t talk to you like an ordinary student. You see things with a more mature perspective than others. Look," the principal leaned over the table and took off his glasses, „Miss Wurm is a fixture of our school. She came here as a young, single teacher, and that‘s how she stayed. She has no family. Only this school. This is her family, and she guards it closely. She‘s already retired. She was also a principal. Maybe you don‘t know this, but when she retired, she recommended me as the principal. She has an indefinite contract. She can only leave voluntarily. Otherwise, we would have to let her go with all the bonuses and pay she‘s entitled to. For a small school like this, it‘s a lot of money. We need every penny. But I promise you that if any opportunity arises to change this situation, I will be the first to initiate it. For the sake of both of you. If the situation becomes unbearable, the doors are open for you. I want the students of this school to feel good. We are a small town and a community, and we shouldn‘t cultivate so many negative memories even in school. I want everyone to remember this school in a positive light. That‘s why I‘m addressing this situation. You‘re not the only one fighting this battle," the principal smiled briefly at Kirsten.

„But I‘m curious why your writing angered her so much. Can you give me some of your work? I would like to read them," he said eagerly, leaning on his chair. Kirsten rummaged through the folder she had with her and pulled out a few papers, timidly handing them to the principal.

„Thank you, I‘ll return them to you after I read them," he said, impatiently reviewing the papers.

„You can go," he said calmly, going through the papers. Kirsten bit her lower lip and walked towards the door. She was waiting for a verdict, whether it was directed towards her or towards Miss Wurm. But it seems that nothing will change after this visit either.

„In order not to forget... Miss Wurm wanted to announce over the intercom for you to come to the principal‘s office. It would be theatrical, I disagreed. Your piano playing brings joy to our school," said the principal, looking at Kirsten with papers in hand.

„Thank you," Kirsten replied, turning around and closing the door behind her.

Chapter 18

- ILLUSION -

The afternoon sun bore witness as Angela and Kirsten played a duet together. Both were breathing quickly. Angela smiled as if she had won a race, while Kirsten looked somewhat uncertain.

„Was it good?" Kirsten asked Mrs. Miller.

„You were perfect, let me tell you," Mrs. Miller smiled.

„I hope so. I don't want to mess up the competition. I can't evaluate myself well enough," Kirsten gasped at Mrs. Miller.

„Stop doubting yourself so much. Why are you unnecessarily modest? So many nobodies walk around this school with their noses sticked up in the air for no reason. And you doubt yourself?!" Angela exclaimed angrily and blinked her eyes quickly.

„Are you afraid of failure? It's like being afraid to take a step. Do you know what happens to people like that? They stay in one place their whole lives. Stuck and desperate about their own uselessness, they try to grab anyone passing by to not feel so hopelessly alone. Oh no... You don't belong with them. Ahem, no! I try every rehearsal to convince you of that. To show you that I'm better than the average, and that you're just the ordinary mediocrity we encounter every day on the street. And I'm not succeeding. It's a challenge for me. There are few people and opportunities in my life that allow me to grow. That's why I cherish every moment when we play against each other. A detective is only as smart as the criminal he's chasing. A bricklayer is only as skilled as the complexity of his construction. And do you know why I want you to accept that you're exceptional and talented? So that I can be even more exceptional myself. Yes, I can leave this town now and be better than the surrounding world. But if I'm not better than you, then I won't be better outside of this town either. Failures will be stepping stones on the sidewalk that will give you a solid ground to walk on towards your goals. You'll walk over them towards your destination. To fail is to learn something new. Only dead fish swim with the current, and only a strong current gives birth to a strong fish that will swim against it. Don't let yourself be carried away by your own doubts in this current," Angela looked Kirsten straight in the eyes.

„I have no doubt about myself, I just want to know the truth. I don't want to spend my whole life living in some illusion by chance. It would be like someone locking me up in a box and telling me how good it is in there. I want to know the truth, no matter what flavor it may have. Everyone around us tries to create some illusion. I don't want to live in any fantasies, neither my own nor others'. What's more important is that I'm learning to recognize whether someone is manipulating me for their benefit and only throwing me breadcrumbs. How do you know if your friends are talking to your money and not to you? You're wealthy, but what if money has locked you up in its own treasure chest, an illusion. Aren't you afraid that you could have lived a completely different life?" Kirsten asked and settled more comfortably on the piano stool.

„What's the difference between living a life in illusion, unfulfilled dreams or everyday reality? It's all in the mindset. You can be happy anytime. You can buy that reality. Or illusion, if you like. If you're happy with it, then it's all good. I like to be in control, so I buy illusions. I'm not so foolish as to not know that many people around me are only here because of my money. But it suits me," Angela stated dryly and stretched herself as a sign of victory. Kirsten could have pinned a medal for merit on her chest by now.

„And what if you could compare the life when you weren't wealthy yet, and the life in wealth? Would you know what you lost and what you gained? Do you know now what you've missed out on?" Kirsten asked further.

„I was born wealthy. I will never know the answer to that. And I don't miss anything. If you were as wealthy as me, these questions wouldn't bother you either. Why should they?" Angela continued to smile.

„I would be afraid that they would change me and change everything and everyone around me," Kirsten added softly.

„I was already born changed - wealthy. Nothing has changed in my life," Angela stated dryly and adjusted her hair clip.

„But you would learn the whole truth if you suddenly became poor overnight. But I don't know if it works the other way around. While you're poor, you live with truth, honesty. And when you become wealthy, can you carry them into that new life, or are they simply not compatible?" Kirsten pondered.

„Surely it is possible to be wealthy and still live a life as if you didn't have the money. To have the best of both worlds. However, it requires great humility, experience, and a strong personality. Not everyone can do it. And not everyone wants to be that kind of person. Money can buy everything today. It‘s easier than working on oneself. Money is a shortcut. When you pass through it, you may have muddy and battered legs, but you‘ve saved time and energy. And in the distance, you see all the others who can‘t catch up with you. But yes, I admit, it‘s possible to live both worlds and both lives at once. Who knows what one must go through to be able to merge these two worlds. It must be a profound experience or an ordeal. Something that breaks your life in half. You may bandage that fracture, but your life is already moving in a different direction. That crack is certainly very noticeable..." Angela pondered.

„I have no reason to connect these two worlds. I have no motivation. This world is not worth it. Do you know why good people suffer? Because they live in a broken world. And bad people are happy because they feed on that negative energy. And I use money as a shield. As a filter. And I live in my own world," she added contentedly. Kirsten reflected on Angela‘s words. Angela was right. What she lacked was motivation. She kept looking at herself in the mirror. But all she needed to do was step out of the house and look around. So that she wouldn‘t end up closed off in her own world like Angela. That was what scared her the most. And as it seems, it‘s quite possible that it could happen to her too. Mrs. Miller was silently jotting something down in her notebook at her desk and listening to their conversation with one ear. Today‘s exam had gone well again. It meant a lot to Kirsten.

Chapter 19

- PLAN -

Kirsten parked the car on her usual spot. She crossed the road and passed by the display with a piano. Today, she didn‘t stop to enjoy the thoughts. She had something better. She had an idea. For Belinda. She hurried to catch up with her, hoping to save her.

Kirsten entered the café. The smell of coffee surrounded her. Several people were sitting at a table, in a good mood. Belinda was placing cups on the shelf behind the counter. Kirsten quickly went to change in the back. As she passed by, Belinda smiled at her. Kirsten stopped for a moment, surprised, and looked in her direction. A surprised smile appeared on Belinda‘s face as well. Kirsten heard her changing quickly in the back and coming back behind the counter.

„Well, spill it. You have a new friend!“ Belinda didn‘t wait for an answer. Kirsten walked past the refrigerated box and tied on her apron on the go.

„Well, not exactly. Something better,“ surprised Belinda with her response.

„You talked about how times have changed. That there aren‘t as many people sitting in the café as before. Not that they don‘t like your coffee. But they don‘t have time for it. Am I right?“ Kirsten inquired about the details.

„Well. Yes. I think you‘re right,“ Belinda nodded skeptically.

„If you‘re aiming to sell takeaway coffee, we‘ve already tried that. Unsuccessfully,“ Belinda guessed with a bit of skepticism.

„I have a different idea. What if we gave your customers the option to make their coffee exactly the way they like it? So they wouldn‘t have to think about whether they have honey, sweetener, dried creamer, or whole milk at home. And we also offered them other flavors. Just so they know that our coffee buffet will be a complete solution. No matter what kind of coffee they want, they‘ll know they can find it here. So they won‘t feel like making it at home in the morning. Because ours will be just a quick stop. Always fresh and always at hand.“

„Well, do you think you could find the time for that? Isn‘t it the same as takeaway coffee?“ Belinda continued to ask.

„We'll move their kitchen corner with the coffee maker from their homes here. We'll offer them something they'll never have at home. Like I said... Complete coffee pleasure."

„One day you may feel like a strong coffee, the next day a decaffeinated one. Another day a nutty flavor, and the day after, for example, a coffee with whipped cream and honey. All of this you will never have at home. And you won't have to. They will come to us, take a cup and make their own coffee as if no one else had ever made it for them. I think that thanks to our coffee buffet, many people will stop making coffee at home," Kirsten smiled.

„There are some thermos flasks for pumping in the back. We'll use them. We'll need about ten," Kirsten contemplated aloud.

„Yes. I've had them there for a while. We used to take them after Sunday church for tea," Belinda recalled.

„We'll place these thermos flasks right by the door. We'll remove one table. Anyway, they haven't all been used at once lately, right? We'll utilize every inch of the café that doesn't generate revenue to increase sales. Please order flavored coffees. Nutty, chocolate, vanilla, cinnamon. And also Colombian, Brazilian, dark and light roast. Let's see what they like. We'll provide them with polystyrene cups with lids. Stirrers, white sugar, cane sugar, whole milk and low-fat milk, cream, artificial sweeteners, whipped cream in a bottle, and flavored syrups," Kirsten continued enthusiastically.

„Do I have time to think about it?" Belinda laughed in surprise.

„Well, I'm afraid we don't have much time left with the café," Kirsten raised her eyebrow.

„First of all, order that coffee and we'll get the counter ready. And on the first day, the coffee will be free. It will cost less than an advertisement," Kirsten contemplated aloud.

Belinda was amazed at Kirsten's energy. She felt a little touched by her approach. Kirsten treated the café as her own, and Belinda sensed her optimism resonating in her body, giving her hope. That's why she liked Kirsten so much. She didn't see her as just another helping hand, but as family. They were friends, despite the significant age difference.

The afternoon passed for both of them in the spirit of preparations for Kirsten's new idea. Belinda herself kept thinking about the red house the whole time. She was looking forward to meeting everyone. Perhaps her life was starting to take the right direction, even if only a little.

They felt it this way while realizing their plan with the café. Kirsten was preparing coffee, and when she reached down for sugar under the counter, her nose landed right above the cup. She inhaled the fresh aroma. Every cell in her brain played a symphony of senses. Kirsten paused for a moment, looked around, and surveyed the café. There were a few people sitting there. She desperately hoped that her plan would work and Belinda wouldn‘t have to close the café. Of course, there would be a few buyers who would purchase the chairs, walls, and counters. But they wouldn‘t buy the spirit and atmosphere of the café. Everything had to remain exactly as it was. The café still had its face and its life. It lived for itself and shared its cakes and carefree life with everyone. It was a delicate balance that any wrinkle on Belinda‘s forehead would disrupt. This café represented everything for Kirsten that couldn‘t be bought with money, and that money could destroy. If someone brought a few thousand to Belinda‘s table tomorrow so that the café wouldn‘t have to close, it would have the exact opposite effect. It would be the beginning of the end, when Belinda would admit that her child is dying. They had to strengthen the immune system together so that the café could recover from this flu season and smile again in the summer sun to passersby. It was a delicate balance, and there wasn‘t much time left.

Kirsten was amazed at all the thoughts that came to her when she had to rely on herself. This kind of thinking enriched her greatly and taught her a lot. And these experiences were priceless to her. She would likely need them soon, and she was grateful for every new idea that propelled her forward on her journey.

She placed the last cake on a plate, carried it to the table, smiled at the customer, and quickly went behind the counter to tidy up. „Well, I‘m off, see you tomorrow," she smiled at Belinda and took off her apron. „Okay, enjoy your afternoon. And thank you for the encouragement. Your ideas really gave me optimism and a little peace," Belinda nodded to her, unable to wait for the days ahead. Kirsten smiled hesitantly and hurried out onto the street. The inflatable lifebuoy was inflated. She just had to throw it to the drowning.

Chapter 20

- (NO)HOPE -

Adam sat on a chair next to the piano. He had a nice view from there through the large sliding doors to the lake. Sofia sat opposite him, paler than usual. She was reading Kirsten's texts. They were papers piled up without any order. A bit crumpled, folded, but Sofia devoured them one after another. Occasionally she smiled and seemed to enjoy what she was reading. Kirsten sat at the piano and occasionally pressed a key, as if slowly playing out a composition.

„What did the principal say? Miss Wurm is such a beast... I don't even know why she sent you to the principal's office. Maybe it made her feel better," Sofia asked a bit annoyed.

„The principal was okay. He's trying to navigate in a way that won't collide with me or Miss Wurm. It was frustrating for me, and I don't want to make decisions like that. I'm not afraid of responsibility, but no matter how he decides, sparks will fly. And some will hit me or Miss Wurm. I'm thinking about how I would handle it in such moments. To have such responsibility and hold the fate of other people in my hands. And every decision won't go unnoticed in a dark corner, but will affect everyone involved. It could be a concrete wall or a silk scarf. And silk is precious. I won't have it at hand all the time. I won't be able to waste it. This world is not perfect. So, my decisions won't be either. No matter how hard I try, I can't make it faster. Acquiring experiences - so that I can make only the right decisions in life. Especially when I have that power, position, and responsibility. Until then, I have to be prepared," she pressed another key.

„Don't lose hope. Miss Wurm will surely get tired of it someday. The whole class knows she's wrong and supports you," Adam added.

„Hope? Hope is not good. It gives you energy that you don't have a way to use. Then it burns you from the inside. Hope is what you wish and should be, but you're not. It shows you what you'll never become and where you may never get. Hope is maybe good for breakfast, but not for dinner. That's why I'd rather have no hope of ever getting into a good school."

„That I will become a veterinarian, even though I have my own plan and goal. And I work hard on them to leave as little room for hope," Adam countered Emie. Kirsten understood that she was talking about her two lives. One that she lived on the farm, and the other outside of it. How many times she studied while others were still asleep, or already asleep. She didn't know weekends or Sundays off. Every free moment was spent in books because she knew that soon she would have to put on her work gloves. Many times she looked like a mess in the morning. They made fun of her for it at the school entrance, of course. But Kirsten saw the fatigue in her eyes. But also the spark that drove her forward. Her life had made her resilient. She certainly didn't feel like she had it as a punishment. But as a gift. And Kirsten liked that about her. She deserved the life she longed for, and she had already decided to combine the pleasant with the useful.

She was awakened from her thoughts by the sound of papers falling to the ground. They fell to the floor and scattered to Adam's feet. Silence fell in the house by the lake. Sofia slipped off the armrest and fell unconscious with her face on the bench. Her face was covered with a black fringe. All three of them rushed to her. Adam dialed emergency services and in slow motion saw Kirsten holding her with her face in her lap, trying to bring her back to consciousness. Emie was pouring water into a glass with trembling hands. Sofia opened her eyes disorientedly. Everyone wished it wouldn't happen again, but it did. The situation was serious, and neither Kirsten nor anyone else knew how to handle it.

Chapter 21

- THE DARK PASSENGER -

Kirsten stood by the window. She remembers it as if it were yesterday. Time seemed to stand still for a moment, even though she felt like she was living five lives at once during this period. Sofia lay on the bed and looked as if she had just woken up. That place did not suit her at all. Kirsten was expecting her to uncover herself and run together to the farm. What illness? How? Until this moment, Kirsten had no idea that Sofia had such a deadly secret from her. She knew that some ailment was gnawing at her, but the speed of its progression surprised her. Sofia always walked around with a smile, as if nothing hurt her. Sometimes she was exhausted and tired, but her fatigue never weakened her knees. She had read enough about the illness on the internet. She knew there was no incubation period, no specific date of no return. And that scared her the most about the illness. She was afraid that the balance had been disturbed and the illness would now have the upper hand.

„I didn‘t want to talk to you about it. I wanted to live as if it didn‘t exist. I felt so good with you. I didn‘t want anything you did or said to be influenced by my illness. I wanted to experience you as genuine, always with my feet on the ground, with a sober view of everything ordinary around me. So that your words wouldn‘t be a consolation, but another inspiration. I want to live to the fullest. So that people accept me for who I am. Do I deserve a harsh word? Then say it! If someone wants to comfort me, let them do it because of who I am. Not because I might not be here in a moment,“ Sofia spoke up.

„You will always be the Sofia I first met in that café for me. You‘ve left such a deep mark on me that nothing else can cover it up. I don‘t know multiple Sofias. You don‘t wear masks. Neither will I. I promise you that this is the first and last time you will hear words of sympathy from my mouth to make this situation hurt less. When you leave from here, you will continue to be the blossoming apple tree under which I seek shelter when the sun is scorching or the rain is falling. I won't let any feelings or thoughts cloud this view of you."

„No pink or black sunglasses... Between us, there will be nothing else but friendship. It will forever be the bench that you can reach me on," Kirsten spoke, looking down at the floor by the bed.

Sofia smiled, „They say there are no medications for this disease, only experimental ones. But I can live with it my whole life, or die anytime. It's my dark passenger," she raised an eyebrow until it disappeared under her black bangs. Kirsten shuddered. Just like Sofia, she also had her own dark passenger, of course. After Sofia accepted hers, she realized they stood between them. They stretched their arms and separated from each other. What if one morning they woke up and were so distant from each other that they couldn't find their way back? She couldn't allow that to happen!

„No," Kirsten finally lifted her gaze and locked it with Sofia's eyes. „Between us, there will only be friendship. Nothing else. No one else. There is no room for any stranger who would push elbows whenever it suits them and separate us like that. We will fight! I will fight! No one will suffer or die here. To reconcile means to agree. And I do not agree with that! I will sacrifice my life for you to be healthy. I don't care about myself right now. When you die, I will die too. My life will change anyway. I have no reason to stand in one place. The fear of losing you is greater than the fear of losing my life," Kirsten squeezed Sofia's hand, as if to signal her to be strong and hold on.

„Now it's just a matter of time. And I believe we will reach the finish line before death does. When my dark passenger dies, so will yours," Kirsten looked into Sofia's eyes. She couldn't hold back. She closed her eyes and held back tears of anger and despair.

„Come on, maybe a cure will be found. I will believe in miracles. That one day this disease will disappear as it appeared," and Kirsten also squeezed her palm.

„You are the miracle! And miracles don't die. Miracles are believed in," Kirsten felt a rising inner strength and energy as she looked at Sofia weakened. She felt that Sofia was helping her shape a new Kirsten, which she desperately needed now. The doctor entered the room. He looked exactly like the ones from the TV shows that both of them knew well. Tall, with a wise expression on his face, a long white coat, and papers attached with a clip to a plastic board. Sofia's parents also entered the room with him. Kirsten briefly greeted them and left the room. She heard them discussing Sofia's health condition with the doctor. It seemed like no one on the planet had a solution.

No amount of money in the world could solve this problem so far. Sofia stood helplessly in the hallway, and all she could give Kirsten now was „just" support, positive energy, and hope. However, she felt that her dark passenger was pushing her weak and indecisive Kirsten into a corner. Trying to growl and take control of her. She felt stronger and more determined with him. But she felt sorry for the little Kirsten, the girl who was dying inside her more and more every day. The door to the room opened, and the doctor walked in with Sofia's parents, heading to his office. Kirsten felt like hope for recovery was leaving with him. She entered the room. Sofia sat on the bed, looking helplessly at all the notes left by the doctor.

Kirsten clenched her teeth to hold back her tears. Sofia stood up and headed to the wardrobe to change. The time until she received the expected news was crushing. She looked at Sofia as she changed out of her hospital gown and into cotton pajamas. She could swear she saw a healthy, cheerful girl in front of her, who lacked nothing. Except that she carried her dark passenger in her heart. She was already looking forward to seeing each other again at school soon. She didn't even entertain the thought of any other possibility. Let both of them be distracted again by the everyday life of a student with its joys and worries. She wanted to think positively. However, every time she managed to do so, her dark passenger would speak up. Her mother's death and coming to terms with a new life. A life without her, where she won't be able to rely on her helping hand, but make her own decisions. And the dark passenger was waiting for every decision she made since her mother's death. Sitting beside her like a court jester, and every time she made a decision, he chuckled sarcastically. Until recently, she fought against him, but soon she will have to join forces with him. Collaboration is probably inevitable. Until then, she has to learn more about him.

Chapter 22

- TURNAROUND -

Several long days passed without Sophie. Without emotions. Kirsten seemed to have turned off all her doubts, joys, and worries like a button. She leaned against herself with the dark passenger on her back and waited. The positive thing was that Sofia finally returned to school after a week. She got an appointment for an examination at another, larger hospital. They said they might be able to help her there. Kirsten didn‘t want to talk to her about it. George still hadn‘t called, so there was no other solution yet. And Kirsten hoped he would show up before Sofia had to leave. She stood in the middle of the classroom, looking at the work she had just finished reading aloud. That‘s when Sofia reached out to her and grabbed it. Kirsten leaned back and read it again. She looked at Miss Wurm. She felt empty. She knew that no matter what she wrote on paper, it didn‘t matter. That‘s how Miss Wurm probably felt too. She was just waiting for her evaluation so she could sit down.

„I‘m looking at your grades. It‘s between an A and a B. You didn‘t convince me. Today it will be a C and finally a B," she said, calmly writing down the grade. More than Kirsten, the whole class felt aggrieved. Wurm attacked their weak spot again. If she had chosen someone really irresponsible, it wouldn‘t have stirred up so many emotions. But the fact that she singled out Kirsten didn‘t leave anyone in the class indifferent. Everyone wished that one day Wurm would simply not appear at their classroom door. Surely she felt these moods too. That‘s why she fought against them in this way. After all, this didn‘t just happen in their school. There‘s always a teacher on every school who is a thorn in the side of all students. And they are thorns in her eyes.

Sofia went through the lines and couldn‘t understand how this work could be graded as a C.

She read these sentences and saw Kirsten in each one. She read the whole work. She couldn‘t understand how this work could be graded as a C. It was like a confession of her inner self. And Wurm trampled on it like this.

„Madam teacher, I will speak on behalf of everyone, but we liked it. We also liked Kirsten's previous work. We don't want to feel fear in class, but rather joy in learning something new. Kirsten doesn't deserve the way you're talking to her," and she looked down at the floor in front of her. Not because she was afraid of Wurm's gaze, but because she didn't want Kirsten to see that it bothered her. She knew she had just earned a visit to the principal's office and probably even a call to her parents. But she would regret for the rest of her life that she didn't stand up for Kirsten. That she didn't support her, as Kirsten had supported her. No matter what happens, she doesn't know how long she'll be here, so what else should she care about?

There was a moment of piercing silence in the classroom. Even Wurm herself was surprised and quickly searched for words. But her thoughts were interrupted by the screeching of a chair. Second, third, fifth. One by one, the whole class stood up, as if they knew this was the moment to express a collective opinion. Now or never. To show solidarity, friendship. Regardless of the consequences. Everyone stood up gradually, and Sofia looked around in surprise. She looked at Kirsten and saw a smile through her sad eyes. Surely, Kirsten didn't imagine it this way. Everyone stood up one by one, except for Angela. Wurm just watched in silence, as if waiting for Angela to join the rebellion as well. Angela looked at Kirsten and got up from her chair. She could only hear Wurm loudly closing her book, collecting her things, and leaving the classroom.

„I'm telling you, there's something about you. Deep down, something that the whole class stood up for just now. Not everyone has that," Angela smiled, her cheeks dimpling as she gracefully sat next to Kirsten like a Victorian lady.

„But I didn't ask for it..." Kirsten wanted to object to Angela, but Angela cut her off: „Exactly! You didn't ask for it, and yet it happened! I buy these moments. I have people standing behind me whenever I need them. Rich people don't have that. They don't need it. They have their money. It's faster and more practical. But I will never experience this feeling that you just had. If the same thing happened to me, no matter how sincere everyone's actions were, I would know that money was partially behind it. Not who I am. You can't have both. Be rich and exude this kind of energy. One excludes the other. Even if people didn‘t know you were rich, they would eventually notice. Money oozes out of rich people. I don‘t know if I‘m resistant to such sensitivity, but it doesn‘t bother me. I probably don‘t know what I should be bothered by,“ Angela smiled.

„Do you know why I didn‘t want it to end like this? Because Miss Wurm has already been punished. She is punished by every glance in the mirror, at the ceiling of her bedroom, in the fridge. She is searching there for what she have never found in life and missed. And she wants to take it away from anyone who found it. We can‘t live forever. But we can create something eternal. And she knows that nothing will be left after her. She didn‘t write any books, she doesn‘t have any children. No one is as afraid of death as they are of being forgotten. You can die, but you will live on. How good it is to die for old people when they are surrounded by grandchildren, sons and daughters whom everyone says are just like their father or mother. If you are published in books or if your books are in many libraries and bookshelves, then you never really die. You will live on in words, thoughts that you left behind. People may quote you, use you as an example. You will live forever. People seem to feel that it will be their energy in the other world that will never let them die. Miss Wurm could not be punished anymore. If you have a burnt hand, the fire will not burn you there anymore,“ Kirsten finished and looked Angela in the eyes.

„Well, you see, balance exists. Either everything balances out in this world, or one scale is in our life and the other in the afterlife. But... what will remain after you? It‘s a pity you don‘t have as much money as I do. You could do great things. You‘re not spoiled by them. You have the personality, heart, and energy that you don‘t want to release from yourself. What are you still waiting for? Can you die tomorrow with a smile on your lips? Or will you thrash about like a fish out of water with a twisted expression on your face, saying that you still can‘t die? Like Miss Wurm,“ Angela looked reproachfully at Kirsten and blinked her eyes as if she wanted to emphasize the question several times. Have you ever felt that life is passing you by? It flows around you, and you can‘t engage with it? And that it‘s only up to you to do something exceptional, to make it happen?“ Angela looked at Kirsten reproachfully, and Kirsten knew what she meant.

„I don't wait. I know exactly what I want. And I know exactly what sacrifice I'll have to make for it. And that I'll have to make that decision myself. But some decisions need time. Proper timing brings the most effective results. They need to ripen to have the right taste. Or to fall at your feet, because they hang over your head where you can't reach them. You can't pluck an apple from a tree until it's ripe. I don't want to pull the trigger until I learn how to shoot. I have my gun loaded and aimed, but I think I would miss this time. I want to be sure of hitting the bull's-eye," Kirsten calmly spoke.

„I just hope that perseverance doesn't turn into eternity," Angela replied, getting up from her chair. She saw a confident girl in front of her, who carefully plans every step. That made her feel uncertain. Kirsten was always one step ahead, even though she herself always seemed to be stumbling.

From that day on, two things never happened again. Miss Wurm never returned to the classroom, and Kirsten never received a lower grade than an A for her compositions.

Chapter 23

- CHESTNUTS -

„I want to go with you," muttered the little pigtailed seven-year-old Kirsten to the boys on the street.

„You can't go with us. You don't know how to ride a bike. Our base is in the park. Right under those big chestnut trees. So we have a supply of chestnuts right at hand. They'll be ripe in a week. We've already found some on the ground."

„I will learn how to ride a bike. Mom will teach me, and then I can go with you!" Kirsten refused to be discouraged as she watched a group of four or five kids on the street checking the valves on their bikes.

„Even if you learn how to ride, you're not a warrior. You don't belong in our gang," the boy retorted, pointing at Kirsten's knees. Unlike the other knees adorned with badges of toughness and bravery, scars and scabs, her knees were smooth and resembled the shell of a white egg. Suddenly, everyone hopped on their bikes and took off. Kirsten watched them disappear at the end of the street. She turned around and looked at her bike lying in the grass. It was now her biggest enemy, always knocking her off the saddle like a wild horse. Her mom was already walking towards her along the sidewalk.

„Still not listening? You'll have to tame it. In life, there will be many bikes that you'll have to earn their attention. Until you do, you'll form a relationship with them. And that relationship will be more important to you than the result. The result will be just the cherry on top. If you want to impress those boys, you have to do what they did. I assume they learned to ride on their own. Without help. That's how you get into their field of vision. They won't look down on you or up at you. You'll look into each other's eyes. But you can sit on the porch and avoid scraped knees. Unfortunately, also without experiences... But remember, knees will heal, but experiences will remain. No scraped knees, no experiences," her mom finished and slowly walked back to the house. Kirsten looked at the bike once more and hoped she would learn how to ride by the end of the week. By then, the chestnuts would be ripe, and she could gather all those round brown ammunition and supply the gang when they would be attacking their common enemies from the neighboring street. They had been chased out of the park, and this was their open declaration of war.

A few days passed, and Kirsten limped with scraped palms and bruised lips as several bikes whizzed by her. „Still can‘t ride a bike?“ yelled one of the boys, laughing, as they disappeared into the distance. Kirsten clenched her fists and approached her bike. She lifted it up and started running again. Two more days passed, and the end of the week was within reach.

The bicycles measured the same route the next day. The gang from the neighboring street gathered in the park. It was the right time for retaliation. They raced through the streets to make it to the park on time and prepare their ammunition before the enemy arrived in full force. Minutes were ticking by. Everyone took risks with broken knees and fractured arms on the bends. But now it was all or nothing. Slingshots were prepared under the leaves. They just had to collect chestnuts and wait for the enemy at their positions. The bicycles returned to the park. They all jumped off while still moving, until the bicycles piled up in a heap. But suddenly, the gang came to a halt as if on command. The enemy was not standing in front of them. There was one more bicycle by their base on the grass. Kirsten was standing behind it, and a large pile of chestnuts towered above her bruised knees.

ര

Kirsten ran her hand over her knee. It was smooth, and the wounds had long healed.

Chapter 24

- COFFEE TO GO -

Kirsten stood on the sidewalk and watched Sam. She quickly checked if the ladder was stable. She knew Sam was skilled and had already stood on it several times during the week, and he would stand on it several more times. However, when you care about loved ones and friends, such thoughts always creep into your mind. They couldn't be suppressed. The sign was bold and clear. Sam stretched and hung its right corner on the nail. Now it was clearly visible that Belinda's café would have free coffee tomorrow, on Friday, and you could mix it yourself to your own taste. 10 types of coffee, 10 flavors, 100 ways to brighten your day! At least that's how the big white sign above the café expressed it. Sam came down from the ladder and looked at his masterpiece. Kirsten smiled briefly. She felt a slight flutter in her stomach and some hope. She was glad they had finished before they got cold sitting on their butts with Belinda. She looked at Sam and entered the café without a word. Right opposite the entrance was a big table with 10 thermoses of different types of coffee on it. Decaffeinated, double dose of caffeine, Brazilian, dark roasted. Next to the table was a refrigerated stainless steel counter. It contained various types of milk and cream: full-fat, low-fat, whipped cream, nut milk, chocolate, vanilla. On the top shelf of the counter, there were several types of sugar. White, dark, cane sugar, artificial sweeteners, packets, and napkins. Above the table hung a large blackboard with the inscription: Life consists of years. Years of months. Months of days and days of hours. Hours of minutes and minutes of seconds. A second is one moment. This one moment can change your whole life. What coffee are you in the mood for in this moment?

„Come and have coffee," Kirsten called to Sam, who was still looking at the signboard with his hands on his hips in front of the café.

„You're our first customer, help yourself," she said to him as he approached the counter with the large thermos flasks. What Sam didn't know was that he was a test sample. Kirsten wanted to see if everyone could easily prepare the coffee they desired. Sam took a polystyrene cup and read the names of the coffees on the thermos flasks. He held the cup under the one labeled „Dark Roast" and filled it up. The aroma filled the café, and a small, fragrant steam cloud rose above the cup. He looked at the counter next to him and grabbed some whole milk. He poured it into the cup and added an artificial sweetener with a stirrer.

He stirred the coffee and took a sip, saying, „Hmm, it could be a little sweeter," and grabbed another sweetener. Kirsten smiled at Belinda and went outside. People here and there read the signboard. Tomorrow would show if Kirsten's plan had worked.

Chapter 25

- RAIN – BUT THAT LIBERATING ONE -

Kirsten looked at Adam. He made a grimace, smiled, and shook his head. She pressed another key and the piano produced a long hypnotic tone. She waited a few seconds and pressed the same key again. The atmosphere inside the little red house was exactly the same as outside. Adam leaned back in his chair.

„You know, I understand that my life is not entirely ordinary. But it‘s getting on my nerves. What would two young people do alone in this place, huh?“ said Adam, spreading his arms, looking at the beams of the little red house. The question was, of course, rhetorical, and they both knew it.

„It‘s still about money. They give you one and take two. I‘m just glad that we both are going through a complicated period and it wouldn‘t be appropriate to show feelings. And I‘m really glad that you‘re not like other girls. I don‘t know exactly why you‘re different, more mature, but that‘s why I noticed you in class. I would like to tell you why I‘m distant towards you, but I can‘t. But I know that someone like you understands it,“ Adam finished and looked at Kirsten.

„We all have our reasons for behaving the way we do. It‘s definitely not out of recklessness. Believe me, you will soon learn my reasons, and I will learn yours,“ Kirsten replied, looking out of the little house. It was raining heavily. But even if the sun was shining, it probably wouldn‘t have affected Kirsten‘s mood. In fact, she was glad that the sun wasn‘t forcing its rays and pleasant warmth on her. She was troubled. Sofia would be in the hospital until tomorrow due to tests, and Emie hadn‘t been to school for a week. Apparently, during this period, the farm required her hundred percent presence. And her relationship with Adam hadn‘t moved forward.

„Yes, money is our master. It keeps us on a leash and occasionally pulls us and changes our direction. That‘s why it‘s good to hold them by the leash. If you let them run freely, one day you‘ll find out that they ran away somewhere and won‘t come back, or that they bit you in the ass,“ Kirsten replied, and she wanted to smile, but couldn‘t.

„I know it won't last long. But do we know what we'll do with our relationship afterwards? I really wish I could just hold your hand. But for the two of us, that would mean prison with the highest security," Kirsten added sarcastically.

„Seems like Sophie hasn't changed, huh? Which is actually good. She looked the same at school. Just like any other day before," Adam finished and looked at the empty spot on the couch.

„I talked to her yesterday. She wants to go to the farm. Be with us. And I actually want to go too. If nothing changes, we promised Emie to help her this weekend," Kirsten replied and shifted on her elbow.

„Will you come with us? We can repeat our production process from last time. And the corn will likely be ripe too. Emie's mom always cooks a full pot, they say. We'll bring butter, spend a nice afternoon together again," Kirsten tried to conjure up some pleasant feelings in the midst of a rainy day.

„That farm is one of the few things that bring me joy and where I can relax. Of course, I'll come. I'll pick you up and we'll go together. I don't know how I'll make it until then. I can't seem to organize my life despite so many options. I can't wait to be officially grown up and have control over my life because it's tearing me apart. I feel very underutilized. We shouldn't be sitting here like two soaked chickens," Adam remarked. „I feel like a hostage thrown into a lake, unable to drown. Like when you step out of the door, onto the street, and a storm starts. And I stand there in the middle of the street drenched with problems, cursing that I didn't take an umbrella again to avoid them and stay dry. And this rain always binds me unbelievably. It prevents me from leaving the house," Adam finished and looked at the impenetrable wall of water from the little house.

„You know what? This is pointless. I might not be able to handle it. I can't just look at you with all that's in my head. I can't let it out of my head, and it's killing me. Damn money! We'll see each other tomorrow. I probably need a good night's sleep. Today is not a good day. It would be good to end it as soon as possible. Take care!" Adam said, threw his coat over his head, and ran to the car.

Kirsten was left alone in the red little house. She looked out the door and felt like crying or something. But she knew it wouldn't change anything. And she didn't want to feel weak. It wouldn't help her recharge her already drained batteries. She looked at the rain. It was drawing her in. She got up from the couch and walked towards the door. In her brown sandals and light dress, she walked towards it. She stepped out of the door, and a drop rolled down her contorted cheek, reaching the corner of her mouth. It slid down her neck. She instinctively closed her eyelids and felt that all the others, which the sky had given birth to, were rushing to fall at full speed somewhere tens of meters above her.

They were flying through the air, one beside the other. Silently. They were cold and choosing their targets. With a corner of her mouth turned up in a smile, she noticed how hundreds of others were falling on her. She stepped out of her little house and suddenly half of the dark sky crashed down on her. She started getting wet. Her clothes caught every drop. She felt them sliding down her back and more sliding down the backs of those, and finally falling to the ground. In a few seconds, she was completely soaked. The rain was pleasant, it cooled her a bit, but on a muggy day, it felt like redemption. She felt thousands of drops. Tens of thousands. They created entire watery worlds on her body, where they met again and disassembled the pleasant flight through the cool air. They crashed into dozens of others, but many streams met again in one point. And when they joined, they were no longer the virginal drops that fell from the clouds. They had a long journey behind them, full of experiences. And even though they fell hard, they managed to reconnect and fulfill the cycle of Mother Nature. Their fate. Many people cannot do that. She let them fulfill their goal, their task. She slowly tried to open her eyes. A small stream flowed over her eyelashes, preventing her from fully opening her eyes. As if it wanted to let her develop her imagination with half-closed eyes. It embraced her entirely. Kirsten played along. She imagined Edwood. She looked at empty streets. How everyone was running under the roofs of their homes, trees, umbrellas, and tunnels. Suddenly, many realized that not everything was as important as it seemed a few minutes ago. Many women were losing their make-up faces at the moment. The black stream was running down their cheeks, taking away their dignity. Hairstyles turned into mounds of soaked hay, and hair salon money flowed through Edwood‘s drains. Those will now smell and be liked. Umbrellas multiplied, walking speed increased. People decreased, roads were empty. Lights started coming on, nostalgia and depression were depressing nostalgically, the earth was darkening, and people were growing pale. Now, in many Edwood households, they were considering whether there really were so many things missing in the refrigerator. Pasta could do without olives and garlic now. Entrances of buildings suddenly became the coziest places for love. The number of members in Edwood households dramatically increased, and suddenly familiar voices could be heard. Lightning cut through the sky, and it echoed with thunderous voice. Kirsten‘s heart jumped to the rhythm of the storm. The atmosphere was palpable. The flash revealed her face, which was no longer grim. Raindrops smoothed her. Her consciousness revived. Again and again. The one that, despite everything, fell into another bout of nostalgia after a few seconds. And it took so little. To expose oneself to the storm. To not open the umbrella and try that feeling. She felt free...

Chapter 26

- NEW BEGINNING (?) -

Kirsten took off her apron. She folded it and looked at the closed door, on which Belinda had just turned the sign from Open to Closed. She turned towards Kirsten and confirmed with a glance the expectations of the next day. It was Thursday evening. The next day, they would find out if the „coffee to go“ plan had worked. Belinda had left everything up to Kirsten. She herself felt that she couldn‘t keep up with the fast pace of this era.

„You came into my life out of the blue, Kirsten. What can I say...“ she surprised her with a compliment. „You‘re the daughter I never had. Oh God, I‘m talking like the main character in some book. In any case, I‘ve lived a beautiful story with you. I hope it doesn‘t end with tomorrow, but rather begins,“ she finished and sat down on the nearest chair. Belinda looked around the café. She adjusted a small glass vase on the table and ran her fingers over the flower inside it. Kirsten noticed the wrinkles on her forehead. They were like that one tree in the forest that has been there from the beginning. Its rings represent the years it has grown in that forest. Belinda‘s wrinkles were like the years she had spent in the café. Kirsten wished that they wouldn‘t increase anymore, but rather smooth out and disappear. So that only the ones acquired over time remained, not the ones caused by worries.

„I have no idea if it will work. But when I took all the variables into account, it certainly can‘t hurt. I‘ve been going through all the supplies all week. We should have everything. The thermoses are ready, the counter is set up. All we need to do now is make the coffee in the morning and put the milk and cream from the fridge into the cooler box,“ Kirsten thought out loud. The café looked like a hungry monster in the dim light of the street lamps, ready to devour all the customers who come close to it. Kirsten remembered that she hadn‘t finished the coffee she made an hour ago. She looked around and found the cup next to the paper napkins. She had left it there when she went to pick them up and distribute them to the tables. She walked out with the cup in front of the counter, put her hand on her hip, and took a sip of the cold coffee. Next to her buzzed the cooler box she had bought second-hand from Belinda. The café smelled pleasantly and the set tables peeked out from the darkness, ready to welcome regular and new customers.

„I'm going to change and then I'll check the supplies," Kirsten interrupted Belinda from her reverie. She smiled and walked away. The café was filled with a fragrant silence. Kirsten leaned against the counter and felt as if time had momentarily stood still. She felt good. Not amazingly, exceptionally happy, just good. She was in a delicate balance that could be tipped by a single word or thought. Would she be here now if she hadn't taken the time to think? Or would she be at some boring party out of obligation? She cherished this moment. Perhaps a similar one wouldn't come along for a long time. She finished her cold coffee and placed the cup on the counter. The sound of porcelain echoed through the café. She had doubts. But doubts were good. They kept her on her toes. She didn't know if the plan would work. She didn't preconceive any outcome. All she wanted was to help Belinda. For her sake, she hoped her assumptions would be correct.

„We can go," Belinda exclaimed and walked towards the door. Kirsten left the café and watched Belinda lock it.

As the lock clicked in the door, Kirsten's heart skipped a beat and she felt a warm rush in her stomach, like a bottle of honey pouring out. These feelings would probably stay with her tomorrow morning as well. Feelings that no amount of money could buy.

„You know... these are the moments that stay with a person for life. We'll remember this even eight years from now. Even twenty. This is my treasure. Not to mention the experiences I gained while preparing our plan. I've already received my share of reward. I really hope you'll get yours too," Kirsten finished and headed towards her car. Belinda descended two small steps to her own car. She got in and rolled down the window on the passenger side.

„I'm glad you see it that way. It's an honor for me. You work for the café as if it were your own. I have nothing to add. Let's get some rest. Tomorrow is a new day. Hopefully a new beginning. Goodbye!" Belinda said, and started the engine.

„Goodbye, I have nothing to add. Get some rest," Kirsten waved and started her car. She watched as Belinda drove away. She shifted gears and hoped that the café also shifted to a higher gear and wouldn‘t stay idle in neutral with a sputtering engine that would run out of gas and stall soon.

ᔕ

Friday morning was a typical day for the café, except for the fact that if they received a coin for every question about whether the coffee was really free, they would probably earn enough for two new handbags in a day.

„Transparent really attracted people. It was still a bit cautious on their part. Occasionally, someone would take a coffee to go and stop by the counter to pay because they couldn‘t believe that the coffee was really free. The day passed fairly quickly for both of them. It couldn‘t be said that the new idea was a bull‘s-eye, but it wasn‘t a failure either. Kirsten knew that one swallow doesn‘t make a summer. She understood that people needed to get used to the new product and incorporate it into their lives and needs. Saturdays and Sundays were traditionally the busiest days when believers came to the café after mass and families with children. Even fewer coffees to go were sold than on Fridays. Belinda and Kirsten had not evaluated their plan yet. Kirsten herself saw tension in Belinda. She knew it wasn‘t too late, but it was still too early to evaluate. She knew that the answer lay in perseverance. She had learned to see opportunities, not obstacles. Profit instead of loss and reward instead of risk. That‘s why she kept her cool. The week passed fairly quickly for both of them. There was a steady buzz in the café even during the week, and neither of them felt that anything had changed. Kirsten occasionally realized that she had put a new thermos of coffee on the table again and that the supplies were slowly disappearing from the storage room. Days went by until Belinda realized it was Monday again. She locked the doors and flipped the sign from Open to Closed. Kirsten was collecting thermoses from the counter and taking them to the sink. Belinda went to the cash register and did the closing. She fiddled with the accounting software for a while. Kirsten was interrupted by a soft „oh." She stopped washing the thermoses and looked at Belinda. „Do you know what happened today that has never happened in the café before? What‘s different today compared to other days?" Belinda exclaimed in surprise, still looking at the computer screen. „Well, I don‘t know. It doesn‘t seem to me that anything unusual happened," Kirsten stated. „Today is the first day when we sold more coffees to go than for consumption in the café,"

Belinda replied and turned the monitor towards Kirsten. Both of them were so absorbed in their work that they hadn‘t noticed this change. Sales of coffees to go had been growing slowly but steadily. People had apparently started getting used to this new product. Kirsten looked at Belinda in the dim light as she gazed at the monitor. She could tell from her face that the café would remain open in Edwood for another year. She was glad she chose this more complicated plan first, rather than the simpler one. Thanks to it, Belinda doesn‘t have to share her child with anyone and won‘t fall asleep feeling like a stepmother.“

Chapter 27

- JUDGMENT DAY -

Adam hung his coat in the small office right behind the door. Angela was already sitting at the table, inputting data into the computer. She sat upright, and every movement seemed like a rehearsed gesture. Perhaps her expensive navy-blue blazer seemed unnecessarily ostentatious in these surroundings, but Angela took pride in these little details. Adam sat across from her in jeans and a leather jacket, looking more like a bystander than a co-owner of the factory. Angela looked like a true economist and commanded respect. Despite the factory being a large warehouse with numerous machines, corners, and storage areas, the accounting office was just a small room. The desks were against the wall, there was a water dispenser in the corner, a couch, and a coffee table. Opposite the desks, there was one large window divided into two parts. Adam kept looking out of it at the production halls below. He watched the employees running around with semi-finished products. He felt responsible for them. But he also felt that he was sacrificing his freedom for the sake of his responsibilities. The factory was one large organism, and for them to survive, all its parts had to work together. However, now their survival depended on Angela‘s family. They had already tentatively agreed to buy a share. Every Friday, Adam and Angela met in this small office to process the accounting documents. Both families wanted them to gradually familiarize themselves with the operation of the factory and gain experience they wouldn‘t find in school. The families probably planned for this to bring not only their accounting together but also their souls. Adam walked past the window and sat down at his desk. He didn‘t even start working; he leaned back and gazed at Angela. She felt his gaze on her left cheek.

„What‘s wrong?“ she asked, puzzled. She was still the one who scrutinized him with her gaze or words. She had never seen this kind of look from Adam before.

„I‘m just thinking about how everything will evolve. My life, yours. The life of this factory, our parents‘. What do you expect from it? Some happy ending where everyone is happy until death? You know yourself that real life doesn‘t work that way,“ Adam replied, averting his gaze.

„And do you think that your feelings will be saved by some coincidence? Miracle? Kirsten?“ Angela retorted, and Adam looked at her slightly defensively.

„Unlike you, I believe in emotional ownership. Moral values. Not just principles and rules,“ Adam retorted.

„So, Kirsten then,“ Angela smiled and briefly closed her eyes to stop the moment before her response.

„It leaves a bitter taste in your mouth, doesn‘t it?“ Adam smiled back.

„You know, I would also like to believe in fairy tales. Just like my life and yours, it‘s a winding road. Both of us would like to get off this road and get lost somewhere in the forest. Maybe you want to find a lost damsel there who will turn out to be a princess with half a kingdom later. And you will live happily ever after. And I will be bewitched by some good deed and we will all live happily ever after,“ Angela replied with a smile and ran her worried fingers through her hair. She sorted the papers on the table and continued with her work. Adam also paid attention and inwardly, though reluctantly, agreed.

„Well, of course, my dear evil queen, who is not really to blame for her wickedness. It‘s the curse. Wealth has overshadowed your perspective,“ Adam said and laughed too.

„I understand that we are currently working on our future. We are responsible. We are adults. Were you ever a child yourself? You know, little Angela, who once broke a window with a ball or dropped freshly painted bread on the floor and started crying in the kitchen?“ Adam asked.

„I think money was like a bridge for me, and thanks to them, I skipped from diapers straight through the childhood that I could experience, to a life that most people will never experience. Do I regret it? I can‘t judge that. Since I never experienced it, I don‘t miss it. You can‘t miss something you‘ve never had,“ Angela replied, inputting data into the computer. Adam felt a chill. He felt a certain empty space within himself, but couldn‘t define it. Probably some unfulfilled childhood memory.

Something that could have been there, but never came. He missed the fact that he didn‘t miss it. He felt as if a certain part of his brain had died off. Or as if it had never been activated. Like a piece of rotten apple that no one would ever be able to eat.

„And you do this job voluntarily? Wouldn‘t you rather be somewhere else? Doing something that truly interests and fulfills you?“ Adam continued asking questions.

„I wouldn‘t want to. Why? I‘m not here, unlike you, against my will. I‘m doing the right thing. I‘m working on myself. I can‘t think of it any other way. I‘m already financially committed. On one hand, to money and a life of wealth. I stood in front of them, turned around, spread my arms and fell into them like the softest bed. And they‘ve been spoiling me my whole life. And on the other hand, I‘m committed to defending, improving, and progressing in this life,“ Angela spoke as she typed on the keyboard. She talked about it as if it had always been with her. Adam didn‘t feel that way. The idea of financially committing his life made him feel like a hostage. As if he would still be driving his life, pressing the accelerator, shifting gears. Just not holding the steering wheel anymore. On the other hand, he was afraid that if he held on to that steering wheel, his life might come to a standstill and he would look like a little child with the wheel in hand, imagining that he had already passed through three states and had incredible adventures behind him. Just like poor people live in their rich fantasies. He was looking for a compromise. Some wise solution that would put him between these two worlds and allow him to enjoy the benefits of money and the freedom of the poor, who are not tied down by tax returns and interest rates. He understood that he shouldn‘t avoid or minimize problems and challenges, but grow into them. He felt that he was growing every day during this period. But not fast enough. Kirsten was a catalyst for him. The way she thought, her actions, and the unknown that always walked with her, forced him and stimulated him to reevaluate his own actions. He simply realized that Kirsten inspired him, even though she didn‘t know it herself. He looked at Angela. She looked truly committed. She worked as if this job was endless. She was like a machine. Yes, that was it. She looked and acted like a machine. Not like a human being. When she committed herself, she left behind a lot of emotions at the door that now had no place in this life. She was like a backpack with limited space. You can‘t fit a whole house into it. A traveler takes this backpack with them on a trip and only packs the essentials in it.

The team of travelers were the money. They took Angela on a trip. But before that, they took away all unnecessary and useless things from her at home, such as feelings and emotions. She liked the journey of the backpack. It was adventurous, and she didn‘t have to walk. She just let herself be carried. She just didn‘t know where this journey would lead. What if the traveler didn‘t notice the cliff and both fell to the bottom of the abyss? Adam stared out the window in front of him, work stood still. Angela interrupted his train of thought.

„Do you know why you will be poor for the rest of your life? And I don‘t just mean money. Because you don‘t know what you want. You‘re not sure about your choices. You don‘t know which way to run, so you‘re standing still. I am fulfilling my dreams and goals because I don‘t emit mixed signals around me. I go after them directly. I have accepted that I am and will be wealthy. I give a hundred percent to my goals. Not ninety-eight, not ninety-nine, but a full hundred. You scatter your hundred percent around you. You waste energy and time. Or... Or maybe you haven‘t even started fulfilling those dreams and goals yet. You gather energy into one point. You hold your breath and aim at that goal. You want to make sure it‘s a direct hit. That would be the better case. I‘m curious to see how it all unfolds. But for now, I don‘t intend to stand still. We bear the responsibility for the lives of many people, even though we are still not considered adults according to societal rules. But my dear, we are more mature than all those who work in this factory. We are already in full force. And that is a gift, not a punishment. Of course... nothing is free. We had to sacrifice something. Something that society or life will return to us someday. Balance exists. That‘s why you may feel like you‘re at the bottom of the scale right now. That life has the upper hand now. You feel like a stone. But believe me, the feelings of your own work, successes, and achievements will refresh your mind, and suddenly your side of the scale will go up. And one day, you will realize that you are in balance with your life,“ Angela spoke, and in the meantime, the large lamps lit up in the hall. They timidly illuminated the small office. The light momentarily awakened Angela. She got up and walked to the water container. She poured herself a glass of water, stood by the window, and watched the hustle and bustle in the factory. She sipped from the glass, not moving a hair. Adam watched her. She looked so mature that she seemed lonely. Long dress, perfectly groomed hair, subtle makeup. Adam didn't know if he was looking at a teenager or an adult woman. Under different circumstances, he would have found this sight attractive. But now it raised more questions than answers.

„Do you know where Kirsten is now? She's playing the piano around the city. In a nursing home, in a restaurant... She's doing exactly what we are doing. Something that she enjoys and fulfills her."

„But there is a difference. Between us and her. She experiences it, enjoys it. We all do the same, and yet differently. Happiness comes with giving, not receiving..." Adam didn't finish his sentence and Angela interrupted him: „Money comes and I can't wish for more. I'm living my dream, fulfilling my dreams and achieving my goals. I probably just have to start singing," she concluded, smiled and sat back at the table. Adam pulled his chair closer and continued his work with his back straight. He momentarily surrendered to the finances again. It didn't make sense to debate further with Angela. But he was glad this conversation took place.

Chapter 28

- RICH AND RICHER -

To Belinda's surprise, sales increased every week while she worked less. More and more customers visited the coffee buffet, which had become a favorite spot for starting the workday among the town's residents. Belinda gradually started making new flavors using local, homemade ingredients. People stopped buying semi-finished products as much. Belinda herself felt like she had caught her second wind. In addition to cakes, she started making syrups and experimenting with coffee. She listened to her customers, and in a short time, the coffee buffet had a stable assortment, and every customer could mix their favorite coffee. Customers started coming to the café from more distant towns, and even those who planned their trip just for Belinda's café. This success reached beyond Edwood's borders, and one day, two mysterious gentlemen with expensive black manager briefcases entered the café.

„Good afternoon, can we speak with the owner?" one of them asked Kirsten as she prepared coffee.

„Belinda! Can you come for a moment?" she shouted towards the storeroom and took coffee and pastry to the table. Belinda came to the counter. They all chatted for a while. Kirsten wiped the tables and glanced at their conversation from the corner of her eye. Belinda smiled strangely and occasionally looked at her. She took the tray with used cups and was about to head to the counter when Belinda pointed at Kirsten, and both gentlemen turned towards her.

„Can we talk to you for a moment? The owner sent us to you. Is the coffee buffet your idea?" one of them inquired. Kirsten put the tray back on the table and sat down.

„Well, yes, it is. Sort of. We came up with it together with Belinda to bridge the gaps in revenue," Kirsten replied nervously.

„We would like to turn this café into a franchise. We like the idea. We are ready to invest in this company and expand Belinda's café beyond the borders of this town,“ the unknown man said and leaned back in his chair. Belinda placed plates with pastries and coffee in front of them. Kirsten didn‘t know what to say. All she wanted was to help Belinda. She cut a piece of cake and put a fragrant bite in her mouth.

„This is Belinda‘s café. I don‘t know why you‘re asking me this,“ she didn‘t understand.

„Because we want you to be a product and marketing consultant in this franchise. We want a complete package,“ the unknown man replied and took a sip of his coffee.

„I can help Belinda, but I don‘t want to be involved in this plan. I will do everything in my power to help her, if she decides to work with you. But I don‘t want to commit or promise anything,“ Kirsten replied and took a bite of her cake.

„You will be wealthy,“ the other man whispered and leaned towards Kirsten.

„But I am already wealthy,“ she replied and looked around the café.

„I understand,“ smiled the investor, „But you can be even wealthier. Building a franchise will take a year or two. Later, you can even go public and sell your shares,“ he added.

„And how long will it take?“ she asked.

„It depends on how much you want to earn. But I think about ten years from now,“ the investor specified.

„And then what?“ she asked further.

„You will be financially secure for life. You can come to this café anytime and enjoy the cakes for the rest of your life,“ the investor replied.

„Like now?“ Kirsten smiled and took another bite.

„Yes, like now,“ the investor smiled as well.

„Well, I can do that without losing ten years, whether I am wealthy or not,“ she pointed out.

„I don‘t mind. If many other people have the opportunity to taste Belinda‘s café, I will personally be very happy. It has a lot to offer,“ she smiled.

„Yes, it does,“ agreed the investor. Both men finished their coffee and left for the counter. Meanwhile, Kirsten continued serving customers, giving Belinda time to negotiate.

With a corner of her eye, Belinda saw that the men handed her an envelope with papers and left. A surprising smile mixed with fear and excitement lit up her face. If someone were to take a bite out of her now, she would taste like a strawberry-vanilla-menthol-lemon cake with a hint of chili. All her emotions were at play.

„Kirsten...this is not what I asked for. I was hoping we could still save the café, but I got so much more. Honestly, I don‘t know what to do. A room has just opened up for me that I didn‘t really want to peek into," Belinda said hesitantly as Kirsten washed the dishes. She knew she was talking about retirement. Leaving this world and making room for others. She didn‘t know anything else, just her café, baking cakes, and the smell of coffee.

„I understand. You feel like a prisoner being released after forty years in jail. Suddenly, you won‘t know what to do with your life. Behind these café walls, you have your life. You don‘t know anything else. Everyone in town knows you. You‘re somebody. And now you‘re afraid that your life will be emptier, even though it will be richer, with almost unlimited possibilities," Kirsten tried to guess Belinda‘s feelings. She just nodded her head to the side and gave Kirsten a faint smile, agreeing with her.

„Look, you can just pass on your know-how to those gentlemen. Or you can keep a small share in the company. You‘ll have enough money to open this café every day and keep baking cakes. There‘s nothing wrong with your motivation not being money. That you‘ll feel better when you unlock these doors in the morning rather than counting the sums that come into your account every day," Kirsten tried to reassure Belinda.

„Yes, the thought of any wealth doesn‘t satisfy me. It actually scares me. What would I do with all that money? And I also think I would have less time for myself and the café. And at my age, that time cannot be bought with any amount of money. The value of my time increases with each passing year. It‘s not for me anymore," Belinda sighed and wiped the already clean counter. Kirsten watched her and knew that no matter how Belinda decided, the coming days would be different. Ones they had never experienced before. From that day on, whenever Kirsten locked the doors of the café behind her, she knew that the café would be here tomorrow. And that the doors of this café would likely slam shut in many other places all over the country every evening.

Chapter 29

- MUSIC -

„Can you help me get the piano onto the sidewalk? Sam will be here soon to pick it up in his van," Kirsten couldn't wait to play it. In that one word, all her inspiration and motivation were hidden. The whole short story, from the moment she found the piano until she earned enough money for it, was contained in that word. During this story, she had formed a relationship with that pile of wood and keys. A relationship that couldn't be bought. While saving up for it, dozens of stories played out in her head. How she would bring it home, where she would place it... She must have changed the first piece she would play on it at least fifty times. She imagined days, mornings, and evenings in the little red house by the lake. And how she would transfer it from the house to the living room in her house. The piano wasn't even home yet, and she already felt like she had played it a hundred times. She would lose all of this if she had bought it on the first day. She would create many real stories and beautiful moments for today anyway. But they would taste even better. The whole story, months of work and patience, fit into a single word. The word that would express this story. Mr. Newton smiled. He knew how much time Kirsten had spent in front of the display or in the store. In that time, he also got to know Kirsten. He knew she was very patient and determined. Since the first day she asked him to wait for her with the piano until she earned enough money for it at Belinda's, he put a „sold" sign on it. And even though people wondered why it had been standing there for a month, he didn't sell it to anyone, even though some people waved banknotes in front of his nose... He just repeated to everyone that when it's sold, it's simply sold.

Today was the D-day, and the piano would leave its honorable spot. With the help of his assistant, they carefully maneuvered it out of the store through the door, quickly looking for a place to put it.

In front of the store, there was a wide sidewalk with benches arranged in a square. One side of this square was not occupied by a bench, creating an optimal spot on the street where the piano would not bother anyone. Kirsten looked around the door to make sure that the piano wouldn‘t accidentally crush anyone‘s foot. They crossed the sidewalk and stopped at the chosen spot. The piano surrounded by benches looked interesting on the street, as if someone had set up a mini concert hall and was preparing for a mini concert. Kirsten looked at it from the side. It was the first time she had seen the piano in daylight. It looked even more beautiful now. She walked around it and remembered when she had seen it for the first time. That‘s when she realized that by saving up for it, she had not only gained many of her imaginary stories, but had actually helped Belinda with the café. Without this particular piano and Kirsten‘s patience, who knows how it would have turned out with the café. She was content with her decision and had no regrets about not buying it on the first day. She would have lost more than just the time she would spend playing it anyway. Now, thanks to it, people were looking forward to the new service at the café, the new coffee selection, and the café was experiencing a second lease on life instead of slowly fading away. Her patience had formed a connection to it and to Belinda. Maybe it wouldn‘t mean as much to her today and wouldn‘t have any story written in it. Today, it had a value for her that simply couldn‘t be paid with money. Today, the last puzzle piece fell into place.

Mr. Newton shook his head, smiled, and went back into the store. Kirsten stood in front of it and ran her hand over the keys. A dream come true. Now she was experiencing exactly the feeling she fell asleep with. The atmosphere was magical. The world around her ceased to exist for a moment. People walked by on the sidewalk, looking at the piano and Kirsten. Many of them had never seen such a sight before. She was like the title of a book: The Girl with the Piano on the Street.

Mr. Newton woke her from his daydream: „Oh, the stool. We almost forgot. Every piano has its stool. You surely know that," he said and placed a small, worn-out swivel stool in front of Kirsten. It was worn from use, soaked with music. It must have known the piano for decades. Kirsten blushed and realized that she had completely forgotten about it.

Probably because she had several of them in her house. But the piano is complete only with this one. It is an inseparable part of it. They are family. And now Kirsten had become a part of this family. She almost felt like a stepmother. She placed the stool closer to the piano and sat on it. She had plenty of time and was starting to get bored.

Kirsten adjusted the height. She opened the dictionary again and scanned the scribbled notes that had been rewritten several times. She closed it and placed it on the piano. They waited for the moment when the notes would spill over her hands and then onto the street. She remembered Sofia. She wanted to play the piece she had composed just for her so badly now. Every note was a part of her personality. Each part of the melody depicted in her mind a facial expression or a memory they had shared. If the composition could materialize, it would become Sofia. In fact, Sofia had become the composition. Whenever she wanted to be with her, she played it. And now she wanted to be with her. She forgot she was on the street, lost track of time and weather. She was in love with the composition and couldn't control herself anymore. She started playing. Kirsten felt a magical bond that was beginning to form between her and the piano thanks to the composition. Or rather, it was strengthening. As if someone had brought her a newborn baby. The street remained a street. People passed by her, the hustle and bustle of the busy hour slowly subsided. It was late afternoon and the sun itself was lazily crawling towards the horizon. Without preparation, she struck the keys. She had played each note in her head a hundred times. She didn't need to think or concentrate. She just needed to place her hands on the piano and listen to her own composition. To her inner self that had been playing it to her all along. She didn't even need to repeat the notes. It was like when a child digs into an ice cream. They know exactly how it will taste. She wanted to have her ears filled with music here and now. Her inner self was filled with the familiar melody and Sofia. She felt a surge of inspiration. Her hands couldn't be stopped and they literally flew over the piano. Notes poured out of it like a geyser that had broken through to the surface after millions of years and erupted. The city seemed as if it had just been washed with cold water. People stopped thinking for a moment and rushing somewhere. The melody flooded the small square and stretched around the buildings, bending at their corners and playing even behind them. Mr. Newton stopped counting money in the cash register, the coins slipped out of his hand and he stepped out of the shop onto the street. He saw a sight that, despite his advanced age, he had never seen before. A young girl, completely detached from the surrounding world and a world that was trying to merge with this phenomenon. People stopped next to Kirsten and listened. And those who couldn't stop just slalomed through the street lamps, keeping an eye on her. It's a pity he only had two ears. He really liked the composition. He had never heard it before. He looked around and noticed that the people who had stopped looked just as surprised as he was. Everyone had an unconscious optimistic twitch on their faces. The music had completely tied their feet and they stood there, unable to move, entranced by the melody...

He only now understood the meaning of the words when someone lives through music. Music lived in Kirsten. It played as if it wanted to save Sofia's life. Kirsten looked intently at her hands, which pointed to the notes. They flew from side to side, and the piano gradually filled the entire street with music. It stretched down the street just like the scent from a nearby bakery. Several people across the street from the shops were drawn to it. Mr. Newton looked around. He observed with interest all those peaceful and positively inclined faces. Just one composition. And he saw how many people would end their day a little more beautifully. He was glad that he had sold the piano to Kirsten. She even gave him an extra reward. He could feel the experience forming in him, one that he would never forget for the rest of his life. Like many other people who happened to be on the street at that moment.

Everyone looked somewhat bashful because they didn't know who the composition was intended for. They tiptoed past her, as if they didn't want to disturb her at any cost. They wanted the composition to last as long as possible. Kirsten just played and played. In contrast to the street, she seemed to be the only person there. She repeated all the notes in her head a thousand times. They were prepared for this piano, for this moment, and for that particular person who was not there. She was with Kirsten, in Kirsten.

With every strike of the piano, she realized that nothing would be the same as before. With every strike, she felt that she was getting closer to something. And with every strike, she was also moving away from something else. While playing, she felt that time had stopped. And right now, she needed it to stop. Or at least slow down. So that she could gradually find answers to her questions. So that she could prepare for the next stage of life.

The music spreading in the middle of the city briefly changed everyone's daily routine. It disrupted the habits and stereotypes of everyone who was absorbed by the music. Many paused just to absorb the atmosphere and take it home with them to their homes and offices. They watched her hands as they pressed the keys gently, deliberately, and precisely. Occasionally, her hand would rise up and emphasize a tone or a fragment of melody. Some people took out their phones and recorded this private concert. But they couldn't capture how the tones crawled out of the piano onto the street. How they climbed up the trunks of trees to their crowns and then crawled onto the roofs of houses. They fell into gutters and raced over their edges, pouring over windows that opened under their vibrations. And the tones slowly crept into the interiors of human dwellings, into the ears of their inhabitants, and then sent them, mesmerized, to the windows.

She played as if it were to be her first and perhaps last composition. She had waited so long for this piano that she couldn't peel herself away from it now. She had almost bought it on the first day and silently took it home. Now she wouldn't play on this street anymore, and she wouldn't even change the mood of one inhabitant of Edwood on this day. In the flood of emotions, Kirsten herself didn't realize this moment. She just listened to the music that flowed from the piano. Schizophrenically, she realized that the girl needed to let her emotions out. For someone else. She didn't want to keep them to herself.

Kirsten noticed Sam's car. She stopped playing. She stood up from behind the piano when an unknown boy approached her: „What's the name of that composition?" he asked, recording her on his phone.

„For Sofia," she replied. She didn't care that a stranger was recording her. There is a story hidden behind every favorite composition. And Kirsten had just told it without opening her mouth. Everyone heard it, but only she understood it. A coded message that everyone decoded according to their own interpretation. She smiled and walked towards Sam. Today she fulfilled one dream. Even the dark passenger momentarily stopped haunting her, comfortably settled in and listened. In this moment, he was considerate and didn't hold the image of her mother's death in front of her. Maybe she just wanted to play. And maybe she played now to feel free again. To not feel the fate that impatiently taps its fingers on the table and awaits the final answer.

Chapter 30

- CARROT AND HISTORY -

Emie walked towards the greenhouse. It was one of those ordinary days when she wouldn't have time for books again. It was time to harvest another crop. At this moment, she felt torn. On one hand, she enjoyed working in the greenhouse, touching the plants she had been observing all the time. What a miracle happens in it every day. How colorful vegetables grow „out of nothing" from the ground. She loved the moist smell, tasting juicy fruits. On the other hand, she knew that by doing this, she was moving further away from her dream of becoming a veterinarian. The grades in school suggested that she would be a good farmer rather than a veterinarian. This year was important in school. Grades were taken into account for future admissions to further education. And that school was supposed to be veterinary school. Every good grade meant a step closer to her desired future. However, Emie knew that if she was not making progress, she was taking small steps backwards. There would be a lot of exams and studying ahead. And some year-end project. And Emie would have very little time for all of that. She was interrupted from her thoughts by a sound coming from the greenhouse. She quickened her step curiously.

„What are you doing here?" Kirsten asked curiously, carrying empty boxes into the greenhouse.

„Well, I sent you a message that I can come and help you today. You didn't answer the phone. It's a nice day today. I felt like spending time on the farm," Emie replied, taking a deep breath of the vegetable scent coming from the greenhouse.

„Hmm, oh. The phone... Where did I put it?" Emie laughed and searched her pockets.

„I'm glad you're here. The work will go faster. At least I won't be so exhausted in the evening. And maybe we'll even have time to look into some books," Emie mused out loud. They entered the greenhouse side by side. The boxes were already prepared on the sides. They just needed to go along the rows, picking the fruits and weeding out the weeds.

„You know, Emie, did you know that the test is next week?" Kirsten asked from across the two-meter wide bed and continued pulling out weeds from the vegetable patch.

„Well, I know. But I already know how it will turn out," Emie replied with a slightly sad voice and threw a handful of weeds into the trash.

„I know you don't have time to study. So at least when I occasionally come over, I'll help you with chores around the house," Kirsten stated.

„But you don't just come here for that. I would feel bad. I don't want to waste your time, and I don't want to feel like a burden," Emie said in a harsh tone.

„Well, alright. Yes, I come here selfishly for myself too, because I simply like it here. The connection with nature. With you. Does someone really have to force themselves into such a pleasant day?" Kirsten laughed.

„Well, I'm glad you feel good here. I'll probably be here for a very long time. You can come and visit me here. Visiting hours for relatives and friends of inmates are every afternoon," Emie laughed.

„I just don't know what to do with that test. And then the next one. I managed to read some, but it's not enough for the test," Emie stated.

„How many pages did you manage to read? At least up to the fifth point?" Kirsten asked while continuing to pick vegetables from the patch.

„Well, only up to the second point," Emie replied.

Kirsten leaned against the bed and looked into the tilled soil. „Well, that's not good. You know what? I'll be your textbook..." she didn't finish her sentence and Emie added, „You already are!" Kirsten laughed and continued, „I reached the seventh point. Just three more and I'll be done. So I can tell you the material we'll be tested on while we work. I'll review it myself, and maybe you'll remember something. We can quiz each other. Or bring the textbooks here to the greenhouse. That way we'll make use of all the time at 200%," Kirsten pondered aloud and looked up at Emie.

„Do you think it will work like that?" Emie asked in surprise.

„Why not? If I keep drilling the same thing into you for two hours straight? Maybe something will stick! It's still better than not looking at the books at all. And we can chat during breaks at school," Kirsten gradually revealed her emerging plan.

ω

From that day on, instead of regular teenage conversations, the greenhouse was filled with educational texts on history, geography, mathematics, and literature. Kirsten often studied ahead, covering material she didn't have to, just so they could go over more multiple times a week in those few hours. And the difference was noticeable. Sometimes it worked out and Emie got a grade on a test or quiz that she herself couldn't believe. Sometimes it didn't work out and Emie found familiar old grades in her student book, but progress was evident. Over time, Kirsten noticed that it brought her more joy than Emie herself. She was grateful for these genuine feelings. This mini project helped her make her own decisions and she hoped it would give her strength before the arrow was shot. So that it would reach the target and hit the bull's-eye. So she wouldn't miss. Underlined, calculated, Emie had to write the upcoming test for the best possible grade to have a chance to get into the coveted school. In the days leading up to the test, she held a book in her hands more often than vegetables or pulled weeds in the greenhouse. Kirsten tried to do all the work for her, just so she could have enough time to prepare for the test.

D-Day was approaching. And it was within reach. In a few hours, Emie would find out where her life was heading. Tomorrow after the fourth hour.

„You know, I've often considered paying for tutoring. But it would be a waste of money. I wouldn't have time to go there anyway. Working on the farm really takes up most of my day. But then you came up with that brilliant idea. And it really worked. You bought me something that money can't buy. Time," Emie spoke up and played with the earring in her ear.

„Well, we'll see tomorrow if we bought enough of it," Kirsten replied and bit into a carrot.

„It would be amazing if a miracle happened tomorrow. But it will still be a small step. I'll still have to prepare for the veterinary exams. They're not until next year, but I already know where I'll spend that year," Emie said hesitantly, crumbling a clump of clay in her hand.

„You don‘t know what will happen in a year. Trust me. That‘s why it‘s not necessary to focus on it right now. Focus on tomorrow," Kirsten reassured her and looked through the glass door as gentle cool rain soaked the trees around.

„We could, I still feel like I need more of those hours. But I‘m grateful for every single one we managed to steal," Emie replied, leaning against the wooden railing next to Kirsten. They watched the rainy theater together, which so melancholically soothed them both. Kirsten reached behind Emie and hugged her around the left shoulder, pulling her close to her side. Emie let out a deep sigh and rested her head on Kirsten‘s shoulder. The patter of raindrops and the crunching of carrots filled the air with their glasses. Cool drops trickled down the growing fruits of the fruit trees outside the window. Today, they took another step towards fulfilling their cherished dream."

Chapter 31

- FINAL EXAM -

Kirsten sat down at the piano. She ran her hand over the keys as if she wanted to dust them off. She caressed them like a kitten that would start purring in a moment. Angela sat opposite her at the piano. Her white blouse, white stockings, and dark skirt matched perfectly with the bright piano. She immediately played a few simple melodies on the keys, carefully listening to see if the piano was in tune. Not a single false note escaped her attentive ear. Mrs. Miller stood next to them, picking a piece from the stack of papers that they were supposed to play today. They couldn't see each other from behind the pianos. Mrs. Miller put the sheet music on the stand for Angela, then went to Kirsten and handed her a music notebook with the pages already turned.

„I don't want to be the judge again today. Just focus on your playing. Angela, we already know from the previous lesson that you're a piano genius. So please, don't destroy the piano too much. It will be enough if the performance is flawless and played from the heart. In the final round, you'll be competing against the best of the best. If one of you fails, you both fail," Mrs. Miller gave her introductory speech before the exam to avoid a repeat of the previous „performance." It was always the same. They both started playing according to the sheet music. But then Angela started adding her own variations to the piece, and Kirsten reacted to them. They didn't play any wrong notes, and every piece sounded amazing. However, with this improvisation, there was always a risk of making a mistake. Mrs. Miller didn't know how they would handle the pressure at the competition. After all, in the classroom, they felt at home. It was their refuge. A small slip-up in front of the audience would be enough to waste weeks of rehearsals. And all for personal reasons. Mrs. Miller wanted to avoid that. Although she admitted that improvisation would take their performance to another level and guarantee victory. That's why she always let them play until the end, even though she didn't approve of this kind of exam. She herself had a mixed opinion of their playing. Maybe Angela would leave Kirsten alone today, and they would practice the piece without any mistakes.

Kirsten placed her hands on the keys. Mrs. Miller always laughed at how such small and modest hands could play such complicated pieces. Short fingers were a disadvantage for Kirsten, but that‘s precisely why they were so agile and nimble on the piano.

Her nails were not specially manicured. Any polish she applied would inevitably chip from her constant playing. She kept them neatly trimmed with a layer of sheer polish. The first note resonated through the hall. Three or four students stood by the door. The doors closed behind them. Kirsten added more notes to the composition. Miller felt the emotions coursing through her. She counted the beats. Two, three, four, now Angela. She placed her hand on the piano keys and already knew that the composition would be as perfect as her perfectly done manicure. Her long and slender fingers could play the chords without needing to shift her hands on the keys. Angela added her first notes to Kirsten‘s. The transition was seamless, as if a single pianist was playing the entire piece. That was the goal of the competition, to make the composition sound seamless despite the transitions between pianos. Angela played her part and gradually caught up to Kirsten. They played the same composition, but swapped passages with each other. Miller listened intently with closed eyes, checking for any false notes and ensuring that every note was played. She opened her eyes and saw that both of them were playing like machines. They were completely calm, and she would swear that they looked bored. They played the entire composition. The first time. Miller always had them play the same composition three times in a row without a break. Kirsten started playing the composition for the second time. But Angela didn‘t wait for her passage, she started adding a few more notes to it. Miller frowned, „Here we go again," she thought. Kirsten glanced at Angela. Angela didn‘t smile, she just kept playing. She was fully concentrated. They slowly approached Angela‘s passage. The composition was still the same, but it sounded somehow more colorful and interesting. Angela played her passage, and Kirsten joined in. However, unlike Angela, her notes were not aggressive, but rather subtly emphasized Angela‘s melody. Angela reacted to the change and started playing Kirsten‘s game. Miller didn‘t try to say anything or interrupt them. She knew what was coming. They both warmed up and the composition started to become musically aggressive. But they still didn‘t make any mistakes. This musical battle would have a winner only if one of them made a mistake, which hadn‘t happened yet. The beautiful composition filled the hall, and the students in the back of the classroom jumped from their chairs. They even skipped several rows of desks to make it to the hall before the composition ended. One of them rushed out of the classroom and shouted, „Kirsten and Angela are playing against each other again!“ and ran into the hallway and back to the hall. About fifteen students were sitting in the classroom. They looked at each other for a moment and then bolted from their chairs to catch up to the hall before the composition finished.

Angela was pounding on the piano keys, hoping that Kirsten would make a mistake. The atmosphere in the room was tense, akin to a competition, and everyone watched in silence. Finally, they both finished playing the piece for the third time, and the room fell silent. Only their rapid breathing could be heard.

„I know what you‘re trying to do. But I don‘t understand why a mistake means something bad to you. The mistake is being afraid to make a mistake. That‘s when you make a mistake. But I‘m not afraid to make mistakes,“ Kirsten said, pushing her chair away from the piano to get a better look at Angela.

„The mistake you make will be the small difference between you and me. I‘m only annoyed by one thing. The later you make it, the better you‘ll become at playing the piano. Because I am the motivation and muse that helps you improve,“ Angela pointed out, straightening her posture and running her hands over the keys, playing an imaginary passage.

„Well, what if I never make that mistake?“ Kirsten smiled, still catching her breath.

„Well, then it would be a disaster. Because then I would be just as good as you,“ Angela frowned.

„But isn‘t it amazing that both of you are so talented? That you found each other and have a real chance to win the competition? Our school has never achieved that before. You will bring visibility to us, to yourselves, to the city. Isn‘t it childish to throw all of this away for personal gain? In today‘s rehearsal, you don‘t even have to continue. You‘re excellent, technically prepared. I just don‘t know if you‘re emotionally prepared. I hope that through this competition, you will find your way to each other, not away from each other. Do you want to throw away your friendship?“ Mrs. Miller interjected.

„Our friendship?“ Angela raised an eyebrow and wanted to say something snarky, but she was surprised by the emotions that this sentence stirred in her. Until now, she hadn‘t had time to reflect on their relationship. She had always seen it as a battle, with two sides pitted against each other. But what if they were fighting together on the same side? For themselves. For both of them. Such feelings were unacceptable and unknown to Angela. They meant weakness and distraction. She wanted to stay focused. Mechanical thinking suited her. She could march straight and efficiently towards her goals with it. Any emotional distraction was unacceptable.

Kirsten was unreasonable. And Angela was unapproachable. And she wished it would stay that way. Does everyone else really see their relationship as just friendship? Could she have not noticed? How is it possible that it spontaneously arose without her involvement? She felt like she was swimming in unfamiliar waters.

„We don‘t have time for friendship now,“ she added quietly. The exam was over. She got up and walked out of the classroom.

ꕤ

Kirsten looked at the empty seat where Sofia was supposed to sit. She wasn‘t there. She was at the hospital for tests. Again. She turned her head and watched Emie. Nervous and full of anticipation. The test that could change her life. Just one of many for the others. One of the last for Emie. The grade that could turn her report card into an invitation to exams or just another meaningless piece of paper with scribbled words. Emie couldn‘t do more. Not yet. She tried to cope with her thoughts. Did she do everything she could, or was she being selfish and refusing another option just because she wasn‘t ready to make an important decision...? She couldn‘t judge. Maybe she didn‘t even want to. She filled in the blank spaces of the written work and didn‘t notice the time. The silence in the classroom hypnotized her and gave room for the endless flow of thoughts and emotions. She knew that she wouldn‘t find the answers to her questions on the ceiling of her bedroom or in the fridge among the yogurts. How many times has she tried! She needed another hour of figure skating. What would her mom do? One thing she knows

- what she shouldn‘t do. Board that plane that took her away and never brought her back. She didn‘t know that she waved goodbye to her old life for the last time back then. One of the most clichéd metaphors happened right in front of her eyes. With the plane, everything she knew flew away. And without preparation, a strong wave of cold ocean hit her from behind, in which she‘s been trying to swim and not drown to this day. It seems to her that she‘s right in the middle of it, and all the harbors are equally distant no matter which direction she swims. And no matter which way she chooses, it always seems like she‘s taking the longest and most exhausting route. If life has any logic, it doesn‘t need any more lessons. She has exhausted all the hours of theory and should be ready to take control of her life.

„We‘re done, put down your pens and hand in your exams!“ Kirsten was pulled out of her thoughts. She felt like this sentence teleported her from a different dimension back to reality.

She sighed and looked at her paper. Some parts were scratched out, but the answers shone next to each question. She quickly got through them. It seemed to be all right. She looked at Emie. Emie sat quietly, staring at her paper. Kirsten raised an eyebrow. She knew that if her teacher had let her take a pen in hand, the paper would have danced from one side to the other. She probably hadn‘t managed to write the essay the way she wanted to. Kirsten handed in her work and sat back in her seat. The teacher lined up all the papers and left the classroom amidst the chatter of the students. Kirsten groaned and pushed her chair back as she walked over to Emie‘s desk.

„It‘s hopeless. I will die that farm!“ she said, tossing her books into her bag.

„Sometimes, miracles just don‘t happen. I should just accept it so I‘m not disappointed for no reason,“ Emie replied, tossing her pencil case into her bag, zipping it up, and looking at Kirsten. She wanted to say something else, but she herself was currently searching for the motivation not to burst into tears every morning after waking up. Emie shrugged, tied a red plaid shirt around her waist, and left the classroom. Despite her words, Kirsten couldn‘t shake off her mood. The verdict would be executed only after the grades were announced.

Chapter 32

- SACRIFICE. AGAIN -

Kirsten sat in the red little house, watching the surface of the lake ripple with the gentle afternoon rain. She didn't know where to go. Her mind was filled with Sofia. The illness was progressing, and a solution seemed out of reach. She was willing to sacrifice herself just to cure Sofia. But so far, no amount of money could help her. She pressed the same key on the piano with one finger at short intervals. It sounded monotonous, almost hypnotic, along with the sound of the rain. She wanted to focus and think. About everything she was going through right now. She felt herself slowly drying up like a puddle on hot asphalt at noon. Maybe when she was completely dried up and her emotions were suppressed, she could make the decisions she was currently afraid of. She would become like a machine. Like Angela. She would become her clone. Then everything would supposedly be easier. She wouldn't hurt anymore if she lost something. After all, she would be able to buy anything then. Even friendship and love. She didn't even feel like crying anymore. She just thought about Sofia and kept pressing the keys in a monotonous rhythm. Her thoughts were interrupted by footsteps on the wet grass. She heard someone's shoes sinking into the sponge-like ground. The footsteps approached, and she was sure it wasn't Sam. She didn't even have her phone with her. The footsteps came right up to the house, and Adam appeared in front of the wide-open windows.

He ran a hand through his wet hair. „Hello, I was hoping you'd be here," he said and sat down in a chair. He looked at Kirsten, and he didn't even need to ask what was troubling her.

„Can you help her in any way?" Adam inquired.

„You can't," Kirsten replied dryly.

„How do you know? There's always a solution. Medicine, treatment. Anything," he responded.

„I know. I just know. You can't do anything," Kirsten said and continued to press the keys on the piano.

„You know, I wanted to say that this is a story with a happy ending and that Sofia will definitely recover and blah blah... But as you can see, that's not the story," she concluded and leaned back in her chair. She looked at Adam. He had no answer for her. And she had no question for him. They gazed quietly out the window.

„I'll go see Emie. I need to distract myself somehow. Maybe a few hours on the farm will clear my head. At least I can help her have a few hours to herself this weekend. Today is Friday. Weren't you supposed to be at the factory?" she asked, turning her head to get a better look at him. She squinted as if trying to figure out what brought him to her.

„I was. I told Angela I was coming to see you and that I'll be late," Adam replied.

„Oh, so you've caught her attention. You could have just called me... Oh, right, I don't have my phone with me," she replied in return.

„I feel like we're all going through a strange and complicated period," Adam said, still looking out at the lake.

„Yeah, we're growing up," Kirsten stated. They heard footsteps behind the house. More feet trampled through the soaked grass. The footsteps were quick, and the person emerged from behind the house right in front of them.

„Do you know we have an important deadline today? Why didn't you take your phone with you?" Angela burst out, blinking rapidly three times. Her long black coat, gloves, and boots hinted that she was getting ready for a business meeting.

„I just wanted to stop by Kirsten's. Sofia isn't doing well," Adam replied.

„Yes, I understand and I feel sorry for Sofia, but that's how the world works. We can go, or you can stay here sitting?" Angela retorted, nervously biting her lip.

„Why? Does it bother you that I'd rather be with Kirsten than with you? That I prefer her?" Adam said, and Angela cut him off.

„Just say it outright that you love her and you just want to be with her. Why make excuses? Go pursue your desires and goals. Enjoy the consequences of your decisions," Angela replied, and everyone knew what she meant. She could intervene in the ongoing investment in the factory at any time. Everyone knew that without this investment, the factory would die. However, what Angela and Adam didn't know was that Kirsten knew about it. Directly from Adam's mom.

„What do you know about my feelings or our emotions..." Kirsten interrupted Adam, jumping in. Adam turned to her and raised an eyebrow.

„You can relax. We're not together. We're just good friends," she looked at Angela.

„We're just friends," she added, looking at Adam. He looked disappointed and stood up.

„You know what? I'll make it easier for everyone. Each of us needs some time for ourselves. All three of us are all struggling with our demons and decisions that we can't make right now. Maybe we're just getting in each other's way or something. We can't all be in the same place, and it's best if we stay as far away from each other as possible. I still feel like everything is weighing on me. If I die tomorrow, will all the possibilities die with me? Am I only important for your selfish needs? I'm your catalyst. But I'm running out of fuel. We're not getting anywhere like this. I'm sorry, but you'll have to figure things out on your own for a while. I don't know how long it will take, and I don't care what happens. Because I feel like everyone around me doesn't care about what's happening with me," he finished, looked at Angela, shook his head, and left without a word. Angela stood in surprise in the small house, listening to his footsteps as he walked towards his car. She could only hear the rain drumming on her elegant umbrella.

„I don't know what to say to that. I hope Sofia recovers," she said, and Kirsten could swear she sensed a hint of empathy in that sentence. But now, she didn't really care. Something inside her was dying. Even though several kilometers away in the city hospital. Love for Adam wouldn't solve it anyway. So let the Earth spin as it needs to. It won't save or salvage anyone. Kirsten leaned back in her chair and watched Angela leave. Adam didn't wait for her. He got in his car and drove off. Angela just shrugged helplessly, looking up at the sky. As if she needed to refresh herself after the previous conversation. She folded her umbrella, got in her car, and left. Kirsten wanted to feel like their relationships were moving forward, but it seemed like everyone was content with just treading water. Time was their most loyal friend now. So she didn't force anything and let it flow.

Chapter 33

- ANSWER -

Days in Edwood were just like any other. Belinda no longer had to worry about the café, Emie spent more time on the farm than at school. Sofia was more often at the hospital than at home. Adam didn't show up at school after their conversation in the small red house. Several days had passed and no one knew where he was. He wasn't at home, nor in Edwood. Kirsten wasn't surprised by his absence after the last words she had said to him. When it came to investing in the family business, he seemed uneasy. She didn't want to hurt him or give him false hope. Kirsten felt like he was from a different world. He had the right to leave and take time for himself. He didn't even respond to her calls or messages. She felt uneasy because of his past. She couldn't tell what state of mind he was in and whether he would fall back to where he was before rehab. She didn't regret what she had said, but she regretted having to say it. She asked herself if there hadn't been enough sacrifices for the greater good. Sacrifices were supposed to bring satisfaction, but it still didn't come. The competition was approaching and her relationship with Angela hadn't moved forward even by a small step. She couldn't decide if it was a moment to let go of all the problems and take a break from her life, or if it was time to strike now. She was searching for motivation and the only person who could give it to her was Angela. No one else had the experiences that she needed right now, and no one had managed their life like she had. Not even Adam.

The class was slowly emptying. Kirsten looked out the window at the faded nature and the gloomy weather. Melancholy embraced the empty streets. Kirsten felt like she was looking into her soul through the window. Angela was packing her bag and watching Kirsten with one eye.

There were only a few people left in the classroom, and Kirsten still had all her things on her desk. Angela put her bag down and walked over to Kirsten, sitting across from her.

„Why do you think that your problems or your life are the hardest? I see that you‘re standing at a crossroads in your mind. And all the traffic lights are red. You‘re an easy target this way. I think it‘s time. You asked me for advice, so I‘ll give it to you now. But please, never come to me again asking for more. All the answers are already in your head, and you just need to hear them from someone else as an alibi. You‘re not just an ordinary girl, like the ones I meet in this town. More or less... I don‘t understand why you still haven‘t realized that. I don‘t know what you‘re waiting for. Miracles only happen in fairy tales. In this world, you have to take the first step. You won‘t change your life overnight. But you can change it in small pieces. That‘s the difference compared to all those who think that one attempt is enough. Maybe two. And after the third, they‘re disappointed and blend into the crowd. They bite off more than they can chew, or they don‘t even have mouths big enough to take a bite. And you know why I‘m even talking to you? Because there‘s something about you. I can‘t define it yet, but you‘re worth noticing. Sometimes I even struggle with the feeling that I should like you or something. You get under people‘s skin. You really do. And the best part is that people like it. Just the way you‘re unshakable during piano exams. Do you know how many I've sent out crying into the hallway? But not you. You even enjoy it, and it annoys me. I won‘t be satisfied until I figure out where you draw your energy from. Your perseverance drives me crazy. Thanks to it, you can achieve great things,“ Kirsten finished and stared into Angela‘s eyes. Angela listened attentively, waiting for some ultimate thought that would open the last doors that she had been hesitating in front of for so long.

„No, your life is not harder. It‘s just as hard as everyone else‘s. And when I say just as hard, I mean to the gram. Everyone feels like others are ahead of them, and they can‘t catch up with the crowd. Let me tell you something. Our family has assets worth tens of millions. Maybe over a hundred million. Do you think I don‘t have problems? Oh, I do. And I experience them just the same. And that‘s something you need to realize. That this won‘t change with money, relationships, or the passage of time. So don‘t act like you‘re the only one getting kicked by life! It‘s selfish and narcissistic towards others," Angela spoke as if she didn't care about Kirsten's thoughts.

Angela leaned over the table. „Do you think someone else is responsible for how you feel? Do you think someone else brought you to this situation and this room other than yourself? Hmm," Angela finished, smiled, and leaned back on her chair.

„What if you stopped sulking in that dark room, got up, and looked for the light switch in the dark? How long will you wait for someone to open the door and turn on the switch for you? And what if the room is locked and you have the keys inside? But if you only see obstacles instead of possibilities and focus on what you don't want instead of what you truly want, then I'm just wasting my time here. You asked for advice on how I managed to stay human and grounded even though I'm so wealthy. So here's my answer: I didn't stay the same. I am a different person now, and I will never be the person I used to be when our family was wealthy, just not this fairy tale kind of wealthy. The answer is in adaptation. You have to level up your entire personality. If you can't do that, then your own life will suffocate, smother you. It will murder you. And when I look at you, I wouldn't blame it if it had a hundred reasons to do so. That's why I told you not to be needlessly modest. You're just lowering yourself to the level of others who are several steps below you. Look up at the sky, not down at the ground. Because that's the only way you'll see how high you can grow. So the answer is: No, I haven't stayed the same person. I still have my feet on the ground, but I've grown. I've outgrown my problems. You know how they say: I used to be arrogant, but now I have no fault," Angela finished, grinning, folding her hands palm up and resting her chin on them. If Kirsten didn't know her, she would have just dryly nodded at that last sentence. But she knew that Angela could say this sentence without caring about what anyone thought of her. Because she had matured beyond any opinion. And that many people around her hadn't reached their opinions yet, so Angela didn't feel the need to bother with them. Few of them would recognize that it was sarcasm.

„You answered me. I felt the same way. That I probably won't be able to hold on to who I've become and am becoming. And that I will have to accept the fact that my life has changed," Kirsten replied, trying to identify with the idea of adapting to her new life. Not fighting it, but accepting it as a fact. The Dark Passenger just nodded silently, as if pleased that he had just sold all his powers to manipulate her. She couldn't figure out this world on her own. He drew his energy from her uncertainty. Angela stood up and shook her head. She walked across the classroom, grabbed her bag, and left without a word. Kirsten started packing up. Her question had been answered, so there was nothing left to do today but visit Sofia in the hospital.

Chapter 34

- HUMILITY -

Posters promising a cure for any ailment were plastered all around. Smiling staff walked from room to room, creating a peaceful atmosphere in the hallway. Kirsten couldn‘t even believe she was sitting outside her best friend‘s room in the hospital. She wanted to stay there as long as she could. She sat in the hallway with her hands resting on her knees, hiding her tear-streaked face in her palms. But she didn‘t want to cry anymore. She thought and sniffed. There must be another way, another possibility. She couldn‘t just wait like this. What if it‘s too late in a moment? But at this moment, she knew she couldn‘t do anything else. Time was against them. She thought about her conversation with Angela and realized she was doing something wrong. Otherwise, she wouldn‘t be sitting here alone now. She understood that there were actions thrown into life that conjured up the ring. It was spreading in all directions now. She just had to wait for it to come back and read the information it would bring. Why it came back and what pushed it back. In these moments, she embraced humility - that not everything in her life was within her reach. And it never will be. According to Angela, realizing one‘s weaknesses is not weakness, but a strength. And Kirsten needed to be strong now. Instead of helplessness and incapacity, she felt humility. It gave her space to reflect on herself and breathe. Otherwise, all those heavy emotions and recent experiences would have overwhelmed her. She got up from her chair and looked around the hallway. Several doctors were walking from room to room and the atmosphere in the hospital was calm. That reassured Kirsten a little. She peeked into the room through the gap. Sofia was sleeping. She looked like Snow White or Sleeping

> Beauty. Kirsten ran her fingers through Sofia's bangs, which mischievously fell back into place. Even in her sleep, Sofia gave her motivation and inspiration.

She couldn't wait for her to open her eyes and spend more moments together in the little red house. She rested her forehead against her, as if trying to read her thoughts, to know how she was feeling. It seemed like everything was in order, and Sofia was just waiting for a miracle to lift her up again, to get back on her feet. Or would she remain trapped like this forever? She kissed her on the forehead and quietly left the room.

On the way home, she pondered which state suited her better. The effortless solitude she was experiencing right now, or the presence of all those kindred souls she had met over the past few months. She couldn't distinguish between the two feelings. It was as if it was still the same feeling. It emanated from within her, and she tried to analyze it. Why did she feel the same even when she was alone or with friends? Was it because she felt good in her own company? Was she her own friend and support? These schizophrenic thoughts wandered through her mind, and she chased them in that labyrinth, trying to catch them by the hand and look them in the face. However, she realized that this feeling was the perfect building block for everything that would come her way and that she probably couldn't avoid. And that was very important to Kirsten.

The journey passed by, trees flickered before her eyes. It was evening, but Kirsten felt as if it were those calm Sunday mornings before the storm, which she loved so much. She parked the car in front of her house. Sam was still somewhere in the city, fixing something, and the house was empty. She headed straight for the little red house. Alone with herself. She walked on the grass and imagined how they had walked together so many times. She raised her hand and ran her palm over the tree flower whose branch bent directly over her head. Below the hill, she saw the red walls that hid the piano. Her steps led her towards it. Maybe its tones would sort out all her thoughts and align her, like when the nurse at the hospital organized the files so that she had an overview of all those diagnoses. And Kirsten would finally recognize her own diagnosis and find the cure for it.

Chapter 35

- RESURRECTION -

Kirsten entered the classroom. Everyone fell silent. It felt strange to her, but she walked to her desk. She started picking up her things and looking around. Everyone had a mysterious and ambiguous smirk on their faces. She could swear it was some hidden imperfect smile. She leaned against her chair. It became clear to her that she didn't know something that everyone else in the class knew.

„You really have no idea, do you?" Angela asked, lifting her chin. She looked like a teacher asking a student why they didn't do their homework. She sat down briskly right next to Kirsten, and Kirsten caught a whiff of her perfume. She shook her head in surprise and couldn't take her eyes off her. She didn't answer. Angela took out her phone and started searching for something. On the touch screen of her phone, she only heard the tapping of perfectly manicured nails. She shook her head and handed her phone to Kirsten. She looked at the screen and furrowed her brow. It was a video of her playing the piano. On the street. She looked at Angela. „I didn't record it or upload it to the internet," she said, surprised.

„I know. It's some unknown guy. But he was obviously there when you were playing, and he recorded it," Angela said, leaning back as if she was expecting an explanation. Kirsten then noticed many people on the street with their phones in hand. She didn't pay much attention to it.

„So now people know where Edwood is. Some cities spend millions on it, and you managed to reveal it to thousands of viewers," Angela added, and Kirsten noticed that the video had indeed garnered several hundred thousand views. Every time she refreshed the page, the number increased. She read the comments under the video. One question dominated: Who is Sofia? Kirsten didn't understand this popularity. She just wanted to play the piano.

„I don't know how much money I would need to become so popular. You just play the piano in the middle of the street and boom!" Angela retorted.

„I have to say, it impressed me. Should I start getting inspired by you again? Exchange my direct shot for the goal with these selfless acts? Or just become completely perfect and simply combine these two worlds."

The worst part is that we either both win or both lose the competition. I can't beat you, and that annoys me. A Trojan gift," Angela recounted, squinted her eyes, and looked out the window at the schoolyard. She seemed to be searching for answers to her inner questions out there, which were gaining in quantity and intensity with Kirsten's arrival. The yard was empty. The tables were waiting for their regular diners.

„You don't always have to win," Kirsten interrupted Angela's thoughts.

„Have you never gained anything by losing? Because losses, just like wins, have their value. It's strange, but they taste the same to me. One cannot exist without the other. Every loss is like a step back. But what if that step back always means a longer run-up for the long jump athlete, to extend the distance for the jump. You have to first pull the bowstring backward to shoot the arrow forward. The further you pull it back, the farther the arrow will fly. What if you only allow yourself half of the emotions, experiences, and half of life with wins?" Angela finished, watching Kirsten with a disheartened expression.

„For you, even a loss is a win," Angela sarcastically repeated. For Kirsten, this sentence would have been another stab that would pierce her. But this time, she didn't feel it that way. For the first time, she felt like she could see and hear beyond Angela.

„The feelings you're talking about, I haven't experienced them yet. But maybe that's because I've never lost," Angela said firmly, and Kirsten felt how this fact calmed her down and filled her with new energy in an instant. She watched Angela walk back to her desk and desperately wanted to find that energy within herself. She felt like she had been losing for the past year. She wasn't afraid to take those steps back and prepare for the upcoming big jump. She was afraid of taking too many steps back and falling into a chasm from which she would never escape. That's why after every step back, she always looked back to see if the chasm was already within reach. And it was precisely that looking back that disturbed her the most. She felt like she had taken enough steps back. Now she was looking for the strength to start running.

ೞ

Kirsten walked towards the hall. They didn't have a rehearsal today. She wanted to distance herself from the noise in the corridors for a while and be alone. In her hand, she again flipped through her tattered notebook with notes and scribbles. She was still improving the composition, rewriting the notes. The pages in the notebook looked like encoded messages from World War II.

And only she could decipher what was written on that paper. She entered the room and saw Mrs. Miller sitting behind the desk. She was looking at the computer screen and seemed like she had been crying a moment ago. She was smiling. Kirsten slowed down and looked at her with confusion. She didn‘t know whether to back away and leave her alone. The door was open, so Mrs. Miller probably wouldn‘t mind being interrupted at this moment.

„Kirsten, come here for a moment," Mrs. Miller said and smiled. Kirsten changed her direction and walked towards the desk with a surprised expression on her face.

„Look," Mrs. Miller pointed at the screen. Kirsten put down her bag and looked puzzled. There were several unread emails on it. They all came yesterday and today. Quite a lot of mail for someone who is not very active on the internet.

„They are all offers. And there is one among them that I thought would never come back. A chance that the same person doesn‘t get twice in a lifetime," Mrs. Miller added, and wrinkles appeared on her forehead. As if she remembered the moment when she had to give up this life opportunity. Kirsten sat in front of her. She still didn‘t understand why Mrs. Miller made her feel like she was part of what was happening around her. Several crumpled napkins on the brown table hinted that it was a very emotional moment for Mrs. Miller.

„Someone mentioned your name in a discussion under a video. He must have been from our school. Do you even know that there‘s a mini discussion about you? And, of course, everyone wants to know who Sofia is. Our competition is even mentioned in it. This year‘s visitors are probably going to be more than last year‘s. And it all started with this comment: ‚Hey, Kirsten is going to rehearsals with Mrs. Miller. She‘s preparing her for the competition with another classmate.‘ And when I opened my mail today, I found these unexpected gifts. Your talent makes this world a better place. I didn‘t ask for this opportunity and I took life as it comes. I‘m not passive and I don‘t expect things to fall into my lap just like that. But I‘m not banging on closed doors either. And yet it happened. Something I didn‘t even hope for, and I missed it so much," she finished, looking at the screen with shining eyes. She hadn‘t even read the emails yet. She looked like a little child admiring all the gifts under the Christmas tree and not wanting to unwrap them so as not to lose the magic of Christmas itself.

„It means now that you‘re leaving?“ Kirsten asked hesitantly.

„Yes. Probably yes. My life will change. But I will definitely stay for the competition here. It will be my last one at this school,“ she replied, and Kirsten felt slightly nervous.

„So, I guess it‘s my fault that there will be an empty space here after you. No one will be able to fill it like you do. I feel guilty towards the other students. I didn‘t mean for this to happen. But I‘m glad you‘re happy,“ Kirsten said, and Mrs. Miller felt sorry for inadvertently involving her in unwanted fame.

„I‘m not dying. We can still meet anytime. Maybe I‘ll even have time for private piano lessons. I would like to... It‘s my life. But now it‘s time to move on. I like it here. I like my job, and I‘m grateful to have met you, Angela. Don‘t worry, you‘ll do well here without me. What if one day you wake up and don‘t have all those crutches by your bedside that you rely on? Did you consider that possibility? So, tomorrow, get up from that bed and stand on your own two feet. Start using them. And you can go as far as you want. Not just until your last crutch breaks,“ Mrs. Miller concluded, and Kirsten lowered her gaze to the floor.

„But I‘ll miss having you around, won‘t I?“ Kirsten lifted her head and smiled.

„Will you miss it? You have to!“ Mrs. Miller replied, and they both laughed heartily.

That day, under the roof of Edwood School, one story ended and several exciting ones began.

Kirsten walked home from school and couldn‘t stop thinking about what her video had caused. And how little it took for that to happen. Mrs. Miller would probably say that it wasn‘t little at all, but her entire musical talent. But Kirsten didn‘t feel like she had so much talent. None of it would have happened if she had bought that piano on the first day. For the first time, she felt like she hadn‘t taken a step back. She held her head high and looked ahead. She was beginning to understand that she wouldn‘t change her life alone, but with the help of all the people close to her. She felt that thanks to them, she had patched up the holes at the bottom of her cup, and her energy was no longer draining away. It was time to fill up the cup. She quickened her pace to meet Sofia as soon as possible.

ꕤ

„Hello. Did you know that you're currently the most wanted and famous girl in Edwood? Oooo, I bow to you!“ Sofia laughed. She sat on the edge of the bed. Kirsten stopped at the door, surprised to see Sofia sitting up instead of lying down. But Sofia took advantage of that moment of surprise to tease her.

„How...?“ Sofia wanted to ask so many questions at once, but she couldn't put it into one sentence. However, Sofia knew what Kirsten wanted to ask, and she had an answer ready since morning.

„No big deal. I watched your video. Once, then again. And I watched it all day long. It improved my mood, like a miracle. I feel better now. Even the doctor said I can go home,“ Sofia smiled. Kirsten knew she was joking in some places, and that the medication had kicked in again. She also knew that this moment would surely repeat. And this fact choked her up. The solution was still out of reach. Now it didn't depend solely on her. She really hoped it would come sooner than this moment repeating at the bedside.

„Is that song really for me?“ Sofia asked shyly.

„Yes. For whom else? And only for you,“ Kirsten replied, smiling, and handed Sofia a small dictionary.

„Is it what I think it is?“ Sofia asked in surprise. „Oh, I hope not,“ she laughed.

„And why not? It's already written. I need something new. I won't lock it up in some bottom drawer of a messy cupboard. I want it to be with you. I don't know who else I would give it to. It belongs to you. Most of the lines and thoughts were about you anyway,“ Kirsten replied and took a step towards Sofia. She held her hand and placed the dictionary in it. She hugged her gently, as if she didn't want to break her. She looked into her eyes and kissed her on the forehead: „It's yours,“ she sealed her decision. Kirsten hoped that if her song helped her get out of bed, this dictionary would be like an endless bottle of antibiotics that wouldn't let her return to this hospital bed. And she also hoped that Sofia would read it when she wasn't feeling her best. It would improve her mood and give her positive energy until news of a new medication arrives.

Chapter 36

- ROOM WITHOUT DOORS -

Sam packed lunch for Kirsten. He put it on the table and sat on his chair. The house was quiet, with fog creeping outside the windows. He took a knife and sliced a piece of bread from the plate in front of him. He spread some butter on it and ran the knife over the slice. Even though his mind was filled with many thoughts, he heard the soft sound of the butter filling the pores of the bread. He ran the knife over the slice a few more times until the surface was smooth and white. Almost perfect. He wished the same could happen with his and Kirsten's lives. That somehow they could smooth out all the pores through which emotions seep in. That they could be like a blank white paper again and write their own story. He took a bite of the bread, bit into a tomato Kirsten brought from the farm, and stared at the empty chair in front of him. It was starting to feel strange that Kirsten hadn't come out of her room for breakfast yet. He put the partially eaten slice of bread on the table, wiped his mouth with a napkin, and stood up. He grabbed the railing and slowly climbed the stairs to Kirsten's room. He knew something was wrong because Kirsten never missed a beat. She had an internal clock. She always kept to deadlines and daily routines. He put his hand on the doorknob and quickly ran through various scenarios in his head. He wanted to be prepared for any question or answer. He opened the door. She was sitting on the bed. Still in her pajamas, holding a picture in her hand. Sam raised an eyebrow and wrinkles appeared at the corners of his eyes.

„I miss her too. That empty space will never be filled. And I don't want it to be. I'm learning to live with it," Sam replied and closed the door to the room. He had encountered this situation in the house from time to time.

„What happened is a double-edged sword. I'm tired. I don't feel well. I'll stay home today. My body would only be at school anyway," she said, still looking at the picture.

„She gave me a lot. I understand that I can't ask for more. We were so close to having all my thoughts come together within me. This is how I miss that most important piece of the puzzle," Kirsten said sadly.

„But what if that piece is so important that you have to find it yourself and put it into the picture that is emerging in front of you? So that it makes sense to you and no one else. You have packed lunch downstairs. If you need anything, just call. I'll come running," Sam reassured her.

„I feel like I'm getting closer to making a decision. But I'm missing some decisive impulse. I still can't open the doors in front of me. But when I look back, my previous life remained closed behind other doors and I'm treading in some connecting corridor, in darkness. The corridor is small, I feel cramped there. There's no light, it's cold. No one can hear me cry or rejoice in there. No sentence or laughter can pass through the thick walls. The problem is that only one of those doors is unlocked. I should open it," she finished and wiped the tears from her eyes.

„Should I stay at home instead?" Sam asked anxiously.

„No, no. I don't want to waste your time. I'll figure it out on my own. I have to figure it out on my own. I just need time," she replied firmly.

„Take as much time as you need," Sam said, placing his hand on Kirsten's shoulder.

„I'll go now, rest. I know it's hard to face each new day. But remember, they are a gift, not a punishment. And mom won't die as long as she continues to live within us. Think about what she would do if she were in the same situation as you. Maybe you'll find some answers. Life takes something from us so that it can give us something else. Or it gives us something so it can take something else. You know, heaven doesn't have visiting hours. And they're not necessary. After all, mom is still with us. When it rains, go outside and turn your face to the sky. In all those raindrops that fall on your face, some will be from mom. But she won't be crying from sorrow, but from happiness," he finished, placing his wrinkled hand on Kirsten's bowed head.

She was only focused on the picture in her hands. The sound of a car engine starting finally broke her concentration. She lifted her head and looked out the window. She saw Sam's van disappearing behind the trees on the bend. She went downstairs in her pajamas, grabbed her lunch from the table, put on her sneakers, and went out to the terrace. She headed towards the red litle house.

The lake was calm. She entered the small house, took off her shoes, and unpacked her lunch. She chewed on bread and looked at the sheet music on her bent knees. The dictionary had changed hands, so for now, she stored her thoughts on any paper that was within reach. Her pink-painted fingers pressed into the couch as she played some notes. In her pajamas, wrapped in a blanket, with her hair tucked behind her ear, she looked like a newly hatched chick. She was surprised by how many papers she had written during that time. She held a bundle of papers as thick as a phone directory for a medium-sized city in her hand. Her mind was neutral. She finished her meal and continued to look at the sheet music, notes, and short stories. The first page of „Composition for Sofia" appeared in her hands. She continued to work on it and never left it untouched. It was crossed out several times, scribbled on, and melodious, just like Sofia. She closed her eyes and a tear rolled down her cheek. She clenched her hand into a fist and threw the papers into the corner with despair. They scattered on the floor and created a white carpet full of notes and sentences written in black ink. Silence multiplied every breath and every heartbeat around her. There was no crying in the red house. Not even a whimper. Just the wind. The leaves slowly fell from the treetops and dropped into the lake. She lay bundled up in her blanket, half-closed her eyes. Time passed slowly, as if waiting for Kirsten's next step. It seemed to her that she was running again on their old familiar street. Like a child. Without problems, without plans, without responsibilities. Without the dark passenger. Her eyelids weighed heavy with nostalgia and exhaustion.

„Kirsten? Are you in the red house? Kirsten!" Sam's voice woke her up. She looked around to orient herself. She closed her eyes for a moment, but it must have been at least five hours. She had slept half the day in the red house.

„Yes, I'm here," she shouted and rubbed her sleepy and still heavy eyelids.

„I heard Emie got a B on that test. I thought you might be interested. I'm going inside. Come for dinner!" he yelled, and Kirsten only heard the door slamming on the veranda.

„She did it! The first step," Kirsten rejoiced. The sleep had given her some strength. She looked at the papers underneath her. They depicted an imaginary solid ground beneath her feet. She sat back on the couch and looked at them with her chin on her knees. They gave her inspiration and motivation. They were like a map. She searched for answers and a way out of the maze in them. So, her actions were leaving a positive trail behind her after all.

Chapter 37

- SURPRISED? -

Days passed by and looked like cloned sheep. They couldn't even be counted. Sometimes she couldn't tell which day it actually was. It was similarly curly and bleated the same. One big enclosure of sheep, constantly mingling among themselves. If she approached the enclosure, she could easily name the first sheep by some name and come to the same spot the next day and greet the nearest sheep with that name. It would bleat the same. George still hadn't called, but someone else did. Something was going to change in the coming days.

„Kirsten... Kirsteeen, you have a call!" Sam shouted from the veranda. Despite the mobile era, they still had a landline at home. She liked sitting by it. It had a long cord that she could walk around the house with while cooking. Many times she would talk to Sofia like this and tell her what she was cooking. She rushed from the red house. She looked surprisedly at Sam.

„I don't know who it is, but they want to talk to you," Sam raised his eyebrows in surprise. She entered the kitchen. There was a handset on the table and the cord stretched all the way from the refrigerator. She picked it up and glanced briefly at Sam. She held it to her ear. Sam stood in the doorway, curious to know who was on the other end of the line. The voice was very serious and confident. Kirsten watched as she nodded into the phone. One emotion after another passed through her. She smiled, frowned, raised her eyebrows in surprise. Several times she tucked her hair behind her ear, and Sam could swear she even blushed.

„Goodbye," Kirsten said, took a few steps and hung up the phone. She stood by the refrigerator and pulled the cord back from the table so that Sam wouldn't trip over it. She looked like she wanted to buy some time. She stared thoughtfully at the floor, as if hypnotized.

„They called from a small music publishing company. They want to buy the rights to the song I composed for Sofia," she said, surprised, and looked at Sam from the refrigerator across the entire kitchen.

„Is that the one that made you famous now?“ Sam laughed.

„Famous... There are and will be more of those songs... It will soon fade into the background.“

„Fade or not, someone has dug it up into the spotlight now. What did they say? Aren‘t you excited?“ Sam continued to inquire.

„The gentleman wants to meet me to negotiate the terms,“ she replied. She walked past Sam and headed back to the red house. Sam followed her to the veranda. He watched her walk slowly and trip over a clump of grass. He sighed and stretched his face in anticipation. He didn‘t know what decision Kirsten would make.

Chapter 38

- ABOUT GRAY BEARDS -

Emie stood in her rubber boots in front of the greenhouse. In one hand, she held an empty box, and in the other, her phone on which she was reading a message: „I won‘t come today, I can‘t.“ She scrolled further, but the message didn‘t contain any more words. It seemed strange to her. This wasn‘t Kirsten. It was as if someone else had written it. She sighed, put her phone in her pocket, and looked into the greenhouse. For a moment, she felt like an orphan again. When Kirsten and the others were helping her on the farm, she didn‘t feel that way. But after those few vegetable sessions with all of them, she had probably gotten too used to feeling like she belonged somewhere. That she had real friends. Not just those with roots and stems. She heard the sound of potatoes being poured from the adjacent shed. She didn‘t want to keep her father waiting. Emie rolled up her sleeves and entered the greenhouse.

Sam parked in front of the house. He walked past Kirsten‘s car and found it strange that she was home at this time. Since Belinda‘s café started, she hadn‘t been home that often, but she spent more time at the farm. Or at the piano. He walked past the withered flowerbeds. The creaking stairs on the veranda would probably alert her, and she would come to greet him, as she had done so many times before. He walked into the kitchen. It was dark and empty, devoid of any soul. It looked like a refuge. It was waiting for someone to turn on the lights and the stove. It needed to have the scent and color when it was time to cook dinner. He put his things on the bench and went upstairs. He opened the door to Kirsten‘s room and expected a similar sight. The room was empty. He raised an eyebrow. Maybe she‘s in the red house. He went back to the kitchen, went outside, and checked the red house. No sign of Kirsten. He was returning to the veranda when he noticed a pair of legs dangling from the bench behind the house.

„Mmmm," he groaned when he leaned his back against the wall of the house. Kirsten sat silently beside him. He didn't want to ask her anything. Sam knew Kirsten didn't have a question or an answer ready yet. He had to be patient with her many times.

„I'm thinking that I might be selfish," she started and kept looking straight ahead. „I like being there for others. It makes me happy to help, to give advice. If someone has a better day because of me. But I wonder if I'm doing it for selfish reasons. To gain energy for my own decisions that I can't make on my own. That I actively seek out situations where I can recharge like this. I wonder if I'm pushing others into these situations just to drain their energy for myself. And all because I'm weak myself. I want to ask them about it, but I'm afraid of the answer. I know how selfishness looks in others, but I don't know if one can recognize it in oneself. Negative traits are cunning in that way, that one doesn't perceive them in oneself. And maybe then one surrounds oneself with people who are afraid to tell them that they have those traits. What kind of person one really is. We keep smiling, everything is fine. It started to seem suspicious to me. And of course, selfishness can't realize that it's selfish. Because it's selfish. Just like I'm afraid of accepting my next life, so that I don't close myself off in some bubble, maybe I'm already living in one. I don't even know if I helped Emie with school just so I could claim her victory as my own. And maybe I just used Emie like a parasite. Belinda's café... Was it my project, or did I want to help Belinda? Because I acted as if it belonged to me. Bold and arrogant, a self-proclaimed savior. I'm like kryptonite to Superman for Adam. He's a rebel, but with me, he can't muster up any revolution. And you know when I realized that my decisions are probably selfish? When I was angry that I couldn't help Sofia. But my anger should have been disappointment that I couldn't help my friend. And not anger because I didn't achieve something I had set my mind to. Because it's not about me, it's about Sofia!" she concluded and fell silent.

„One day someone will tell you the truth, someone you least expect. And that's when you'll know it's really true. It will come to the surface at the right time like a geyser. Right now, you're probably pushing your way out. But it's unstoppable. It will burst out right next to you and soak you completely. Every day, every minute, every action or spoken thought, you're building up pressure that will one day be strong enough to bring it to the surface. And don't be angry that you have flaws. That you make mistakes. So you're perfect ninety-nine percent of the time. And it's that one imperfect percent that makes you one hundred percent. How many around you pretend to be one hundred percent flawless people?"

„And that's why they can't be one hundred percent. This formula always works. So don't blame yourself for anything. Life has already put enough on your shoulders. I'm proud of all the good qualities. Even the bad ones. And all the imperfections and flaws. Personally, I call them Kirsten," he laughed.

„Yooou," Kirsten muttered...

„It's good that you can acknowledge these things. That's a good start to change them. But you know that if you change them for the better, some other bad quality will fill that vacant spot, right? We're just born that way. We'll always have bad qualities. It's pointless to fight against them. How do you want to get rid of your stubbornness? With stubbornness?" Sam laughed.

„I should say that you know all of this just because you have a gray beard. There must be something to the idea that old people carry wisdom in it," Kirsten teased him.

„And where do women carry that wisdom then? Like your mom?" Sam smiled.

„In the heart," Kirsten whispered.

Chapter 39

- AGREEMENT AND A FEW WRINKLES -

„Hey, do you have it?“ Kirsten asked as soon as she sat down at the table with Sofia.

„Of course, I do. Losing it would be like losing a kidney,“ Sofia laughed.

„I‘ll borrow it, and I‘ll give it back to you. Like I said... It‘s yours,“ Kirsten replied and took her battered dictionary from Sofia. She flipped through it for a while. She quickly scanned the pages with her eyes, as if trying to remember everything she had written in it over time.

„Don‘t you want to have some ice cream? Cheers! Because I feel like even if the café fell on our heads, you wouldn‘t even notice,“ Sofia replied, widening her blue eyes at Kirsten.

„Everything is fine. Everything is fine... I‘m just thinking. When I know more, you‘ll be the first one I‘ll tell,“ Kirsten replied and put the dictionary in her pocket. Sofia gave Kirsten a slightly crooked smile and started on the cake in front of her.

Sam didn‘t start his delivery truck in the morning. He didn‘t even put on his work overalls. Cluttered closets and clogged drains would have to wait today. At least until tomorrow. Today, Sam and Kirsten took a little trip out of town. Two hours away from Edwood, Kirsten‘s agent will be recording an album with a band he called. He‘ll have some time for her. They arranged a meeting that surprised Sam a little. After seeing Kirsten walk away to her little house with that phone call in her head, he wouldn‘t bet a dime that Kirsten would give this opportunity a chance. He himself didn‘t know how she would decide. He knew she would dictate the terms, so he didn‘t hold much hope for the agreement. He wondered all the way how she would behave. How her experiences and maturity would manifest in her. Or is she still the same little Kirsten who used to collect kittens and puppies from the streets?

They arrived in front of a run-down building. It didn‘t look like the place where talents are formed and musical hits of the next summer are created. Kirsten wanted to go to the meeting alone. Sam was glad they took this trip. He would walk around some warehouses and buy some upgrades for his delivery truck. Kirsten waved goodbye to Sam as he left and stopped in front of the door. She looked up, as if trying to capture the moment. She double-checked the number next to the door and stepped inside. She walked up the stairs, holding onto the iron railing. Kirsten kept reevaluating her decision, even though she had already finalized the plan since last night. She reached the first floor and found herself in front of black double doors, just as the agent had mentioned. She walked in. They were already expecting her. The unknown man approached her without introducing himself and pointed to the chair next to her: „Have a seat. So, you're Kirsten... We spoke on the phone. I probably don't need to repeat what you already know. One of my musicians would like to use your composition in his song."

Uploading videos to the internet was a good idea. You may not know, but both me and musicians go there for inspiration. Why reinvent the wheel, right? Here's the contract. Read it. You can take it home, consult with your lawyer. However, I need an answer within a week. It's a unique opportunity for you, and you probably know that not just anyone gets a chance to sit here," the agent concluded and leaned back on the couch. He ran his hand over his chin and pushed his long hair back. In jeans and a leather jacket, he looked younger, but the wrinkles on his face revealed that he had been in this business for decades. She was not used to such fast negotiations and was a bit taken aback. Just a few minutes ago, she was checking the house number on the street to make sure she was at the right address, and now she was holding some contract in her hand. She looked into his eyes. His experienced gaze reminded her that the man in front of her knew what he wanted. And he had been through this countless times before. Apparently, this process was completely normal for him, and he didn't have time to waste his day on uninteresting debates. He went straight to the point.

Kirsten looked at the contract on the table. She put her hand in her coat and pulled out a dictionary. She placed it on the table next to the contract and pushed it towards the agent. He raised an eyebrow as if asking if she was serious. She knew he could easily be offended, laugh, and thank her for her interest. But from the conversation and body language, she could tell that he was indeed interested in her composition. He reached out and opened the dictionary. He flipped through it here and there. On some pages, he paused for a moment, as if imagining the melody.

„I don't want any money. I'll write music and lyrics for you," Kirsten said, watching the agent flip through the dictionary.

„All of this is your creation?" the agent said, closing the dictionary and placing it on the table. He pushed it towards Kirsten.

„Yes. One part. Everything I liked. I have more at home," Kirsten added, picking up the dictionary from the table.

„And what else could I offer you for your creation? Fame? Contacts? You know there's no room for negotiation here. When you leave through those doors, the same girls and boys who think they have the next hit in their pockets will come in after you," the agent said skeptically.

„Not the same. I don't want money or fame. If we agree, I'll provide you with music and lyrics for free. Probably for a very long time. Because I have a different motivation."

I propose to establish a foundation. There is a certain disease that is not well known. The development of a cure for this disease is progressing very slowly. But if more people knew about it, we might be able to save more lives. You will determine what percentage of the revenue from my songs will go to this foundation. You know that you can write off these funds from taxes. My songs won't cost you anything," she concluded, unsure of the answer.

„But you know that in the end, it could be more money than the amount of your reward?" the agent asked.

„Yes, but how much money goes to this foundation will directly depend on the popularity of my work. The more popular the song, the higher the revenue. And therefore, your profit," Kirsten negotiated.

„You know, there are young people here who have no clue about business? About accounting and marketing? They only have their dreams. Mostly rosy. And many of us have made unfavorable deals, which I am not proud of. But it's business first and foremost. And it has to be beneficial first for me, for the publishing house. I've made many bands famous and wealthy. Many no longer exist. But I'm still here. No one has presented me with such an offer before. You probably have your reasons, and you understand that you can earn a lot of money," he said and looked at his dictionary, „I just want to make sure that we both understand each other. You can manage the foundation yourself. In the contract, we'll just agree on the amount and method of money flow. I understand that you will want us to mention its name in every song you write and we publish. In the end, such cooperation will also shed a positive light on our publishing house. You're not silly, so I want us to be straightforward. I can confidently say - like adults. There are three, maybe four potential hits in that dictionary. Can you play them for me?" he said and pointed to the piano, which stood in the middle of the hall among other musical instruments. From the leather couch, he was clearly visible. Kirsten got up and walked through the hall. As she walked past all the cables and equipment, she felt like a star for a moment. Unfamiliar. She knew this wasn't where she wanted to stand. Kirsten sat down at the piano. The agent sat on the couch so he could see her better. He ran his hand over his chin again, making a sound like sandpaper rubbing against wood. She started playing. She didn't play for the agent. She didn't play like a star. She played for herself. She didn't try to impress or overdo it. The piano was tuned and had a beautiful sound. Within a few seconds, she completely merged with it. Kirsten loved trying out new pianos. Getting to know them.

To find in them those musical nooks and how they sounded. It was like discovering an island where a boat had just anchored. She played relaxed, as if she didn't care that a famous music agent was sitting next to her. Suddenly, he rose from the leather couch. His big leather boots sounded on the wooden floor like a metronome. He sat behind the drums and tried to tune them lightly with the piano. Kirsten liked it. She smiled at the agent and kept playing. He settled in even more comfortably and added the complete repertoire of drums to the composition. Suddenly, a hint of a new composition echoed through the studio. It had rhythm and the drums gave it a gentle rock atmosphere. They both liked it. The agent suddenly stopped playing. Kirsten finished the passage and put her hands on her knees.

„I could make you a star," said the agent, placing the drumsticks on the drums.

„I don't want to be a star. I prefer to stay in the background. Where not even the stars can see, but they know that without those people there in the dark, behind the curtain, they wouldn't be stars. What can the best soldier on the front lines do if the supply doesn't work and he has nothing to shoot with? It fulfills me to feel that I helped someone take a step forward. That I stand firmly behind them, and when they take steps back, they can lean on me. And that they can bounce back from me again," Kirsten replied, and the agent smiled.

„I understand. I think we can come to an agreement. I'll send you a new contract home. And I want everything that's in that dictionary for it," he said, standing up. Kirsten approached him and shook his hand as a sign of agreement.

As she descended the stairs, holding onto the iron railing, she kept repeating to herself that the plan had worked. It all happened so quickly and she had no idea how many hours had passed. She had no concept of how much time she had spent in the studio. It felt like an eternity and an instant at the same time. She liked it. Kirsten felt like she was locked in a room after hastily eating a whole chocolate bar. And now, there in her mouth, she moved one forgotten streak of chocolate with her pinkie. She didn't want to believe it yet - until she had the new contract in her hands.

Chapter 40

- DANCES IN PORCELAIN -

She ran up the iron stairs all the way to the top. Under her feet, the factory lived its own life, and everywhere you could hear the whining of wood being transformed into regular pieces of varying lengths by the saws.

„Hey, was Adam here?“ Angela asked and closed the door behind her. The noise subsided a bit.

„Adam? You scared him off so much that he landed who knows how far from here. No one knows anything about him. Maybe just Mrs. Mackenzie. He jeopardized the whole deal. Or actually, you jeopardized it,“ Angela replied, placing her pen on the table dressed unconventionally in a tight white shirt that accentuated the contours of her body, which was becoming more adult.

„Me? It was his decision. We probably both contributed equally to it. But if I‘m the only one to blame, then I‘ll take the entire win. And I can finally tell Adam that I love him,“ Kirsten said, looking out the window into the factory premises.

„And do you think I‘ll run this company, sitting here with him while you two frolic around? Watching you two making fun of me? That you won? I don‘t have to be here. It‘s only my responsibility. This factory was supposed to be my entry into the business world. Something that is fully in my hands. And I have to start like this? I have a choice. I can start my entrepreneurial career elsewhere too. The truth is, this factory suits my start the most. It‘s in our town, it has district-wide significance, interesting money flows through here, and it‘s a size I can manage on my own. And you have no problem prioritizing emotions over reason? I thought you were smarter than that. Would you do the same? Would you be so selfish? Do you know what‘s at stake? The fates of those people outside the window. And you don‘t even know how Adam himself would react,“ Angela stated, blinking her eyes quickly.

„Yes. I won‘t know how he‘ll react until I tell him. What if I, for once in my life, were selfish? Didn‘t care about others? Took what I wanted?! Didn‘t hold back like so many times before. Would it be a shock then?

Would the world be turned upside down? And what if I turned it right-side up for once? What could possibly happen? We'll be together, he'll have some money. We'll leave this town after school and study somewhere far away and forget. What's happening here is not our fault."

Angela interrupted her: „But it's your responsibility. Or rather, Adam's. What if he loses interest in you? What if he becomes afraid of this possibility? Right now, he wants you by his side more than anything. But if that were to happen, he would probably reconsider the pros and cons. What would your relationship be like then? And don't forget that I have a say in this transaction too. I won't work with someone who doesn't trust me, whom I don't trust, and who isn't close to me. This isn't a game of beans. But what would you know... with your small-town life and a few coins in your pocket," Angela retorted.

„So why don't you tell him that you love him then? You wouldn't have anything to lose. It would be a perfect chain of events," Kirsten asked.

„I won't tell him for one simple reason. Because I don't love him. He's so infatuated with you that if he had eyes only for me, I would have to kill you first. Or maybe just humiliate you enough to win him over. Or maybe he'll think about it alone for a while and figure out where he belongs. Then I'll fall in love with him," Angela said confidently.

„So you're just using him foolishly," Kirsten said softly.

„I use, abuse... only as much as he allows. I don't need to throw myself at someone's feet. I'm not a log for someone to trip over, but a crutch that so many rely on. I use all available weapons to achieve what I've set my mind to. On one hand, the smooth sale of the factory, and on the other hand, perhaps his love. But we're getting ahead of ourselves. We have the competition ahead of us. Don't forget," she said, raising an eyebrow.

„Winning the competition could achieve a lot for the school. Money, fame. And you could ruin it all. So go, fall in love, tell him. I'll win either way. I have nothing to lose. But you do," Angela concluded, straightened her back, took a pen in her hand, and continued calculating the forms.

„I won't fight. I'll just be myself. Time will show which path was the right one. For me, it's usually the path of perseverance. If Adam can't walk that path, then it shouldn't be that simple. He's walking it now and thinking."

And that's good. Emotions should not control us. If necessary, I will go those few meters to meet him. But I won't fight with him or with you, or with life. I‘ve already thrown a stone into the water, I‘ll wait for the ripples to return. That‘s when the timing will be right. I‘m not used to losing either. Just my victories need to solidify. They don‘t stand on clay feet. Or rather, they don‘t stand on the value of money like yours. And they never will. And yes, I‘ll tell him that I love him,“ Kirsten finished and opened the iron door.

„You certainly don‘t lack self-confidence. The fall will be all the more painful,“ Angela said without taking her eyes off the charts. Kirsten closed the door behind her. Angela briefly looked away from the screen and rubbed her eyes. This tug-of-war was starting to wear her out. She felt that her arrogance and competitiveness were gradually fading away. She leaned back in her chair, kicked off her heels, and propped her feet up on the table. She still felt the confident Angela inside her, but behind her stood the new one, who placed a hand on her shoulder and spoke to her in a calm voice. If Adam were in the office, she would have handed him over to her, just to get everyone moving.

Kirsten rushed down the stairs, feeling that with each dialogue with Angela, she grew stronger. As if she absorbed her experiences and used them against her. The factory would be saved one way or another. She was just uncertain about Adam. Where he was, how he was feeling. Kirsten wondered if she should pull out the trump card up her sleeve to shorten the distance to him. But it wasn‘t the right time yet.

Chapter 41

- PLANS -

Adam`s place was by the door on an old chair. Across from him, on a comfortable old worn-out couch, Kirsten and Sofia sat by the window. Next to them, on a red fabric armchair with large wooden armrests, Emie sat wearing a cap and jeans with suspenders, looking like a queen on her throne. Her legs were propped up on a dark wooden coffee table. The interior of the little red house was unfinished. The walls were lined with planed boards of light wood, with a few shelves and a piano in the corner. On the makeshift table, there were a few coffee cups. Above the entrance, the house had a black tin roof. Many times, Kirsten stood under it, listening to the symphony of raindrops overhead.

„You're kidding, right?" Emie looked at the contract on the table in disbelief.

„So you're going to be a star now? You'll be rich! I recognize that logo," Emie said with wide-open eyes.

„No, I'm not going to be a star. And I don't want more money either," Kirsten said and looked at Emie. She took the contract and flipped through it. She stopped at one page and seemed to read it thoroughly, as she alternated her gaze between Kirsten and Sofia, who sat next to her. Kirsten knew exactly which page it was. She looked at the headline again: „Sofia's Foundation for..." She shook her head and laughed.

„Do you really want to sell yourself so cheaply? I would understand this step if you were already rich and famous. But isn't it exploitation?" Emie asked, adjusting her earring.

„Believe me, it's not. The condition has more value to me right now than any fame or money. I'm founding an idea that will be a part of me for the rest of my life. And probably my face too," Kirsten added.

„So, if you're not famous, what will you be? A lyricist and musician?" Sofia asked.

„Yes. Something like that. I will write music for artists. I didn't even realize that's what I would love to do for the rest of my life. I mean, I'm already doing it. So why not give it a broader meaning? It's enjoyable, fulfilling," Kirsten replied and hugged Sofia around the shoulders.

„And I thought what will you be when you finish school, and behold! We have a celebrity here!" Sofia exclaimed admirably.

„No, no. I'm not a celebrity. I'm not special or unique in any way," Kirsten wanted to complete her sentence, but Sofia interrupted her: „But you're not like others either," she added.

„What are you going to do now? I mean after school," Emie asked.

„Until now, I didn't know. I'll see how the collaboration goes. But I would like to go the path of philanthropy. And I'll study some art, music. To acquire something that money can't buy and therefore will have great value to me. And we'll keep farming. You'll be a veterinarian, there will be lots of animals on the farm, Adam will successfully save the factory, Sofia will recover, and Angela will be our good friend," Kirsten said.

„And one day, a prince on a white horse will come for you," Sofia interrupted Kirsten.

„Yeah, it sounds like a fairytale. So what. Let something come out of it... It's better to have one big leafy tree so that after the storm, there are still a few branches with leaves left on it. From a distance, it will be clear that the storm didn't break it. Who knows where we'll all be in a few years. Whether we'll still be meeting here, in the little red house. We made a promise to each other in the cafe after that match. Just whether we'll be able to keep it..." Kirsten mused out loud, looking at the empty chair where Adam used to sit.

„Who knows how the relationship between Adam and Angela will develop. Between all of us," Kirsten said, running her hand through her hair, frowning, and looking out of the house window at the lake.

„Well, thank goodness, we brought our grades up to the average so I can take those exams. I really appreciate your help with that. And you can't be with me on the farm forever," Emie replied, pulling her cap down over her eyes, as if trying to hide from reality.

„But I can," Kirsten stated to herself, and continued to gaze out of the window at the lake. It was clear that not all battles had been won yet.

Chapter 42

- ALL YOU HAD TO DO WAS OPEN THAT BOX -

Angela walked down the stairs and headed towards the open doors of the waiting limousine. She was still thinking about the details of the contract. Everything was going according to plan, just as she had intended and arranged. She was pleased that she had deliberately achieved what she had set out to do. Adam would eventually show up. He couldn‘t hide forever. Angelina‘s family had time on their side. Mackenzie, on the other hand, didn‘t, and would likely be tamed soon. She admitted that the relationships and business had gotten a bit tangled, but in the end, money showed its power. She stepped on the sidewalk and tapped a melody on the asphalt with her heels. She passed by the benches and walked quickly towards the car. Out of the corner of her eye, she noticed Sofia sitting on one of them. She took a few more steps and turned around. Sofia was sitting there all alone. She looked around, but didn‘t see Kirsten or anyone else from their group. She took a few steps back, looking at Sofia from a distance. Sunken cheeks, leaning against the bench, staring at the ground without moving. She headed back towards the car. When Sofia suffers, Kirsten suffers too. She grabbed the car door, lost in thought. The idea that both of them suffering brought her no satisfaction, it infuriated her in a schizophrenic way. She tried to get into the car, but couldn‘t. She looked inside the limousine for a moment while the engine was running. She threw her bag in and walked back towards the benches.

„Are you okay? Are you waiting for Kirsten?“ Angela asked Sofia, surprising herself that she dared to do so.

„Kirsten is out of town. She went to sign some papers. I just sat down for a moment. I need to rest,“ Sofia said and gave Angela a faint smile.

„Well, you don‘t seem to be doing well. Do you want to go to the hospital for an examination, just to be safe?“ Angela said, sizing her up.

„It‘s not a seizure. I know that state already. It‘s just fatigue. My body is taking a toll. I‘ll go home slowly,“ Sofia concluded, but Angela wouldn‘t be deterred.

„Like this? You won‘t even make it there. Isn‘t there anyone who can drive you home?“ Angela squinted.

„My parents are at work, and I don‘t want to bother them. They‘ve already had to leave work a few times recently. We can‘t afford that. Emie is already on the farm,“ Sofia assessed the situation.

Angela extended her hand. „Come on, I‘ll take you home. No, not home. You‘d be alone there. First to the hospital, just to be sure. At least get checked out,“ Angela said in such a tone that Sofia had no room to negotiate. She placed her hand in Angela‘s, and Angela helped her up as they walked together to her limousine. They got in, and the driver turned to look in the rearview mirror.

„To the clinic,“ Angela ordered, and the car moved.

They looked at each other silently and felt like two worlds from opposite ends of the universe had come together in the car. The clinic wasn‘t far, and Angela didn‘t hurry to get home. The factory transfer had already been administratively prepared; now all that was left was to meet and sign everything. It would be over by the end of the week. In a few days, the competition would take place. Angela resisted the emotions and feelings that looking at Sofia stirred in her. She didn‘t want them to gnaw at her and make her weak, fallible. She felt like every glance at Sofia was a battle within herself. With herself and with Kirsten. With unwavering resolve, she patiently awaited their arrival at the clinic. The car stopped at the main entrance. They both walked up the stairs to the first floor, where Sofia‘s doctor had his office. He wasn‘t surprised to see her at all; they had been meeting frequently lately. Angela left Sofia in the office and went out into the corridor. She sat down on a bench and pondered what she was actually doing there. It was as if something from Kirsten had stuck to her after all. And she couldn‘t peel it off herself. Or didn‘t want to? She closed her eyes tightly, as if trying to recover from a hangover after a sleepless night.

„We didn‘t find anything unusual. Slightly elevated blood pressure, but with regards to the diagnosis, it‘s within the normal range. We can keep her here overnight for observation if you want," the doctor read out the results of Sofia's tests.

„Just don't stay alone now. Just to be safe," the doctor added.

„I'll call my parents, they'll come get me," Sofia reassured the doctor.

„If you want, you can come with me and my driver will take you home afterwards when your parents come back from work," Angela suggested.

„I was supposed to meet with the girls today. To gossip in the hall while listening to music. But... I would prefer to be with you. If you accept the invitation, that is," Angela narrowed her eyes, almost like dashes, as if she was waiting for the impact of tiny fragments on Sofia's face after a blow from a sledgehammer.

„I'd love to. When does one get the chance to be invited to a millionaire's home?" Sofia laughed.

„But go on! I hope you're not just going because of that," Angela asked.

„No, I don't want to be alone. I'm feeling better now. I'll wait for my parents or Kirsten," Sofia added quietly.

„Alright, let's go," Angela said and handed Sofia her coat. As they got into the limousine, Sofia looked at it with interest. After the tour, she was feeling calmer. Her mood had returned. She relaxed and began to perceive the world around her. During the drive, she ran her hand over the tasteful wooden accents. She didn't even have time to bombard Angela with the multitude of questions that were running through her mind during the entire journey. They arrived at the main entrance, dominated by large wooden double doors. Sofia looked at the endless number of windows and guessed what might be hiding behind them. She looked behind her. A perfectly manicured green lawn stretched as far as the eye could see. She immediately felt the urge to run towards it and roll in the middle of it. Next to her were several expensive cars. Sofia felt like she was in a museum of wealth. Everything beautifully and perfectly arranged. It left her with a preserved impression. Angela ran up the stairs and opened the doors. Sofia slowly ascended towards the doors, observing every detail. She entered the foyer. Marble stairs leading to the next floor, a large chandelier in the middle, hanging high above the ground. The hall was almost sparsely furnished, in a minimalist style. On either side were two purple armchairs with high backrests. They looked like thrones. Behind them, in the middle of the room, between two stone pillars, stood a small white wooden table. Behind it, another room was visible, with large white double doors leading to the garden behind the house. Sofia imagined herself as a little child playing chase with other kids from the street here. The floor with a simple, tasteful pattern shone like a mirror. In its center, a large circle was drawn on the floor, with Angela's last name bordering it.

He looked like an heirloom. Angela walked towards the side wooden brown doors. She opened them and they entered a sort of anteroom. It was entirely lined with dark black wood. There was only a small table and a built-in wardrobe with mirrors. Sofia guessed that this is where all the expensive fur coats are stored, and where the finest champagne is offered as guests step into the most aristocratic party in the vicinity. Angela continued walking and opening more and more doors like a princess in a fairy tale. Sofia was just being careful not to knock over anything and not to break her nose on another column. She caught up with Angela in the kitchen. It was as big as their whole house. She had never seen a bigger refrigerator in her life. Angela took some water from it and handed a second bottle to Sofia.

„I should say something like ‚make yourself at home', right?" Angela pondered.

„We have time until your guests arrive. Come, I'll show you something really valuable," Angela replied and walked towards more doors. Sofia was getting dizzy from all the wealth and couldn't imagine what could be more valuable than everything she had seen so far. They went upstairs. A long corridor stretched out in front of Sofia, like in a hotel. The walls were lined with many doors. Angela walked straight to those at the very end of the corridor. All the other doors on the sides were exactly like the ones Sofia had at home. White with golden handles. But the ones at the end of the corridor were the same double-winged doors as many on the ground floor. Angela pushed them open and they entered the room.

„This is my room. But that's not what I wanted to show you. Come further," Angela winked at Sofia and stood by the door.

„You have your own balcony in your bedroom? And where are your closets? You must have a ton of fancy clothes," Sofia's blue eyes widened as she spoke. Angela walked towards the side doors, opened them, and gestured for Sofia to come in.

„A dressing room? It's as big as my room! I could easily bring my bed here and live here. Do you have a ladder in your closet?" Sofia couldn't contain her excitement about all the details. She moved the ladder here and there as if she wanted to make sure it was real and probably heading towards the top shelves where there were maybe a thousand pairs of shoes. Meanwhile, Angela came out of the dressing room and headed towards the opposite door. Sofia looked in her direction, and if her eyes weren‘t already as wide open as possible, she would have opened them even more.

„Private bathroom! No more morning battles over who gets to use the sink first!“ she laughed. The bathroom was more like a living room. There was a large white bathtub under the window, opposite a shower corner that was perhaps bigger than Sofia‘s entire bathroom. Three large rectangular mirrors were positioned across the door. In front of the middle one stood a small modest stool. Angela washed her hands and watched Sofia.

„I wish I could experience what you do. And close those blue eyes for a moment, because I could drown in them,“ she blinked her eyes and her lips stretched sideways.

„Come on,“ she nodded her head and shrugged her shoulders. She opened another door in the room, and they entered a narrow corridor. They descended stairs and arrived at another set of doors. The passage looked like a secret passage to an atomic bunker. There must have been something very interesting behind the doors. Angela glanced at Sofia for a few seconds and opened the doors. Sofia stepped in, but this time her eyes didn‘t pop out of their sockets. Instead, she couldn‘t quite comprehend what she saw. On the left side was a long table with some tools on it. It looked like someone had been working with it just a moment ago. There was only one chair in front of the table, and a large magnifying glass was attached to its frame. On the wall were various knives, scalpels, and some chisels. The room looked like a workshop and smelled of wood. Only now did she notice the large glass doors, and something behind them that she couldn‘t identify. Angela pulled the doors aside and revealed the interior of the cabinet.

Sofia exclaimed, „Furniture? Is this for dolls? Seriously?“ She walked in surprise towards the cabinet. She found herself in front of dozens of miniature beds, wardrobes, armoires, and tables.

„Is this you?“ she looked at Angela incredulously.

„Yes, it‘s me,“ Angela smiled and picked up a small bed from the cabinet.

„I suspected there was something about you. I didn't believe it, but Kirsten was right. She keeps telling me that what we see of you at school is not your whole face. That there is much more to you. She admires you," she finished, and Angela raised her eyebrow so high that it almost disappeared under her bangs.

„I didn't understand her before. But now I do. How could Kirsten know? You have to show her. It's amazing!" Sofia said as she ran her fingers along the perfectly polished edges.

„She saw a few pieces of furniture at Adam's factory," Angela said and picked up a small cupboard with shelves. The wood felt pleasant to the touch.

The beds had hand-sewn mini duvets and mini pillows. Various patterns were embroidered on them. It required great precision and a dose of patience. Some of them had a similar logo to the one she saw downstairs in the hall. With each touch, Sofia felt like she was touching Angelina's bare soul.

„I promised to show you something truly precious," said Angela and picked up a carved cabinet from the shelf. At first glance, it was very intricately crafted with a multitude of different ornaments and patterns.

„I've been making this cabinet for a long time. It's special. I store all my emotions in it. Whenever I'm angry, sad, or happy, I take this cabinet in my hands and record my emotion in it. Sometimes I even remember the occasion and emotion when I carved a particular pattern. When it comes to the same thing, I continue with that pattern. That's why some of them look really strange," Angela smiled and turned the cabinet in her hands. Some patterns started with beautiful curves, only to be followed by strictly mathematical shapes with deep grooves. Some ornaments were only superficially indicated, and some were even traced. Many of them were inside her. She carefully pulled out one shelf. It was covered with patterns. She slid it back and handed it to Sofia.

„It's yours," she said, reaching out to Sofia.

„What? What are you... I can't accept this!" Sofia exclaimed in surprise.

„I knew you would say that. But I am determined. Take it. Trust me, if you accept it, you'll be giving me a gift that money can't buy. Not with all my money," Angela replied, placing the cabinet in Sofia's hands. Sofia examined it and looked at Angela with incomprehension. It was as if she held Angela's entire emotional and sentimental life in her hands.

She didn‘t know what to say. And she certainly didn‘t expect Angela to confide in her like this.

„Take it. There‘s hardly any space left for new ornaments on it anyway. I‘ll probably start making a new one soon. It‘s amazing when you carve the first pattern on clean smooth white wood,“ Angela reassured Sofia.

„Let‘s agree that you‘ll keep it at my place. Whenever you want to see it, touch it, just let me know,“ Sofia said, turning the cabinet in her hands, examining it.

„I know it won‘t be lost with you. Maybe some emotion, some feeling will stick to it. There‘s still some space left on it,“ Angela added, gazing at the cabinet as if recapping everything that compelled her to pick up chisels and carve all those ornaments into it.

ꕤ

They walked out in front of the house. Angela leaned against the large stone staircase and pulled out cigarettes.

„Do you smoke?“ Sofia asked, surprised.

„Only when I‘m nervous,“ Angela replied and took a drag.

„Are you nervous? Why? Don‘t be. I liked your house, and... thank you for the gift!“ Sofia smiled.

Angela gave her a cold look. She needed to get back to „normal.“ Thanks to Sofia, she had learned a bit more about Kirsten. She was just worried that her competitiveness was fading away. It was as if Kirsten‘s spell was working on her from a distance through Sofia. She felt herself softening, soaking in it. She needed to light up a cigarette to hypnotize her true self and return to her side of the barricade.

„Well, we‘ll have our little secret now. Let‘s see what you do with it,“ Angela smirked under her mustache.

Sofia didn‘t say anything, just winked mischievously and dashed off to the waiting limousine.

Chapter 43

- FROM DARKNESS TO LIGHT -

„Kirsten, close the shutters on the upper floor. There's a storm coming today," called Sam from the kitchen, as he secured all the windows with wooden shutters that had been a part of their home for most of their lives.

„Finally, they come in handy," he muttered to himself and latched the bolt. Kirsten rushed through the upper floor, closing all the shutters, and then returned to her room. She lay on her bed in a gray cotton shirt and loose sweatpants, with her hair loose. In a few days, she had a competition coming up, and it occupied most of her thoughts, vying for the spotlight with thoughts of Sofia. Somewhere in the background, Adam stood in the shadows, watching her. She hesitated, unsure if she wanted to fall into his embrace. Kirsten looked up at the ceiling, just like she had on many evenings before. She knew she wouldn't find answers there, but it helped her clear her mind. The blank white surface was like an unwritten book, where all the thoughts that raced in front of her eyes faded away. Her eyelids grew heavy until she couldn't keep them open anymore, and she slowly closed her eyes.

Kirsten dreamed that she was standing in an empty gray room with a large mirror that covered the entire wall. There were several doors in the room, and a small square gray chair stood in the corner. She felt that someone was standing behind the mirror, someone who had locked her in there. But it seemed to her that she had entered the room willingly, without resistance. The piano started playing from behind the mirror. The composition that she had played with Angela during their rehearsals. She hadn't heard anyone else play it, only Angela. But suddenly, the perfect notes turned into a false melody, as if the pianist was just learning to play. She looked into the mirror and saw herself. When she turned away from the mirror, the melody suddenly became perfect again. She looked over her shoulder and heard the false notes again. „Angela must be playing the perfect notes. Who else?" she wondered. Kirsten didn't like the room and wanted to escape from it, but at the same time, she was afraid of what awaited her behind the doors. She examined all the doors; they were all exactly the same. She opened the first one, to find herself in the same room again. She opened more doors, but it was like chasing her own tail, unable to escape.

She took off her shirt and tossed it to the center of the room. She opened another door. In the middle of the room, her shirt lay there. She gave up. She sat down on the small gray square chair and listened to the composition that echoed from behind the mirror. She didn‘t look at it, didn‘t want to hear that false melody. She wondered why every room was the same and had already realized that she was still in the same room, looking for an exit in the wrong place. Kirsten still hoped that behind the next door, she would find her way out of the room. So, if there was no exit behind any of the doors, the truth must be in the mirror. She looked ahead, directly into it and heard the false melody again. She suppressed the seeds of depression within her and stepped closer. She could clearly see her face and looked into her own eyes, wanted to touch her face in the mirror. She raised her hand and gently touched her cheek. However, her hand went through the mirror and the composition stopped being false. She was slightly startled, withdrew her hand from behind the mirror. She heard those familiar false tones again, extended her hand again, and it disappeared behind the mirror. She didn‘t feel anything strange. Only the melody was pleasant again, soothing her ears. Kirsten realized it was a sign showing her the right direction of her path. She took a step forward, passed through the mirror to the other side. Light flooded her. There was nothing behind the mirror, only bright light. She turned back and saw Angela wandering around the room. Opening and closing doors, just like she did a moment ago. Kirsten quickly passed through the mirror again to lead her out into the light. However, when she entered the room, Angela had disappeared. The false melody alerted her that she was on the wrong side of the barricade. She went back behind the mirror and saw Angela, desperate and lost, in the room. She realized Angela had to find her own way out. She was trapped in her own perception and was scared. What if while she was inside, Angela was outside behind the mirror, seeing the same play. Watching her wandering through the rooms. She shouted at her, but Angela didn‘t hear her. Kirsten realized that if she could hear the melody, Angela must hear it too. If she could play a different melody from behind the mirror, maybe she could guide her to the exit. She remembered Mr. Newton‘s piano. If only she had it there behind the mirror, took a step back and stumbled.

She turned around and saw the piano. Kirsten looked around, but the space was still filled with bright light and the piano stood beside her by the mirror. She felt like she was in her own mind, where she could materialize any of her thoughts. Or where every thought of her subconscious would materialize. Suddenly she realized that if she controlled the situation, it didn‘t mean the situation controlled her. She felt empowered and strong, realized the power of her will.

Kirsten sat down at the piano and played „For Sofia." Angela suddenly stopped and looked towards the mirror. She frowned for a moment. She reached out her hand and gasped, took a step back and disappeared with a jump on the other side of the mirror. Kirsten stopped playing. She looked around but couldn‘t see Angela. Maybe she was inside her own mind right now. Who knows if she sees the same bright light. She stood up from the piano, and it disappeared instantly. In the distance, she heard Sofia laughing heartily. Kirsten didn‘t know why Sofia was laughing, but her laughter calmed her, walked forward, and the mirror gradually moved away from her until it disappeared completely. She found herself alone in the middle of a bright white room, wished someone would hug her. Someone who would help her arrange this big bright room without furniture, emotions, and experiences. Some architect who knows her and to whom she wouldn‘t have to explain every detail.

„Hello," said a figure that appeared out of nowhere, directly from the sharp light.

„Adam?" Kirsten asked incredulously, but at the same time immediately understood that she had been thinking of him in her subconscious mind.

„Wake up!" he said and grabbed her hand.

„I don‘t want to wake up," Kirsten replied stubbornly.

„Kirsten, wake up!" he insisted.

„No, I want to be here with you," she replied resolutely.

„Wake up," she heard again, but not from Adam‘s mouth, but near her right ear. She turned her head and saw Sam. The light suddenly disappeared, and the room gradually came into focus before her eyes. Sam stood right above her, saying something. Kirsten could only hear the sound, still caught in a deep sleep.

„Are you awake now? You slept really tough tonight. Did you even notice the storm outside?" Sam asked in surprise.

„The trees were falling outside, and here you are sleeping like a Sleeping Beauty. You probably won't make it to school today. Let's at least tidy up around the house. I'm going to prepare breakfast for you," Sam added, and Kirsten could only hear creaking stairs in the hallway as he walked away. She leaned back on the bed and ran her hand through her hair. That dream! It had a somewhat melancholic mood. She wondered what she had just seen. It felt so vivid!

„It was just a dream!" she said to herself, got up from the bed, washed her face in the bathroom, and opened the window. A scene of devastation greeted her outside.

A few fallen trees in their garden, with a red house buried under leaves and branches. Kirsten quickly got dressed and ran to the kitchen. She quickly ate breakfast and rushed outside to help Sam. The morning passed by quickly as they worked. They managed to tidy up the area around the house to some extent, but the flower beds were irreparably damaged. All of them were broken and scattered everywhere. She remembered Belinda and the café, hoped that the storm hadn't damaged the storefront. Rushed into the house, changed clothes, and grabbed the car keys from the table. „I'm going to check on Belinda to see if everything is okay. I'll come back in the evening," Kirsten said, finishing her sentence and hurried to the car. Sam nodded in agreement and comfortably stretched out on the couch.

The drive to the city was slow. There were firefighters and volunteers everywhere. The storm had been strong, but most of the houses remained undamaged, with only a few broken windows and fallen fences here and there. Nature had dealt a bigger blow to itself. Broken trees and flooded lawns lined the roads, but the roads were passable, and Kirsten slowly made her way to the city center. She reached the square and saw that a large tree had fallen directly onto the fountain. She couldn't drive any further, so she parked her car near the square. She walked on foot past the shops, and the city was bustling with activity. Electricians and other workers in various colored overalls were repairing faults in both above-ground and underground networks. Kirsten crossed to the other side of the sidewalk and could already see Belinda's café with intact displays from a distance. The doors were open. Most of the square had electricity now. There were a few people sitting in the café, and Belinda was bustling behind the counter.

„Hi, I‘m making coffee for all those hardworking people outside. Poor things, they haven‘t stopped since morning. That was a terrible storm. Did you see it?“ Belinda asked, pouring coffee into thermoses. Kirsten didn‘t remember the storm, but she remembered the strange dream. She left the café and saw Angela standing by the broken fountain, along with her parents, the mayor of the town, and a few others. Kirsten crossed the road and walked towards the group by the fountain and that‘s when Angela noticed her. Angela interrupted her mid-sentence, saying, „Hi, would you like to help?“ Kirsten didn‘t have a chance to finish her sentence before Angela cut in with a sarcastic tone, „And how? Are you going to play the piano? Write a poem? Clean up branches?“

She looked up at the sky, as if trying to gather her thoughts. „Oh! Look, sometimes kind words are not enough, but money has to speak. Our family wants to help the town with the restoration. The damage assessment is currently underway. We probably won‘t be able to cover the entire amount, but together with Mrs. Mackenzie, we will contribute enough to the repair fund to help the town get back on its feet. I don‘t know how you could help. Our world simply functions on money, whether you like it or not. Some things can only be solved with money. It‘s noble that you want to change the world with kind words, but your power ends there. If you want to help, go talk to the mayor and tell him how. Maybe he will like what you propose,“ Angela concluded, tightening her coat belt.

„I think he will like my proposal. Has Adam reached out?“ Kirsten asked, looking towards Mrs. Mackenzie.

„I‘m not aware of anyone reaching out. But you can ask his mother directly,“ Mrs. Mackenzie replied, gesturing towards Adam‘s mother.

„But I can‘t,“ Kirsten thought to herself, and without a word, she walked towards the mayor. Angela raised her eyebrows in surprise and grew silent. Her sarcasm was being replaced by curiosity. Kirsten approached the mayor. They exchanged a few words and separated from the group. Angela squinted her eyes in bewilderment and watched the conversation. The mayor raised his eyebrows in surprise, but then nodded in agreement. The conversation was short, but she could see that it left several questions in the mayor‘s mind. However, he seemed satisfied. Kirsten ran from the fountain to the sidewalk, waved to Angela, pulled her hair from behind her collar, put on her brown leather jacket, and hurried off. She disappeared down a side alley, and Angela walked back towards the group by the fountain. The town was still messy, and she had to watch where she stepped to avoid ruining her expensive high-heeled leather shoes.

ഗ

Kirsten parked her car in the parking lot covered with white pebbles. She knew on the way there that the storm had probably also spared the farm. She got out and walked along the sidewalk full of leaves, empty plastic bags, and branches towards the greenhouse. Several windows were broken, and glass was scattered among the crops. The greenhouse was ankle-deep in water, and the rain had washed most of the soil from the raised beds with vegetables. There was an eerie silence around the farm, as if the wind had blown all life away from it. The doors of the house were closed, and there was no light inside.

In front of the greenhouse, there were empty wooden crates scattered all around, which the wind mercilessly played with during the night. At first glance, it was clear that cleaning up the farm area would take at least a week or more. Kirsten herself hadn't even tidied up around the red house yet. She walked along the greenhouse and turned onto the path that led to the barn and the fields. The only sound disturbing the silence was the squelching mud swirling under her shoes. She emerged from behind the barn and saw Emie. A large devastation stretched out before her. The field looked like a mess - like tousled hair after a sleepless night when one tosses and turns and can't fall asleep. The harvest was ruined. As far as her eye could see, corn cobs were lying in the mud, wheat was broken, and wheat ears were half empty. Emie noticed Kirsten and looked around. She sniffed and looked back at the ruined harvest. Kirsten heard her crying. She approached her slowly and looked at her from the side.

„So many callouses and efforts. Days when I couldn't be at school, the bad grades. And for what?" she said and continued to cry.

„Just before the harvest. We were supposed to collect and sell it in a week. I don't know what will happen now. Maybe the farm will go under. Our parents went to the mayor to ask for help," said Emie, wiping her eyes, which were filled with tears again. Kirsten remembered her conversation with the mayor. The town probably wouldn't have the resources to help the farm. The situation seemed hopeless. Lost time couldn‘t be returned to Emie. And she didn‘t even receive any reward for it. She remembered Angeline‘s words. That brief conversation by the broken fountain in the middle of the town. Even these moments helped mature the thoughts in her head that kept her from sleeping.

„I know someone who could help you with the farm. I‘ll go talk to your parents,“ she added, looking ahead at the devastated field.

„I don‘t think anyone would want to help the farm now. We couldn‘t find anyone to invest in the farm when it was thriving, let alone now,“ Emie wiped her tears again.

„Now it will require twice as much investment. Only a madman or someone who doesn‘t know where to put their money would do it,“ Emie said sarcastically.

„Life takes something away from you, but it also gives you something else,“ Kirsten said in a sad tone, and she hugged Emie‘s shoulders. They looked together at the devastation, both trying to believe that a miracle might be just around the corner.

Chapter 44

- BUSINESS -

After a long day, Angela took a hot bath to relax. As she soaked in the tub, she reflected on what Kirsten had told the mayor. He had only said that she would help with the city's revitalization and promised not to reveal any details. Angela couldn't understand how Kirsten could help the city. She still couldn't fully understand her. She was interrupted from her thoughts by a ringing phone. Angela momentarily stopped grooming herself and looked at the table in the room.

„At this hour?" she asked herself. She walked barefoot in a dark gray nightgown to the table and picked up her mobile phone.

„Adam?" she shook her head in confusion and held the phone to her ear.

„Hello, can we meet and discuss everything? You were right. We need to finalize the transaction. I needed to clear my head, and this is one of the first things I should do. That we should do," Adam replied and paused.

„Well, you're in luck. Tomorrow, I'm going to the capital to meet with our law firm and review and approve the contracts. After tomorrow's visit, they will be ready for signing. We'll have two to three hours in the car together. I'll send a car for you in the morning," Angela thought with excitement.

„No need. I'll wait for you in the lobby downstairs in the morning. Just inform the reception. Bye for now," Adam finished and hung up before she could say anything. Angela looked at the phone in confusion, trying to understand Adam's motivation. Maybe there's really nothing behind it. Just the completion of the transaction. In any case, a point for her. She shook her head, as if she couldn't believe it. She didn't want to think about it anymore today.

ᔕ

The next morning, Angela quickly checked the parking lot in front of her house, but there were no other cars except her family's cars. She fixed her hair in the mirror. Her hair elegantly and neatly combed back, not a strand out of place. A discreet bun on top of her dark jacket, with white sleeves and golden cuffs peeking out.

She was in her military uniform, ready to win any battle, ran down the stairs and in the hallway, Adam was indeed waiting for her. He didn‘t have the suave look of James Bond, but he was dressed appropriately for their upcoming meeting. His hair was slicked back with gel, he wore a dark blue suit, shiny shoes, and a tie. Angela knew from his attire that he was serious.

She took a few more steps and stood directly in front of him. He glanced at her briefly and pointed to the car that was already parked in front of the house. The driver was waiting with the doors open. Angela continued with her folder under her arm towards the limousine, and Adam followed closely. They got in silently, and Angela waited to see if Adam would bring up yesterday‘s conversation. Adam just settled in quietly and watched as the car pulled away from the house. The familiar streets passed by them, and Edwood slowly faded into the distance.

„Tell me, why did you come?“ Angela broke the silence after a while. She needed to know more information, and she could tell that Adam didn‘t care what she thought. It was about business.

„Because of what you said. I want to be responsible. And besides, I don‘t have any other option in life but to move forward. Which direction and when. I could have waited to see how things would unfold, but it seems like they won‘t unfold in any way. At least not until we finish this transaction. You know, I won‘t swim against the current. I‘ve wasted my energy before, and it was all for nothing. It‘s more convenient now to go with the flow for a while,“ Adam replied, reaching for a bottle of mineral water from the mini-bar and looking at Angela across from him.

„Does anyone know that you‘ve returned?“ Angela asked curiously.

„Only you and my mom, of course. I told her where I was going. She always knew where I was. She kept urging me to take this step. But I wanted to make this decision out of my own conviction. I thought about the people at the factory. I couldn‘t be so selfish to only think about myself first. If we didn‘t close this deal, I wouldn‘t be able to look at myself in the mirror. This way, it‘s the right thing to do,“ he finished and took a sip from the bottle.

„You see, you think like we do. Rich and successful. Everything is subservient to the right decision. That‘s why we‘re rich and successful.

We‘re a perfect match. Fairytales are for children. We live in the real world. I‘ll turn the factory into a thriving business without debts. It just needs some healing and modernization now. The crisis has damaged it badly,“ Angela said, looking back at her folders.

Adam couldn‘t say that he didn‘t like Angela. She was a confident young woman, always elegant and beautiful. She was like a mountain stream into which someone poured ink. She was only for those who didn‘t mind that they would also drink unwanted impurities along with the pleasant water in a beautiful environment.

„To be honest with you, I want to tell you that I will look for ways to buy out your family from the factory. As long as you‘re there, I‘ll be there as a fifth wheel on the wagon. And I‘m afraid of what will happen to the employees. I imagined that we would run the factory with someone who has a soul and hasn‘t left it with the devil,“ he finished, and Angela smiled devilishly.

„Edwood is a family town. Everything in it originates from family circles. It‘s a small town, and that‘s why it‘s so charming. Because everyone in it is like family. It annoys me a little that I don‘t know what your plans are with the factory. I understand that you‘re mainly after profit. And that‘s what I‘m afraid of,“ he replied, fixing his gaze on Angela.

„So you‘re afraid of making money? Come on! Do you want to be some kind of samaritan and give away money to everyone for nothing? You‘ll end up on the street, used and poor. It doesn‘t work that way. There‘s no one who has a lot of money and doesn‘t have a guilty conscience, skeletons in the closet, and a list of moral values in place of a paragraph. Money breaks everyone eventually. They have a miraculous power,“ Angela opened her eyes wide and gestured with her hand like a cat‘s paw with claws.

„If I meet someone who has a lot of money and is moral, I‘ll kneel down and pay him homage with a long knightly wave of my hand after I eat a wire brush. But like this... I wish you good luck in finding my replacement. It touched me,“ Angela smiled. Adam knew that leaving Angela out of the game would be the greatest punishment for her.

„And it will be expensive,“ she added and turned the pages further. She was waiting for this moment, but the reward wasn‘t as sweet as she had imagined. She didn‘t understand these new feelings herself. Something was happening in her, changing. And she knew it was because of

Kirsten. She still had the image of Kirsten standing up for her in class. How she could sacrifice herself for Sofia. She wondered if she should accept these positive aspects for everyone and if it would make her even stronger. Whatever she threw at her, she was like a sponge. She absorbed something, and something soft sank and fell next to her. She was soaked with emotions, and Angela currently felt like a sheet of paper on which the sponge was placed. She felt how it absorbed the moisture from her. The journey passed calmly, and Adam was still putting his thoughts together. But what he knew was that he would meet Kirsten tomorrow and be honest with her. He would hug her, and she would agree that their relationship as good friends would be best for everyone. Especially because from now on, they...

Chapter 45

- WRONG RECIPIENT -

Sofia went out to the courtyard with a paper bag containing her lunch. There weren't many students there now in the autumn. Many preferred to spend their breaks in the classroom or on the stairs in the hallways. That's why Sofia always chose this part of the school during this time. She looked around to see if she could spot a familiar face and spotted Angela sitting at a table. She noticed her and gestured for her to join her with her eyes. She looked to the opposite end of the small courtyard and saw Kirsten sitting at a table with a few other girls. Both of them were eating their sandwiches with a mesmerized gaze. Sofia didn't know if they were even aware of each other. She walked towards Kirsten.

„Hi, I'll be there in a moment," she said quickly and headed towards Angela. She sat down with her and took out her lunch from the bag - a sandwich cut into two triangles. Kirsten was observing them and would have joined them, but she knew she wouldn't be good company at the moment. The fresh air and solitude in the courtyard gave her space to think about her next steps. The dark passenger within her was now speaking the loudest since its birth. She couldn't kill it or turn it into a dove, so she was considering how to bring it into the daylight. Kirsten would reveal it to everyone and show them its weakest side. The one that was born from her mother's death. She would introduce it into her life and into the lives of others. Sofia and Angela were talking about something. The two different universes suddenly didn't seem so foreign. They weren't two million light years away galaxies, but planets in the same solar system, orbiting an unknown sun. Kirsten slowly chewed on her sandwich and watched them. It looked like a normal conversation between classmates. Suddenly, Sofia took out a small object from her bag. She placed it on the table in front of Angela and stopped for a moment from biting into her lunch, stared at the object in front of her. She put her sandwich down and picked up the unknown object, examined it as if she were seeing it for the first time in her life. Sofia smiled, packed up her lunch, said goodbye, and walked towards

Kirsten. Angela looked at her for a moment before turning her attention back to the unknown object.

„Hello, I want to give you something. Something that should belong to someone else, someone more deserving than me. Think about it before you say anything. This gift carries beautiful thoughts that I already know. But for someone else, this gift could be an experience that gives them more than it gave me,“ Kirsten concluded and pulled out a worn-out dictionary from her bag.

„I would like the two of us to finally sit at the same table. I hope the moment comes soon when you can give it to the right recipient,“ Angela added, looking at Kirsten.

„I carry this dictionary with me all the time anyway. Even when it‘s sitting at home in a drawer, on my nightstand. It can be safely kept by someone else other than me,“ she said, taking a bite of the second half of her sandwich. Sofia got up and walked back to the classroom. Kirsten felt like she had a similar conversation with Angela. She looked at the dictionary. It was her body and soul. Whoever she gifted it to would recognize the real Kirsten. All those letters arranged in order would help them understand the unknown author to the core. The sentences would reveal what they think and who they are. Angela ran her hand over her gift too. It could also be read. By touch. Under her fingertips, sentences and even entire paragraphs appeared directly in her mind.

Both of them studied themselves in that courtyard. Subconsciously, they knew who the right recipient was. They knew the address. However, they didn‘t know the path to get there yet.

Chapter 46

- TRANSFORMATION -

Angela walked into the classroom at the end of the hallway. She was upright, with her blonde braid twisted, wearing a maroon knee-length skirt and ankle-length leather boots that echoed softly in this forgotten part of the school. She imagined herself playing the keys with her fingers, not giving Kirsten a chance to shine. She couldn't stop thinking about yesterday and about Adam. Did he tell her about his latest plans? There weren't many people left in the school in the afternoon. The hallways were quiet, with only the murmurs of the last students leaving school. The music room was on the other side of the building, so the musicians had some privacy in the piano classroom. It had its charm. Angela walked down the hallway, looking at the floor and rehearsing her piece. The linoleum shone from the neon lights, and the hallway looked like a runway ending in the classroom. The rehearsal was supposed to start in half an hour. Even though they had recently finished their last one, all three of them wanted to meet again and play just for themselves. Angela passed by the second-to-last classroom. The doors of the bathrooms opened. They creaked horribly, as if they were trying to warn her. They laughed with an elderly cackle. She slowed down a bit and got scared. There were still people in the school, so she wasn't that afraid, but she still stopped. There was someone she could hear. She looked around curiously. She looked like a side character from a horror movie. It was quiet everywhere, and she could only hear the faint buzzing of the neon lights overhead. It sent shivers down her spine. If she ran down the hallway now, it would seem ridiculous, but at the same time, she couldn't just ignore it. She walked past the slightly open doors, quickened her pace, and kept looking at the ground. She didn‘t hear any sounds. Suddenly, a figure jumped out of the door and grabbed her shoulders tightly. Angela‘s throat tightened, and she couldn‘t utter a word. In shock, she realized that it was Hans. It calmed her down a bit.

„Let me go! What do you want? Leave me alone!“ she tried to break free from him, but Hans was a strong lad for his age. What used to be a source of mockery for him was now his advantage. She had no chance against his dominance. He dragged her towards the toilets until her notebook fell from her hands.

„Are you drunk? Let me go!“ Angela tried to wrestle herself from his grip. Hans was sweaty and excited that he could touch his idol, the one who showed no interest in him before and with whom he could now spend some time alone. Angela stood there in front of him, belonging only to him. He had no intention of letting her go just like that. He had caught her.

„You‘re disgusting, repulsive, and fat!“ Angela screamed at him, but no one heard her. The sound of a slap echoed through the hallway. Angela grabbed her cheek and froze. She realized what was happening. She was frightened that Hans had a knife on him. She understood that he had planned it. And she realized that he was serious.

„If you scream, I‘ll finish you off,“ Hans threatened.

„Hel...“ she tried to scream, but before she could utter a word, Hans‘ rough hand covered her mouth. She struggled to break free from his grip. Her slender figure had no chance against his large body, which held her like a twig in a pair of pliers. Hans grabbed her by the throat and dragged her towards the toilet. She grabbed his hand and tried to pull it off her mouth, bite him, scream... but it was futile. She realized that this was a situation she couldn‘t handle alone. Her parents‘ money, her status wouldn‘t help her now. It all came down to one thing. Hans lifted her until she came off the floor and slammed her onto the toilet. Her face smashed into the door, and she tasted blood in her mouth.

She still couldn‘t scream. The blood was pulsing in her, and she felt like her heart might burst out of her chest. He turned her around and pushed her to the ground, still with his hand on her mouth.

„Why are you doing this? You dress so nicely and provocatively. You have a beautiful body. I can't resist!" he spoke, looking directly into her eyes. Angela never thought she would find herself in such close proximity to him. Hans certainly didn't imagine it either. And he intended to take full advantage of this situation. Angela was forced to listen to his monologue. She was thinking about what to do and how much time she had.

Hans didn't give her much chances or hope. His body was too heavy for Angela to be able to do anything. She began to realize that the situation was desperate for her.

„You humiliated me. You never even acknowledged me, except when you wanted to insult or ridicule me. I don't belong in your world, but now I will be for a moment. I'll give you back everything you gave me. Maybe you'll feel exactly how I felt the whole time," and he kissed Angela on the cheek. She felt disgusted and tightly closed her eyes, a tear falling from her eye. It rolled down her cheek and fell to the ground. If he hadn't covered her mouth with his hand, she might have vomited.

He grabbed her thigh. She was wearing only a skirt and stockings. His hand moved up her leg to her calf. He was completely aroused and sweaty. He seemed to be unaware of the situation he was in. His hands were guided by hormones, instincts, and adrenaline. He started to breathe heavily. Angela's mouth hurt from the impact of the door and the pressure of Hans' hand. She looked into his bloodshot eyes and was burdened by his sweaty body. Only now did she have the opportunity to really get to know Hans. What he looked like up close, what kind of person he was. Until now, he seemed to not exist at all. Even though they were in the same class every day, she didn't know him at all. And she didn't recognize him now either. She looked around but couldn't see the door. She lay with her head towards it. She didn't know if it was open or if someone might see or hear them. Hans saw it. He was checking the situation. They were lying by the sink. Hans knelt on her legs and held Angela`s mouth with one hand and started to unbutton his pants with the other. She tried to tear his hands away from her mouth, but she couldn't. Angela didn't know if she should free her legs, body, or mouth. Tears streamed down her face from fear and helplessness. She started to feel weak and exhausted. She was waiting for the worst and was drained. Angela looked into his eyes. They were burning, but soulless. She saw an animal in them. And maybe that‘s the last thing she‘ll see. Either he‘ll kill her, or she‘ll go crazy herself.

At that moment, his eyes lifted for a split second and looked ahead. Something flew over Angela and collided with Hans. It threw him backwards all the way to the window. Suddenly, she was free. She got up, rubbed her eyes, and saw Kirsten. She was getting up from the ground, but Hans was faster. He grabbed her waist and threw her against the bathroom door. Kirsten hit her face against the metal door and fell to the floor. Angela recovered a little and realized that this was her chance. With anger, she got up and ran towards Hans from behind, tears in her eyes, and slammed into him, pushing him against the radiator.

He furrowed his brow and winced. He turned around, blood streaming down his face from his eye. With anger, he lunged at Angela and struck her in the stomach. It knocked the breath out of her, and darkness clouded her vision as she fell to her knees in pain. Hans wiped his eye and prepared for another strike. Angela knelt helplessly in the middle of the restroom. Kirsten jumped up from the ground and kicked Hans in the groin with all her strength. He screamed and collapsed onto the floor, holding onto a radiator, his face twisted in unnatural pain. Angela fell onto her side, clutching her abdomen. Hans leaned against the radiator and lifted himself up. He took a few steps, squealing like a little child in agony. His voice revealed that the pain was stronger than his desire for revenge. He stumbled towards the sink and leaned on it, but his hand slipped, leaving a bloody streak on the surface. He fell hard onto the floor but quickly got up, opened the door, and fled. Kirsten and Angela only heard his staggering footsteps echoing down the hallway. Kirsten lay shaken on the floor, looking at Angela. She was still holding onto her stomach. Their gazes met at one point, as they looked at each other, trying to assess if everything was okay, if there was no longer any danger. They listened carefully in case Hans was coming back, but they only heard deep breathing from the restroom. Kirsten propped herself up with her elbow and used her leg to help Angela up from the floor. Angela placed her hand on Kirsten‘s knee and pushed herself up. They leaned against the restroom door, still breathing rapidly in silence. Kirsten wiped her cheeks. It hurt. She rubbed her hands on her shirt. Angela wiped her mouth and looked at her hand, stained with blood. She started to cry softly, from the depths of her heart, in private, where no one could see. It was the kind of crying that comes from trying to release all the pain. Kirsten turned her head and felt sorry for Angela. No young girl should go through what she just experienced. Kirsten opened the door to the restroom and reached for the toilet paper, unrolled it and handed it to Angela. Without a word, Angela took it and wiped her mouth. She blew her nose and wiped her tears. Kirsten rubbed her eyes. She was sweaty and her body was on fire. Her heart was still racing, and she couldn't fully grasp what had just happened. When she walked down the hallway and heard the commotion behind the restroom door, she didn't know what awaited her behind that door, and she didn't know how this moment would end. There was no time. They stood next to each other. Sweaty, covered in blood, changed.

Angela was in shock and still crying. Kirsten grabbed her hand, wanting Angela to feel someone close to her, to have some sense of security now.

ଓ

Angela calmed down a bit. She sniffed again and wiped away her last tear and wasn't crying anymore.

„This is not the life I imagine," the words cut quietly from Angela's mouth. Kirsten raised her head and furrowed her brow. Angela had never shown that she was struggling. She had always been the perfect girl that everyone liked and every boy wanted. She had everything she desired. Was she such a perfect actress? Or was she terrifying? The deeper she sank, the stronger her act became? Kirsten looked at Angela. She didn't see that confident girl in front of her, and it scared her. Whatever they had been through, and no matter how angry she was at Angela, she didn't deserve this. Did this experience reveal Angela's true face? Kirsten had cried several times in the past year. She had experienced similarly intense moments, and she knew that now Angela would have to be strong. Kirsten didn't know what was going on inside her and was afraid to say anything.

Angela looked directly into Kirsten's eyes through the mirror. She was silent. For a moment, they stood there again like two little girls. They wanted to feel the innocence that had disappeared from their lives just moments ago. Kirsten started to see the real Angela in front of her. The one she had always seen in her, the one that Angela had been desperately trying to keep hidden. There was no longer that fiery spark in her eyes, just a sense of peace. Her face didn‘t have that distinct, slightly stern gaze. Her eyes didn‘t shine, they just looked quietly and guiltily ahead. Her back hunched as if waiting for the next blow from behind. Despite what she had just experienced, she exuded a suspicious calmness and felt resigned. She still pressed her lips together, her hair disheveled, streaks on her face.

Angela leaned against the wall opposite Kirsten and slowly slumped back onto the floor. She looked as though she never wanted to leave this room and face the daylight again.

„It had to come someday. Kirsten, you don‘t know what it‘s like. You haven‘t seen the world beyond that window. You only see it as it wants to show itself to you. Just the surface. Because the world doesn‘t care about you. You‘re not like a stone that they want to uncover to see what kind of bugs live underneath. And you, like a stone, have to be very heavy so they can‘t move you. But gradually you become a heavy and hard rock. Emotions and feelings don‘t penetrate you. You simply become an unfeeling stone."

„You didn‘t miss out on childhood, puberty. On all the things that make a young person young, or a child a child. I was born as an adult. My life has always been about responsibilities and money. About what the whole world wanted from me, not what I wanted from the world. My parents, teachers, and caretaker were money," Angela said, still with her eyes slightly closed, tucking a strand of hair behind her ear. She uttered the word „money" with absolute hostility and selfishness, as if she wanted to rule over it. The truth was that they ruled over her. She no longer spoke about them with that light dose of romance and love.

„I wish you never feel the power of money. The power it gives you and the freedom it takes away from you. It gives you power over others and at the same time usurps power over yourself," Angela concluded, looking into Kirsten‘s eyes. Kirsten didn‘t know how to react. She looked into Angela‘s empty eyes, which were filling with tears again. It was like discovering a forgotten shelf in the library with brand new books. Books that nobody knows about, that nobody has read, and that tell a story that nobody has experienced.

Angela sat leaning against the metal door, speaking calmly. And that‘s what made Kirsten very nervous. Until now, Kirsten would have been perhaps the only person to whom Angela would never have said these things. But suddenly, Kirsten was the only person to whom Angela had said them. Angela wiped her nose.

Kirsten rubbed her eyes. „Angela, you don‘t have to tell me this. Even without that, our relationship has changed. I‘ve always felt that you‘re not the same person I see every day in the school hallway. I believed that one day I would meet the real Angela. That it‘s not the hairstyle you want to wear. That your face is just a mask. I felt it that way. And I hoped that one day I would get to know you, your inner self,“ she confided.

„Kirsten, I want to tell you. I want to share this realization with someone close. With you,“ Angela replied, wiping her tears. Kirsten didn‘t even find it strange that they were having this conversation in this place. That they were having it at all. They were sitting on the bathroom. The late afternoon rays were coming in through the window on the right. Next to them was a dirty sink, with traces of a struggle. In a moment, piano class would start. Who knows if anyone would come looking for them. Angela didn‘t seem to care.

Kirsten looked at her and tried to understand what she was going through. Why hadn‘t she stormed out of the door yet, and why was she revealing her deepest secrets to her? It felt like a war zone around them. They were imprisoned by what had happened just moments ago. This was one of those moments in life that leaves a lasting mark. One where you remember every detail and every second.

ග

„Money has controlled my entire life. I was born tamed into captivity. They ride me here and there just for fun. They plan my whole life, day after day. I do things I don‘t want to do and shouldn‘t have to. My life is worthless. If I were to die right now, who would miss me? Those few people? They would only miss my money. I haven‘t accomplished anything important. I just follow orders and spend money. It‘s really innovative. I‘m a contribution to society. I guess I‘ve had too little imagination until now,“ Kirsten looked into her eyes. „You have beautiful eyes,“ she smiled.

„You know, you‘ve become my role model. You probably don‘t know that,“ she continued to smile. It was a calm, almost humble smile. She ran her hand through her hair. Kirsten didn‘t know what to say. She didn‘t expect these words. Angela was emotional and Kirsten didn‘t know how much she was speaking out of shock. Her emotion was a just-born baby, brought in by a burly bear wrapped in a swaddling blanket.

„Angela... Despite what you just said, you have been a role model to me. Persistent, strong, successful. I never felt the power of money in you. I ignored the pretense. Maybe it was those money that drove you towards your achievements. Or maybe it was you who achieved what I admire you for. I've never seen anyone play the piano like you do in person. Your school results speak for themselves, you're really talented. I don't think you had to buy all those A's," Kirsten countered.

„Money has stolen my life. I have no experiences. I'd rather not remember anything. I actually don't remember anything. Whenever I do, I see the truth. That I see nothing. No childhood, no fun. I can't run away from myself. Where to? I would trade my whole life for yours. I've treated you horribly many times. And you know why? Because I envied you!" Angela said somewhat bitterly.

She looked Kirsten in the eyes. „Yes, I envy you. I envy your friendship with Sofia. All those genuine emotions and words that your loved ones shower you with every day."

I envy you for all the things that I couldn't buy with money. You see how money has ruined me. I am an encyclopedia of the world's sins. Be glad that you were spared from the power of money and wealth. Because you don't own it, it owns you. The feeling of having so much money that you won't be able to spend it all in this lifetime is not a liberating feeling, but a feeling of emptiness. It's as if destiny has been fulfilled and all dreams have come true. What will be left for you? When looking at that number in your account gives you a false sense of godliness. That everyone around you gives you that false sense. Willingly, you tear off your own face and in the mirror, you stop recognizing yourself. People stop recognizing you. Until you become a different person. And I started to hate that new person. I look into the mirror and I don't know who that person in it is and what they really want," Angela finished and looked up at the mirror above the sink. Kirsten stared at the ground as if she knew what Angela was talking about.

„Do you think I can look at myself in the mirror for more than a few seconds? I feel sick from what I see there. What my eyes are screaming at me in the reflection. What that person behind my eyes is screaming, the one that is still inside me, only imprisoned there by that other bitch. My eyes tell me the truth, and I don‘t want to hear it. What‘s worse is that I would hear it even if I pierced my eardrums. I would hear it even more distinctly,“ she said, still looking up at the mirror. The hallway was quiet.

Sitting on the floor, she reached for the shoes that were lying dusty beside her. Angela carefully lined them up next to herself, like slippers by the bed before sleep. She pulled her knees up to her chin and rested her head on Kirsten‘s shoulder. „I feel good with you,“ Angela whispered, as if speaking from a dream. For her, it was the most beautiful feeling. The kind that she never wanted to wake up from.

Kirsten felt that Angela had calmed down, but it also unsettled her. She was too calm for what had just happened a few minutes ago. She felt that it was not so much calmness as resignation and felt sorry for Angela. She was disturbed by the truth that she had just revealed. Her confession was terrifying. Kirsten felt that she was sitting next to a person who was dying. She didn‘t even want to imagine what would happen to her in a similar situation. The idea of life with the power of money scared her. Kirsten was grateful for everything she had and achieved. Everyone liked her the way she was. What would happen if the situation changed overnight? Would she turn into Angela? Would her life and destiny be the same? Would she still have control over them?

Angela suddenly stood up from the ground and walked towards the window. „I have often watched birds. At first, I thought I had unlimited freedom. That I was one of them. As if I had no problems, no cage. Like them. But I was just learning to fly. And when I learned and spread my wings wide, I hit the cage with them, and only then did I notice it. It‘s ironic, but money gives you freedom, and then takes it back with interest. And you start living in that golden cage. You adapt. I want to feel true freedom. To be able to do what I want. That my decisions will be mine and no one else‘s. That they will belong only to me,“ she finished and opened the window. Her hair, which had been lying on her shoulders, blew in the wind. Kirsten was still sitting on the ground, looking at Angela. She stood by the window, holding one wing and watching the birds flying around the school. She had never seen her so peaceful, so reconciled.

Angela turned to Kirsten. „You know, everyone thinks that in the position I‘m in, you get wings. That you‘re a free person. The truth is, someone has cut off those wings for you. And I bleed from those wounds every day. I don‘t know where I went wrong,“ she replied and stepped closer to the window.

Angela looked like a fallen angel. Without wings. The one who doesn‘t know how to soar back to the sky and is condemned to live the fate of ordinary people down here. And can‘t adapt to such a life. She suffers. Angela lifted her right leg onto the window.

At that moment, Kirsten jumped up from the ground. „Angela?“ she asked in surprise.

Angela looked at Kirsten and honestly replied, „I want to feel free again, Kirsten. To experience that feeling of making my own decisions at least once more. Not listening to parents, money, directors. I want to step off my path. And for that feeling, I am willing to die. Just to be able to feel it again,“ Angela wiped away a tear and tucked her hair behind her ear.

„I‘ve experienced so many emotions that I‘m lost in them. I don‘t even know how I feel anymore. As you can see, I‘m not as strong as you,“ Angela smiled through her tears.

„Instead of working on myself, creating a hierarchy of values or relationships, I bought everything. I always took shortcuts - money. I felt like I was achieving so many goals and that I could buy even what can‘t be bought. That‘s the illusion of money. At first, it was pleasant and uplifting. Over time, I began to realize that I was buying a facade, and people were only giving me what I wanted.“

Never getting what they wanted. And I will never find out what it could have been. Maybe I missed out on wonderful gifts, friendships, relationships,“ Angela‘s throat tightened and the word that was supposed to come out remained unspoken halfway.

Angela gathered all her strength and continued, „And love,“ she wiped her nose with her finger and brushed tears from her cheeks with her palm.

„And as if that wasn‘t enough, I wanted to take it away from you too! That‘s how I became... a monster. What I couldn‘t have, no one else could. And over time, I realized that there are things that money can‘t buy. And that angered me the most. I couldn‘t get off this path and still keep my face. I realized that I had bought my own world, where it was just me, ghosts, illusions, self-deception. As if I had cut out stars in the sky myself and never seen the real and natural beauty of the night sky.

Those stars of mine shine dimly and I don't like them. I want to tear down this world and build a new one on its foundations. But I can't do it. And the more I listen to myself, the more I hate myself. And the more I love you. Our Kirsten. Oh God!" she raised her voice and sniffed.

A cold feeling ran through Kirsten's body. Angela's words meant only one thing...

„Let's go to the hall. We can talk further there. We can play the piano together," Kirsten tried to divert Angela's attention. She wasn't sure if she could reach Angela in time. Kirsten was afraid that she would startle her and something would happen that she tried not to think about. She wanted to keep a cool head.

„If something bad happens to you, look for something good behind it. That's why bad things happen. I know it's hard in this moment, but try to look beyond and think about why it happened. When you're doing well, you don't notice what's happening around you. You don't have a reason to. But it's these bad moments and experiences that open your eyes. When you walked in here, you were Angela. But now I see a different Angela. You should look in the mirror too. You'll see her too. The other one will come out through those doors. And the one who walked in here will stay here. She'll never leave. She'll stay locked in here forever. I think right now you're putting a period at the end of your previous life. I understand that you're pressing the pen hard to make the end of the last sentence visible. And it hurts. But that period doesn't have to mean pain right away. It can mean rebirth. Believe me. The worst thing is that every story ends with a period. Periods are bad. That's why you have to keep writing constantly. And if not you, then someone else."

Can you write a nice word after that dot? Or even two. Then three, and suddenly you find yourself on the other side of the book, barely able to find that dot anymore. And you won't be looking for it anymore. There will be another story behind it. And another one after that. Let your life be not just a few pages of a superficial magazine, but a novel. And Angela... Trust me, you're not that magazine. I've been reading you for a long time. I haven't finished reading you yet. Every day I open a new page and in the evening, I reflect on those few pages that I've read.

Angela looked at Kirsten with tears in her eyes, „You're kind," she smiled. She didn't know what to do and hesitated. She lowered her look to the ground and bit her lip. One or two tears fell on the dirty pavement. Angela shifted her foot on the ground as if preparing her stance.

„I lived in my own world and thought it was perfect. Don‘t get me wrong, I really liked that world. Everything in it fit together. But when I met you, I realized that I can achieve the same without money. And suddenly I was poor. All those feelings that won‘t warm you up unless you have a banknote in your hand. But anytime. In good times and bad. And that annoyed me. The only drawback of the world of money is that it exists only as long as there are money. I didn‘t see it that way at first, and later I didn‘t want to admit it. If they run out, this world disappears. But your world will never disappear. Friendships don‘t vanish overnight. The changed fates of so many people you‘ve touched. What you‘ve learned over time, all those experiences and emotions are real. They‘re not just a haze through which you can‘t see beyond the tip of your own nose. Suddenly my life seems pointless to me. I paid not for the goods, but for their reflection, the illusion. And when I started realizing that, I began to envy you. To hate you. A dark passenger sneaked into me. I fought with him, but he always won. He pushed me into a corner, I couldn‘t breathe. And what just happened now, it uncorked me and all the emotions flooded out. I couldn‘t keep them inside me any longer. In the end, I would have been like a bottle of milk left in the sun. The pressure would have shot the cork off and the curdled, stinking mess would have spilled all around. I feel sick about it. I feel sick about myself," she finished and leaned over the window. She closed her eyes and took a deep breath. She smiled like a child who just got an ice cream.

„Angela! When you do it, you‘ll change my life too. And when you don‘t, you‘ll still change my life. Trust me, you‘ll make a very deep dot that will be imprinted on all the previous pages of your unfinished book."

„And I want to keep reading... This moment will leave its mark on me and I don‘t know how I will cope with it. I see hope in you now, that anyone can change. Anytime. And that they can change themselves and everything around them for the better. You are my role model, one of my best friends, even though you don‘t know it. If you walk through that window, a piece of my soul will go with you. And that place will never be filled," Kirsten continued to watch Angela intently, trying to read her body language. She wiped her eyes and sniffed.

„Just like you're changing your life now, you're changing mine too. It's your life. You've been given it and it's exclusively your right what you do with it. I have no right to tell you how to handle it. We can remember this moment together in a few years, or I will remember it on my own. We can say that your decision was the best first step in both your life and mine. Or I will be left wondering what that decision could have been. You're like a sister to me now and I don't want to lose someone close," Kirsten finished, tears streaming down her face. She felt like these were the most sincere words she had ever spoken in her life.

„Angela! You're stronger now than ever before!" Kirsten said emphatically, trying to drown out her own tears. Angela looked at her in surprise. She didn't expect these words. Did they catch her at this moment? When she doesn't know if she wants to live or die?

„You're at a crossroads now. You can choose your path. This is not the end, but a beginning!" Kirsten continued, and Angela felt like Kirsten was reading her mind. Her words compelled her to resist her original plan.

„I know that your past life was different. And you thought that it could never be different. That this is how it would end. You were afraid to change it, to try something new. You were afraid of the unknown. Until now, your life has been about what you can't do and what you must do. From now on, it will be: You can do anything and you don't have to do anything! You're stubborn enough to break through that impenetrable wall with your head and make your way through all the problems. Now you'll be able to say ‚I love' without looking weak. You can lend a helping hand, do things that you couldn't do before or were afraid to do. But trust me, I know you, and you have all the weapons you need. You won't lose. Your lips will finally smile and not twist into a fake smile. They won't be bent by pretense or the judgment of others. It will be your private smile. You will utter kilometers of pleasant words."

Your eyes are healthy now. You will be able to see things that you couldn't see before. Your ears will hear words that you have not heard for so long or never heard at all. The tips of your fingers will feel touches and sensations that you may not have felt before. You don't have to be afraid of it. You can start looking forward to it! You will live life to the fullest. You won't just dream about how you could live, but you will have the power to wake up in the morning and turn your deepest dreams into reality. All the pleasant experiences, words, moments, and memories will find you naturally, because you will be open to them. You will let everything flow. You will receive various treats on your table, and it will be up to you what you taste. Every day you will take deep breaths, because you are no longer bound by your own prejudices, the prejudices of others, or fear.

This will sounds strange for you, but sometimes the best thing that can happen to us, is when the world loses interest in us. When you are not swarmed by the crowd, their opinions, actions, or feelings. Suddenly, you step out of the overcrowded waiting room into the fresh air and finally take a deep breath. You don‘t smell anyone, no waft of binding opinions and perspectives. That‘s why you don‘t go to relax in a crowded square, but on a green meadow. And now you need to stand on this meadow alone and start building your own world. Not living in the one that others have built around you. You allowed them to build this world around you. But instead of a cozy little house with a garden, you ended up behind high walls, guarded by armed guards who wouldn‘t let you leave. You heard laughter beyond the walls, and you always knew that there was something out there that you needed to see and know. Until one day, they forced upon you the opinion that leaving these walls is unacceptable. The walls moved every day, and streets were created around you, where you got lost because no one gave you a map. And when you finally walked to the edge of the city, you saw more walls forming in the distance, and another and another tangle of winding streets in front of you. So many times you wanted to take flight and look at the city from above, to give it meaning. To see where the east is or a place where you can hide. But no one taught you to fly, to be free. What if the way out of this maze leads through an underground tunnel? You will have to descend into dark corners, shine your flashlight and look around to see where the path leads. You will have to find it on your own. You will wander in the darkness and maybe feel afraid for a while. But eventually, you will see a light at the end of the tunnel. You will reach it, push aside the bushes with your palm, and your face will be bathed in light and warmth. And when you take a step forward and turn around, you will see that the tunnel has magically disappeared, and you will never find the way back. That city will become a legend and remain in you forever...

Angela looked up as if she wanted to say something and burst into tears. She looked at Kirsten, who wiped her eyes and became attentive.

Angela‘s look exuded determination, a stance. She was completely still, so desperately wanted to hear how Kirsten felt, and yet she was so afraid of what she would hear.

ℭ

Angela wiped her eyes and sniffed, „Kirsten, you just described yourself. I saw you in those words. Your life. Just the way I see it. And others too. The life I‘ve always envied you for. I envied who you are, what you‘ve been through, what you‘ve achieved and how you‘ve achieved it. You‘re a strong personality, one that even I couldn‘t break. You have incredible opportunities and goals within reach, all because of who you are. I don‘t know if you see it the same way, but trust me, you probably haven‘t really looked in the mirror. You have no reason to be scared or desperate. You know...we were like two unsolved equations, each with an unknown variable. We couldn‘t arrive at any result. I immediately plugged you into mine, and everything started making sense to me. And maybe the same thing happened with your equation. You plugged me into yours. And when we write them both together, we‘ll get an equation that explains everything that‘s happening around us,“ Angela wiped her tears and nose. She looked broken, as if she had accepted humility.

ℭ

Angela put her foot down from the window and sat on the windowsill. She looked down at the floor, and it seemed like she didn‘t know what to do with these new feelings and the life she had just stepped into. She seemed torn between two personalities. The original Angela and the new one that had just been born.

Kirsten was confused. She didn‘t expect Angela to return the ball with such a powerful hit. Did she really describe her life that accurately? She had never perceived it that way herself. She always did what she thought was right. No one interfered with her decisions. Was this her true face? Could she describe it so precisely because she was subconsciously describing herself? Did she want to give hope, energy, and motivation to Angela or to herself? She had never stood in front of such a mirror. It was a very emotional moment. Both stood by the window in the restroom as if they had just learned something new. And yet, it had probably been there in them all along, deeply hidden all this time. They didn‘t say anything to each other that they didn‘t already know.

They finally activated it within themselves and realized it. Each of them seemed to be contemplating their own thoughts. Kirsten's thoughts turned outward. She closed the door in her mind and reflected on how she had described her life. Angela's reaction completely caught her off guard. She had been struggling with her inner self the whole time, searching for a way to live her new life. Was she ready to accept her new fate that was impatiently waiting for her? She was afraid to take it into her hands, for fear of breaking it. She had waited for the moment when she would understand that she was ready. There had been many such moments, and in the end, it had always been just a fleeting illusion. But after this conversation, Kirsten experienced a feeling she thought no longer existed and that she would never experience again. And it happened when she least expected it. Only now did she realize how unprepared she had been until this moment. This was the last room she had managed to open with the smallest and rustiest key in the big bunch she always carried with her. She had opened so many doors that she thought she had tried all the keys. And suddenly, the last one was the most important. She found it in the bunch only when she wanted to use it to open the door not for herself, but for someone else. That was the unknown ingredient that acted like a magic powder, and the key turned in the lock.

Angelina's footsteps crunching on a pebble brought her back from her thoughts. She was standing right in front of her now. She was no longer crying. Kirsten grabbed Angela by the shoulders. „Do you know what's best about the fact that you decided to step to this side of the window? It's proof that you're not just thinking about yourself, but about the people close to you. You've shown that you care about someone else more than just yourself. That's the best evidence for you that something has changed today. And that you'll never be ‚that' Angela again. You don't have to be afraid. Now a new life begins for you. Everything will be fine," Kirsten finished.

„Tomorrow is the competition. Can you handle it? We don't have to do it," Kirsten asked.

„We don't have to, but we can. And we want to," Angela smiled and wiped away a tear.

„Of course, we'll go to the competition. For Sofia. And for you. Until now, I thought I was ready. But now I really am. More than ever. And maybe more than ever before!" she added with a trembling voice.

„I currently have mixed feelings. I should feel down, but I actually feel really good with you in this moment. I don‘t understand it. How is that possible?“ Angela said, running her hand across her face.

„Maybe it‘s because you‘ve never really lost before? Not here and now? Even defeat can mean victory,“ Kirsten replied, but Angela interrupted her.

„Kirsten, how can you hug me after everything? Doesn‘t that seem strange to you?“ Angela looked into Kirsten‘s eyes.

„Yeah, I guess I‘m behaving like a love-struck teenager,“ Kirsten pondered aloud.

„I don‘t think so,“ Angela lowered her head and rested her forehead against Kirsten‘s chest. They embraced each other. Kirsten felt as though she was embracing a newborn. As if she had just given birth herself. She didn‘t know if she had experienced an even more intense rebirth than Angela.

They stood in the middle of the mud and darkness like two doves in a war zone who had survived the battle for a key territory. This moment would help them win the entire battle.

Kirsten had tears in her eyes, but she didn‘t want to cry. She wanted this to be Angela‘s moment fully, to let her release all her emotions. She didn‘t want to mix her own feelings into it for now. Kirsten looked at herself in the mirror. Her quivering lips hinted at relief. She held Angela tightly.

„Tomorrow is the competition. We should go home and get some sleep,“ Kirsten said, looking ahead.

„Yes, we should, but I want to stay here with you for a little while longer,“ Angela replied, clinging to Kirsten like a newborn. Kirsten knew that many things would change now. Just as Angela‘s life had changed, hers would too. Something had fallen out of the window today. Two big boulders.

Chapter 47

- WINNERS -

Angela was already waiting behind the curtain, listening to the murmurs of people who gradually filled the hall. Mrs. Miller observed Angela, and it certainly wasn‘t the same Angela who was at the last rehearsal. She didn‘t know what had happened in the bathrooms. No one knew. Hanz never returned to school. No one knew where he was. Rumor had it that the whole family had moved out of town, probably out of fear of humiliation and Angela‘s lawyers. Angela stood by the curtain, impatiently waiting for Kirsten. The only nervous person behind the curtain was Mrs. Miller, who sensed that something had changed. Kirsten opened the door and saw Angela. She smiled. She closed the door quietly behind her and walked towards her. Along the way, she surveyed the organized chaos that was hidden from the stage.

„Hello," Kirsten smiled at Angela and hugged her so warmly that it made Mrs. Miller‘s mouth water.

„Hello, I‘m so excited! Really, very much. We‘ll enjoy it!" Angela grabbed Kirsten by the shoulders.

„I won‘t pretend that I‘m not confused, and I won‘t ask you anything now. Just tell me one thing - are you ready? Do you know what awaits you when you go on stage?" Mrs. Miller wanted to make sure that all three of them would meet the audience‘s expectations.

„Yes, we are. Like never before," Kirsten said calmly. Their names and the title of the piece, „For Sofia," echoed in the hall as the audience applauded enthusiastically.

Angela grabbed Kirsten‘s hand. „Come on, it‘s going to be an experience!"

Kirsten just managed to wave to Mrs. Miller as they found themselves in the hall next to two grand pianos. Kirsten couldn‘t imagine herself standing here one day. She was afraid of what emotions she would experience. Whether she would be able to play against Angela. Now she knew that they wouldn't be playing against each other, but for their recently revealed friendship. She walked towards her instrument and glanced briefly at the stage.

She glanced at Sofia and Emie and could hardly believe under what circumstances she was walking across the stage. Just a few months ago, she was ready to fight. Today, she was here to celebrate. Sofia looked pale. The illness was slowly, but surely, taking its toll on her. Kirsten hoped that the rescue was near. She sat somewhat nervously at the piano, her fingers resting on the keys, and turned her head to the audience. Everyone gradually fell silent. Over 200 pairs of ears hungry for music. She scanned the unfamiliar faces, and then she spotted him standing on the stairs...

„Adam?" she hinted with her lips, as if asking him if it was really him. She noticed that he smiled and winked. Kirsten looked at Angela, who laughed. What Kirsten didn't know was that the night before, Angela had called Adam. The conversation was short, and Adam swore that Angela had set another trap for him. The words she had spoken had never before come out of her mouth. That was also the reason why Kirsten came to the competition, to see if Angela meant what she had said on the phone. Both of them knew that this evening was now complete. Only the most important part was missing. Playing the piece. For Sofia. Kirsten felt like a vessel filled to the brim with emotions. She needed to pour them out to someone. She wanted to be half-empty again so she could be filled with more. She ran her fingers over the keys. White, black, white, black. Like the days of the past weeks in Edwood. She felt like fate was playing a similar symphony with her, and it didn't spare even the black keys. Every time she struck them, they produced an extraordinary tone that, despite being different from the rest of the composition, was not false. It was an integral part of it. Kirsten gradually stopped seeing the connection between these tones and their color. If she removed them from her life, it would be the same as if someone removed the black keys from the piano. They simply belonged to it, and she needed to learn how to play them too. A few months ago, she couldn't incorporate them into her composition. But in the past few weeks, she felt like she was on a crash course. Mainly because she started paying attention and stopped getting bored during practice. Fate had gratefully taught her to play these keys. She no longer skipped pages in the book and didn't just read what she liked. She realized that she would miss many beautiful bright ideas if she only put them against a light background. The hall fell silent. Kirsten looked at Angela, who had her hands on the piano and was waiting with a mischievous smirk on her lips for Kirsten to start playing.

Kirsten pressed the first key. It felt as if someone had lit up inside her. The light spread through her like rays of the rising sun across a dark canyon. She felt warmth, certainty, and comfort. At the same time, she remembered Sofia.

It was like a blender on full throttle, mixing all these ingredients into one refreshing drink that Kirsten was so eagerly anticipating. Her fingers danced effortlessly across the keys, and the first notes filled the hall. Angela listened as Kirsten‘s solo slowly gained momentum. Kirsten glanced briefly at Angela and knew her part was approaching. Angela struck the keys and underlined Kirsten‘s notes. She smiled, as it reminded her of the beginning of their relationship. Two different compositions, each beautiful and unique in its own way, coming together to create perfect harmony. Only now did Angela truly appreciate the beauty of this piece. When they didn‘t clash against each other, but instead held hands and moved forward together. Suddenly, Kirsten struck the piano keys with greater emphasis, and the chorus filled the hall. Majestic and serene, like a bird soaring above the highest peaks on the horizon. She played the first part of the chorus, and then the compositions swapped. Mrs. Miller waited to see if they could synchronize. It was a crucial moment, when the piece would become truly unique or fall apart in a second. No one before them had attempted it, as it was risky and required a great deal of talent and experience. All the previous contestants had played classical compositions, with both pianists playing their own parts from beginning to end. But Kirsten and Angela had to learn two separate pieces and merge them into a third one. To the audience, it sounded like a single piece, but everyone could see when they swapped notes with each other. It was a unique performance. Kirsten played the second part of the chorus, and then they switched the compositions back. Mrs. Miller stood motionless behind the curtain, barely breathing. She hadn‘t noticed a single mistake so far. Both Kirsten and Angela sat at the pianos, completely unaware of what was happening around them. Mrs. Miller, as their piano teacher, was experiencing the most beautiful moment of her life.

She had never had the opportunity to lead two such talented students. She stood there like a little girl, afraid of punishment and at the same time knowing that a great reward might await her. After the chorus, Kirsten began to play a slow melody, and Angela multiplied it with a gentle accompaniment. Every note could be clearly heard. If there was a place in the entire composition where the exchange of notes would be audible, it would be here. Both of them switched hands on the pianos, causing some of the audience to scrutinize closely to see if they had indeed exchanged compositions. If the audience didn‘t notice all the exchanges, the jury did. It consisted of many experts who had been looking forward to this competition all year long. And many others were sitting in the audience. Angela and Kirsten were in their own world. In their castles, where in the courtyard surrounded by high walls, they played their compositions and looked like fairies at the bottom of a well. The hall didn‘t even breathe, wanting to hear every single note.

The final chord. And silence fell. They looked at each other. Time stood still in their eyes, and that second felt like an eternity. They saw each other within themselves. They felt that they had merged into one soul, just like their composition a moment ago. The hall came alive with applause and wild cheers. Kirsten laughed and thought of Sofia at the same time. She stood up and stepped forward from the piano. Angela rushed to her and embraced her. Kirsten hugged her like a plush teddy bear. They looked at each other and turned to the audience. Holding hands, Kirsten and Angela bowed and the audience couldn‘t possibly get any louder. Mrs. Miller hugged them both around the shoulders, and it was clear she was truly proud of them. But only she knew that she was proud of them not just for mastering the composition, but for their friendship. She couldn‘t have asked for a better ending to her time in Edwood.

There was no doubt about the victory. However, Kirsten had already won before the competition. She had won Angela and her friendship. Thanks to her and Sofia herself, she had no more doubts about the days to come. She no longer felt fear, but certainty. Her steps were suddenly clear and firm. Kirsten turned around and walked into the once mysterious forest, which was now magical. In it, the wildest miracles would soon happen and the deepest dreams would come true. Hers and everyone else‘s dreams. She wouldn‘t hide in it, but it would be her home, her sanctuary. And there would be no monsters in it, only stories. She couldn't have done it alone, and the forest would have likely engulfed her eventually. Now she knew she had true friends who would guide her through the forest. And she would show them all the beautiful corners in return. Kirsten was no longer afraid of losing her freedom, herself, or those around her. On the contrary, she was looking forward to discovering a new world that her mom had feared after death.

Chapter 48

- RULES -

Kirsten descended from the stage as if walking on soft moss. Her steps no longer hurt. She was not afraid to move forward and remembered the days when she took steps back to increase the distance between herself and the jumping board. Finally, she felt what it was like to run and jump into the distance. Kirsten had a paved path ahead of her. And she knew exactly where it was leading and what her goal was. She pulled back the curtain. Sofia and Emie smiled and looked at Adam. He grinned at them. They slowly left the auditorium, and Emie pointed east with her finger. Kirsten read from her lips that they would wait for her outside the school. Adam stood in the same spot on the stairs near the exit. Kirsten hesitated for a moment, wondering if she would turn around and leave through the door. He smiled. He descended a few steps and met her and Angela next to the stage.

„I would..." Angela began to speak, but Adam interrupted her: „I think we all have telepathy now, and we all know what the other wants to say. It's not necessary anymore. Really. It will be enough if we all project in our heads the conversation that should happen now and here. We don't need to hear it. We all already feel as if we had and wanted to feel after it. Sometimes words are not necessary. Especially when we are one mind," Adam finished.

„Alright, I'll leave you," Angela said, blinked her eyes, and hugged Kirsten. Adam raised his eyebrows in confusion.

„Hey, a lot of things have changed. And it will change even more," Kirsten said, taking Adam's hand.

„Angelina's family probably won't buy the factory. I understand that they can appoint their own management, but they can't imagine how Angela and I would work together. They say it wouldn't be good for business. My mom doesn't want to sell the factory without me in charge. She has seen the finalized contracts and knows that it would be the end for many employees and their families. There aren't many buyers. Angelina's family is offering the most. They have more companies in this region, and apparently it fits well in their portfolio. And if Angelina's family doesn't buy it, we'll have to sell it to someone else, but at a lower price. And with the same result for the employees," Adam poured out the latest news.

„Don't worry about the factory. I'm glad you're back!" Kirsten smiled.

„Mrs. Miller, can we take a quick detour to the gym? I want to show Adam something," Kirsten called out to Miller, who was walking a few steps ahead of them.

„But no shenanigans!" Mrs. Miller said with a serious yet mischievous expression on her face. Kirsten mimicked her, as if trying to tune into the same wavelength. They both smiled. Finally, Kirsten saw a complete smile on Mrs. Miller's face. One hundred percent smile. All the facial muscles relaxed. Not just the ones that had resigned to fate.

„I'll be in the staff room for half an hour. Come find me there afterwards. We need to lock up the school," Mrs. Miller smiled and turned sharply towards the staff room. Her hair swirled and landed on her left cheek. They both just watched as she disappeared down the corridor past the notice boards.

„Come on!" Kirsten grabbed Adam's hand and ran. He widened his eyes and tried not to step on her heels. She had never held his hand like this before. He couldn't figure out what was happening right now. Kirsten pushed open the doors to the gym of Edwood's school. It was dark, with only a faint light from the corridor illuminating a small part of it. They stood at the doorway like characters from a black-and-white cartoon. Adam still didn't know what would happen next. Kirsten felt for the switches on the wall and turned on one spotlight right in the middle of the gym. The lamp created a private cone of dim light. It was still not enough to fully light up their faces and dark enough to conceal Adam's embarrassment and Kirsten's flushed cheeks. There was a stereo system next to the switches. It still played music from the last dance or the end-of-year school disco. Kirsten approached it and played her favorite song."

Adam was expecting a slow song, but to his surprise, the gym was filled with lively tones. It wasn't a modern composition, but rather a very melodic one from the 90s.

„Can we do this now?“ Adam smiled and looked at Kirsten‘s hand, which held his like a mother leading her child across the main road to school.

„Are we breaking any rules? Not that I don‘t like it. I really do. But I don‘t want to pay too high a price for this moment. Like losing you. Or someone around me losing something,“ Adam aimed at the thoughts that were racing through Kirsten‘s mind.

„We can break all the rules that have applied to us so far and held us back. We‘ve already paid our price,“ Kirsten said softly.

„We can break them now? How?“ Adam wanted to know Kirsten‘s backup plan.

„Because now we‘ll create our own,“ she grabbed Adam‘s other hand and came close to him, so close he could feel her breath on his chin. She looked up at him from under her lashes, smiled, and started dancing. Adam laughed and danced to the rhythm with her. Kirsten moved around him with a mysterious expression, her hand brushing his shoulder. He grabbed her around the waist, dipped her until she laughed. He pulled her back up to him. He saw those beautiful eyes again, the ones he fell in love with on the first day. They were the same, yet different. Still dark and enigmatic, but no longer showing an empty universe and darkness where every gaze disappears. Now he saw a supernova exploding in them. Incredible energy radiated from Kirsten‘s eyes. He couldn‘t help but laugh. Looking into those eyes was contagious. He felt immense strength in them. He always knew it was there, but those eyes were looking in the wrong direction. Now they were the center of a new galaxy being born. And it would expand infinitely.

Her thoughts were interrupted by a hand that reached out and brushed against her cheek, landing on her shoulder. The music was playing, but they weren‘t dancing. They found each other in their eyes, mutually hypnotized. They had known each other for a few months, but both felt as if they had known each other their entire lives. And after all those days of uncertainty, they had finally invited each other on a date. Adam placed his hand on Kirsten‘s cheek, and a tear rolled down her face as she laughed. Adam wiped it away from her cheek, and looked at her as if she were a fairy creature that had materialized right before his eyes. He had read about her, imagined her, thought of her. And suddenly, she had chosen him as her prince. Kirsten stood on her tiptoes and kissed

Adam. The hallway outside the gym was empty and quiet. She didn‘t want to spoil the moment with the noise of students‘ footsteps behind the doors, and she certainly didn‘t want to end it with the sound of the bell. The neon lights flickered softly and blinked at Adam and Kirsten through a small crack in the door. Behind them, new rules were being born. Rules that wouldn‘t harm anyone and would soon surprise many. In that moment, two lives turned 180 degrees. And it wasn‘t just dance steps, but many life-changing moments. Soon, the lives of many residents of Edwood would also change. A fragrant cake was baking in the oven, which everyone would taste and wonder who had come up with the recipe. Fate was no longer lying by the road Kirsten was walking on. She held it tightly in her hands and blew away all the impurities that had accumulated on it over time. It transformed into a crystal ball from which she could now read her destiny.

Kirsten and Adam walked out of the school. Angela joined them on the way. Emie and Sofia were waiting for them outside the school.

ഗ

„So that‘s a shock. The end of the world is supposed to happen tomorrow, and nobody told me? Or am I just losing it and having hallucinations again?“ Sofia exclaimed, widening her blue eyes.

„You‘re not hallucinating. I see the same thing,“ Emie chimed in, her eyes filled with joy.

„And where did they find you?“ Sofia laughed and looked at Adam.

„I found myself. Sometimes you just have to get lost to find yourself. So be right in front of everyone, yet as if you were never there,“ Adam chuckled and nudged Sofia.

„Watch out, don‘t break her,“ Kirsten teased.

„Don‘t worry. From now on, no one will suffer anymore,“ Adam said firmly, tucking Kirsten‘s hair behind her ear.

„And... Is there going to be a nuclear explosion now? Nothing? No Armageddon?“ Sofia added, looking at Angela in amazement, who stood upright next to the couple who had just displayed their affection publicly.

„No, there won‘t be any more Armageddon. We‘ve survived enough of them. It‘s time to appreciate every new day,“ Angela replied, a little embarrassed, looking down at the ground in front of her.

„Do you want to explain something to us? Because it seems to me that we are in some other dimension with Sofia," Emie looked surprised at Kirsten.

„Alright, let's go. We could go to Belinda's café," Kirsten suggested.

„Agreed, come with me. We'll meet at the café," Emie said to Sofia, and winked at Kirsten.

„Well, I've never ridden in such a fancy car before," Sofia said, looking at Angeline's car.

„It's not a fancy car. It's just a car," Angela replied, tucking her hair behind her ear and gesturing towards the car with her hand.

Kirsten still had the keys, although she didn't spend as much time in the café anymore. They all went inside, with Emie entering last.

She stopped by Kirsten and whispered, „I don't know what you said to them, but they told me not to worry about the farm anymore. They seemed very calm," Emie said, looking into Kirsten's eyes in the dim light.

„Where's the light in here?" came a voice from the café.

„Coming up..." Kirsten shouted and smiled at Emie. She locked the door behind her. The light from the street drew several silhouettes on the floor and walls. They were all the same, none stood out. Kirsten turned on only one small light on the opposite wall. The darkness created an intimate, private atmosphere in the café. Kirsten went behind the counter and started preparing coffee. Sofia picked a few pastries from the refrigerator and divided them onto plates. They took the trays and sat at the table. Kirsten handed Adam a cup of coffee.

„It suits you very well," Angela smiled from behind the table at Kirsten and Adam. Sofia almost choked on her cake.

„Oh come on," Angela said with a half-smile.

„Alright, alright. I just have to get used to it. Sorry about that," Sofia coughed and tried to form a coherent sentence.

„These pastries are excellent. I haven't been here in so long. Things have changed here," Angela added, taking another bite.

„Many things have changed," Sofia chuckled.

„I don't know what you two have been through, but your friendship with Kirsten is enough evidence for me that we can all be friends. You won't tell us, right?" Sofia asked Kirsten and took a sip of her raspberry drink.

„Well, it‘s a long story. I think it will be part of my private collection. Some books are written only for a selected eyes. Those who understand the text. But I can tell you that it ended happily,“ Kirsten looked contentedly at Sofia.

„Well, then let‘s seal the deal at the little red house. You should choose your spot to sit. Everyone has their favorite spot in the house,“ Emie Angele said.

„We can meet there tomorrow. It‘s Friday, we can light lanterns, order pizza. It will be fun,“ Emie continued.

„At the red house? I‘ve never been inside,“ Angela replied, remembering the moments when she and Adam dealt with business matters in front of the little red house with an umbrella in hand. However much she thought about it, she really couldn‘t remember ever stepping inside.

„ I had a sort of respect for the house. I know you guys meet there and it‘s not a place where my foot should step in. Yes, because I‘m a jerk,“ she tilted her head to the side and smiled at Emie.

„You meant to say you were a jerk,“ Sofia retorted, pursing her lips.

„Well, I don‘t even fit in there,“ she replied, comparing her blouse with the t-shirts of the others at the table.

„I always liked your elegant style. There are no rules in the little red house. We can be ourselves there. You don‘t have to change for us. You‘ve changed enough already,“ Kirsten smiled.

„At the concert, I realized that something happened between you two. It must be something very private since you can‘t tell us. And I don‘t want to know. It‘s not necessary. But it‘s nice that your relationship has changed,“ Adam replied and settled in more comfortably.

„You played differently. It was still masterful and all that. But it sounded different from the rehearsals. Even then, on the stairs, after the first few seconds, I felt that something was different. And maybe you would have won the competition even without that change. After all, you always played perfectly. But when I heard your performance before at the rehearsals, it was like a wrapped candy playing with all the colors. But today, I could taste that candy. With your music, you let everyone see inside you, who you are. Until then, it was like, listen, applaud, but stay outside the gates. I can‘t describe it any better. I hope you understand,“ Adam concluded and looked at Kirsten.

„I felt the same way inside,“ she agreed.

„I feel everything somehow different now. I can‘t ask anything from you. I can only receive something. You have the right to think anything about me, and you have the right to say anything to me. I don‘t want us to live in pretense. Besides you, my best friend will also be time, when I can prove that something has changed. And no matter what happens, I already know that I will never feel lonely again. Like I have felt until now,“ Angela replied and looked at everyone at the table.

„And Sofia... Kirsten and I agreed that the gifts we gave you found the right recipient. You!“ Angela smiled.

„I guess you don‘t want them back, do you?“ Sofia asked in surprise.

„We agreed to keep them in the little house. A sanctuary must have some precious items that hold the past, right?“ Kirsten reassured Sofia.

„We will try to give you enough time and space. We won‘t make any promises, won‘t dwell on the past. We all have a new life ahead of us. New challenges and opportunities. We are almost grown-up people, and this won‘t be the first bold line we draw in our lives. Honesty, loyalty, and trust should be at the top of our values. That, and time, are the only things we can offer you now,“ Kirsten replied and looked at the others. She could see the same thoughts reflected in their eyes.

„That‘s fair, alright,“ Angela agreed. Outside, night was slowly descending on the city. The street lamps were shining even brighter through the window, and it seemed like the day was not ending, but beginning. At least for the five friends and acquaintances in Belinda‘s cafe. Only time would ensure that all dreams came true and every destiny was fulfilled. The wind whispered through the streets, and a few green balls fell from the tree in front of the cafe. As they hit the sidewalk, they burst open, revealing shiny brown ripe chestnuts. But that wasn‘t the only thing that ripened by the window of the cafe.

Chapter 49

- ENVELOPE -

Two cars stopped in front of the house. Kirsten picked up Sophie's backpack from the trunk. The slightly faded inscription „Winners" was still visible, so the smudged letter H. The five best friends got out of the cars and headed straight for the little red house. They walked on the grass, excited that they were all walking on it together after so long. Kirsten held Sophie's hand on one side and Adam's on the other. Angela walked on the right side and held Sophie's hand. Emie held Adam's shoulder on the other side.

„Kirsten, shall we change the number at the table to five?" Sofia laughed.

„The number at the table? To five?" Angela asked in surprise, as if sensing that she was the only one who didn't know what was going on.

„As soon as I step into the house," she nodded. Kirsten finally found her diagnosis and found a cure for it. She was finally wealthy and knew that she hadn't consciously and directly caused everything, but her actions had set off a chain of events, and the funnel had dropped everything nice right in front of her. They walked past the trees. Kirsten raised her hand and ran her palm over the flower of the tree whose branch bent directly over her head. They could already see the red walls of the house below the hill. She already knew where they would place her dictionary and Angela's box.

Kirsten opened her palms and took a few steps back. „Go ahead, I'll catch up," she smiled and ran towards the house. Adam shook his head in bewilderment, grabbed Sophie's shoulder, and gestured to the others. Kirsten rushed onto the veranda and opened the door. She paused for a moment and looked towards the red house. Kirsten saw the four people who meant so much to her. She smiled and entered the kitchen. The room was bathed in sharp colors, painted by the setting orange sun. She heard laughter from the red house. Everything seemed to be in harmony with the universe. In her hand, she finally had the answer from George, the trustee of her estate. She also received the long-awaited phone call, so she knew that the contents of the envelope would please her. Kirsten unfolded the letter and read line by line.

According to medical records, there was an experimental treatment for Sofia's disease with a high success rate of cure. Sofia's parents were glad that they agreed to this option. They didn't reveal anything to Sofia to give her false hope. The letter contained all the details - the location, contacts, and the clinic where this treatment had been successfully applied. George also prepared an estimate of the costs. At the end of the letter, the total amount for the treatment and associated hospitalization costs was stated - around eight hundred thousand. Almost the value of three houses. Kirsten packed the letter and placed it on the table.

There was another white envelope lying on the table in front of her. It was clearly visible on the brown wood. It was still unopened, but she knew what was inside. She didn't have to open it. But she wanted to. In its sealed state, it evoked feelings of hope. She wanted to open it and feel the change. So that she would never forget those feelings when she picked up the envelope again and again every month.

ശ

Since the last envelope arrived, a lot had changed, and Kirsten wanted to leave it that way. She paid great attention to it, opened it and took out the folded white paper. Kirsten was willing to exchange it for her mom and uncle. She still remembers the day when the plane crash made her the sole heiress of the empire. That number hadn't changed much since the beginning. The summary of her assets still showed over fourteen billion.

26. jún 1980 - **Mark Kollar** - mark_kollar_one

- ABOUT THE AUTHOR -

After many experiences gained from living on three continents, Mark Kollar decided to inscribe what he had lived through into books. Thanks to his travels, he learned a lot; some experiences humbled him, while others left him wiser. He wants to introduce readers to the traces of human destinies he encountered. The lives of people thousands of kilometers away were first showcased in dozens of blogs and articles.

Through his own experiences, he discovered that sometimes, if the whole world abandons you, it can be the best thing that ever happens. Amidst all these experiences, he understood that he won't live forever and would like to leave something behind. His books are intended to be his legacy. "Kirsten" is the first one, followed by "The Chosen" and "The Exceptional," which are already waiting to be published. More are in the works, namely "The Twisted" and "The Chosen Ones."

In his books, he can offer a different perspective on life. Through the main characters, readers can explore what they might attempt if they knew they could not fail. Anyone who reads these books belongs to the author's imaginary club, joining the fans of life.

_Instagram: mark_kollar_one_

- KIRSTEN -

In 2024, JADRO Publishing released:

Author of the text: Mark Kollar

Language editing: Text has not undergone linguistic editing

Cover photograph: Spencer Gurley; pexels.com

Graphic design: Jaroslav Šleboda - JADRO, www.lacna-tlac.sk

ISBN 978-80-89426-58-4 (printed version)

ISBN 978-80-89426-97-3 (PDF)

ISBN 978-80-89426-98-0 (EPUB)

ISBN 978-80-89426-99-7 (MOBI)

www.ingramcontent.com/pod-product-compliance
Lightning Source LLC
LaVergne TN
LVHW012049160826
845678LV00014B/2754